THE PRINCE OF WALES IN INDIA

THE PRINCE OF WALES IN INDIA

OR

FROM PALL MALL TO THE PUNJAUB

J. DREW GAY

GYAN

Published by

GYAN

Gyan Publishing House
5, Ansari Road
Daryaganj, New Delhi-110002
Phone: 011-47034999, 9811692060
E-mail: books@gyanbooks.com

Distribution Network
gyanbooks.com
India, USA, Canada, UK, Australia, France

ISBN : 978-81-212-9448-5 (PB)
First Published, 1877

2nd Impression 2023

Printed at: Gyan Press, Delhi.

THE PRINCE OF WALES IN INDIA
Author: J . DREW GAY

THE PRINCE OF WALES IN INDIA.

THE PRINCE OF WALES IN INDIA

OR

FROM PALL MALL TO THE PUNJAUB,

BY

J. DREW GAY
SPECIAL CORRESPONDENT OF LONDON "DAILY TELEGRAPH."

NEW YORK:
R. WORTHINGTON, 750 BROADWAY.

1877.

THE PRINCE OF WALES IN INDIA;

OR,

From Pall Mall to the Punjaub.

BY

J. DREW GAY,

Special Correspondent of the London "Daily Telegraph."

NEW YORK:
R. WORTHINGTON,
1877.

CONTENTS.

ILLUSTRATIONS.

THE PRINCE OF WALES IN INDIA.

CHAPTER I.

FIRST IMPRESSIONS OF BOMBAY.

It was a bright autumn morning when we landed in India, —bright not in the sense that you in England understand brightness, but with a gleam and a heat which you only associate with the midday glare of a hot summer's day, and not at all the cold calmness of an English autumn. Nothing could be pleasanter to all of us, heartily tired as we were of the sea and its belongings, than at length to descry the long line of hills which told us of proximity to Bombay. Had we not had the incentive to satisfaction which a three weeks' voyage engendered, the prospect which presented itself, as the ship neared shore, would of itself have been sufficiently delightful. Only five minutes ago, and the sky was brilliantly lit with stars; now the sun's rays were shooting up in the east behind the grey mountains, and driving night away with startling rapidity. Like a huge panorama Bombay rose before us. Yonder on the right was the island of Elephanta, with its caves and its jungle; away in front of us Trombay Island with its mountains and precipices. Bombay itself, skirting the bay, was thrusting out, so to speak, from the lingering gloom into the advancing sunshine, its white houses, its palm-trees, its pleasant hills and valleys, and its splendid harbour, and drawing forth, from those who now saw it for the first time, repeated exclamations of astonishment.

It is difficult to say what Bombay looks like. The Bay of Naples, to which this home of Western Indian industry and government has often been compared, is not at all like it. You fail to see the huge mountain overtopping everything. The lines of hills which skirt the water and shut out the horizon from view, fill you with surprise, but certainly do not remind you of Vesuvius. They are peculiar to the place, and are like nothing to which our European eyes are accustomed. Boldly out against the sky stand Matheran and the outposts of the Ghauts, some apparently extending for miles in a hard, straight line, as though, by some tremendous convulsion of Nature, the peaks had been sheared off, and a hard road made in the region of cloud-land. Near by are hills with summits, which look marvellously like ruined temples, columns, and monuments, fantastic results of inexplicable forces. There is scarcely a hill with the orthodox cone—nothing half so respectable as Snowdon or Pilatus. As for the town, it is almost as irregular in appearance as are the hills in the distance. Not that this irregularity is objectionable; on the contrary, the very absence of sharply-defined streets and regularly laid-out squares adds to the charm which the place possesses. The white houses struggle down to the water's edge in most curious fashion; they are huddled together as though every inch of ground was of the utmost value, and it was necessary to crowd as many bricks and stones as possible into the smallest conceivable space. You wonder, as your eyes move along the strand in the direction of the fashionable suburb of Malabar Hill, that some one did not suggest wider spaces between the houses in the valley, instead of leaving the land so comparatively unoccupied in the higher ground. But once you have landed, you find many of your preconceived notions upset. The part which appeared to be crowded and close is, in reality, only so down at the water's edge. Right through the centre run wide roads, flanked on either side by fine houses and grand public buildings, such as on a first sight one could scarcely expect Bombay to possess. There is a magnificent expanse called the Esplanade, with large trees overshadowing its pathways, and parade and cricket grounds on either hand. There are troops in review order on the right, and two cricketing elevens of Englishmen bowling and batting on the left, with the old-fashioned scoring tent, the familiar soda-water and brandy bottles peeping out of ice-pails, and a fashionable crowd of English ladies and gentlemen watching the game and applauding the players. One side represents the fleet, lieutenants, sub-lieutenants, and midshipmen; the other side is drawn from a club which boasts the title of Gymkhana. When the stumps are drawn, the battle is undecided, the officers go to their ships, the Gymkhana to their homes, and the spectators towards the Apollo Bandar, to listen to the band which plays near that landing-stage before dinner each night.

The streets which pierce the strange-looking houses wherein the natives reside are crowded to excess. The vehicle, notwithstanding that its driver shouts himself hoarse and strikes fiercely at passers-by, can scarcely move forward at a good walking pace. Mohammedans, Parsees, Hindoos, Mahrattas, Chinese, English sailors from the flying squadron anchored in the harbour, negroes, Lascars, nondescripts from every known place, are all here, and are dressed in their most brilliant costumes. Before every house is hung a festooned wreath of leaves and flowers; glass lanterns, to be lighted at night, are to be seen everywhere. When darkness comes on, and the lamps are lit, when the coloured fires burn in the courts of the temples, and the light is reflected from house to house by the burnished metal work, for which streets in Bombay are famous, the sight is magnificent in the extreme; even now, in the daytime, it is marvellous to the unaccustomed eye. Robes of vermilion, scarlet, blue, and gold, richly chased jackets and flowing, white burnouses, intermingle and blend with the olive coloured, naked backs of those who own neither ornament or dress worth mentioning, but who are come out by tens of thousands to look at each other. Does the eye fix upon the numberless head-dresses worn? Then there are the Parsee hat, the European helmet, the Turkish fez and snow-white turban, the turban of green worn by the most favoured of Mahomet's own, and that of red or pink, boasted by the Mahrattas of the hills. All kinds, shapes and colours are passing in view like the varied glasses of the kaleidoscope. How silent is the footfall of this mighty mass of athletic men! Occasionally a sandal may grate on the hard road; but, for the most part, the promenaders are innocent of foot covering of any kind, and move along as noiselessly and as stealthily as though absolute quiet were the object of their lives. Ever changing in appearance, the tide of human life rolls on, without the buzz of a European crowd, with scarcely the sound of a single heel.

The rapidity with which colours melt one into another almost bewilders the spectator: he can scarcely note that more than half of those who are passing have marked their foreheads with red paint, and that the ladies who are in the crowd have, in many cases, very large rings passed through their particularly small noses. The fashion of facial ornamentation is not wholly unknown among sundry of high degree at home, only in these Eastern lands it is brought to further perfection. If a dark-coloured gentleman considers that his complexion would be improved by a patch of yellow on each cheek, in front of the ears, paint is not costly, and a friendly hand will quickly apply the pigment. Should a lady think that a ring in her nostril, and a little patch of crimson on her forehead, would add to her other attractions, she follows out her convictions bravely. Even the Nubian at Aden has the courage of his opinions in this respect. His instincts tell him that Nature was not prodigal of beauty when she designed his countenance and hair. Does he rebel? No; he begins where nature left off, and with a knife makes several delicate slashes on his cheeks, while, with a solution of lime, he rubs the top of his head, and colours his curls a brilliant yellow. This is as it should be, and the conclusion is acknowledged by the dwellers in Bombay

Then there is the additional charm that an act of ornamentation is at the same time an act of devotion. It is combining business with pleasure, satisfying conscience, and pleasing the mind—a two-handed comfort which renders the body a thing of beauty, and morally constitutes it "a joy forever." So the people have very generally daubed their foreheads all over, and thus added to their beauty and their piety at one stroke. The Mohammedans have a reason also for joining in the festivities. It is the first day of Ramadan—a time for best clothes and, to say nothing of best behaviour, a moment for sanctified exultation and religious hilarity. And with a firm belief in Dr. Watts' aphorism that "Religion never was designed to make our pleasures less," the Mohammedan brings an extra supply of betel-nut, puts on his choicest turban and robe, and does his best to keep the feast. In this way the crowd is recruited, and before the night comes on the roads are impassable, for the feast of lanterns is an abiding pleasure to the native of India, and the brilliantly-lit houses, temples, and statues may well be gazed at by a people whose faults, whatever they may be, do not include a lack of appreciation for colour and light.

Just when we arrived Bombay was full of Rajahs; and, if proof of this were wanted, nothing would be easier than to copy from the official list a long column of their names and titles. But as at the best life is short, and the cognomens of these dignitaries are not the lightest of reading, I will only give a sample. I will not imitate the official report even in this. Under the heading of distinguished arrivals stands a series of extraordinary titles. Were they alone, they would be grand in their very unpronounceability—if I may coin such a word. But an ingenious official has attempted to make the matter clear to the uninstructed mind, and to that end has prefixed an *alias* to each name. Thus we find admirable and well-born rulers placed on the list, and respectively styled

Gungadharrao Gunput *alias* Bhaoo Saheb, chief of Meerujand; Ramchundrarao Gopall, *alias* Appa Saheb, chief of Jamkhundi.

There is always a pleasure in beholding the inexplicable. Who that has seen them has not gazed with delight upon the Sphinx, the Pyramids, the tablets from Nineveh, or the paintings of Gustave Doré? You cannot understand them a bit; their very mystery makes you happy; if you knew all about them you would give them no more attention than you do to the lions in Trafalgar Square or the Bethnal Green Museum. Why, then, eliminate all pleasure from a contemplation of the name of Trimbakrao Ram Purandhare by telling in plain English who the gentleman really is, or bother people by stating that Luxumon Maharudra Swami is the ruler of Chafal? It may be pleaded as an excuse that very few know where Chafal is, and that the explanation has merely a look of careful attention about it. But it robs the list of all romance, and makes it a dry statement of unintelligibility. The only consolation under such distressing circumstances was that we were informed with great regularity of the visits of the Chiefs to the Governor of the Presidency, and of his visits to them.

There is an old but admirable saying to the effect that "every dog has his day." In Bombay, at festival times, every Chief has his ten minutes. According to the Government statement, the aged Governor of Bombay, Sir Philip Wodhouse, began his visiting at eleven A.M. punctually. From that time till 4.30 P.M. he visited six fresh grandees every hour, winding up this pleasant and entertaining diversion by an interview with Trimbakrao Ram Purandhare. We learnt with some pleasure that betel-nut and the leaf called *pan* was presented by each Chief to his Excellency, and that in each case the Governor was placed by his host in the place of honour at the right. But about the conversation the "Gazette" knew nothing; and it did not even state what weight of betel-nut his Excellency accumulated when he had paid the last visit and received the last offering. One source of amusement was, however, open to those who put their trust in princes. Every now and then some fresh potentate arrived at one or other of the railway stations or landing-stages, and was received with more or less friendly effervescence. Among those who thus came into the town was the Maharajah of Mysore. To heighten expectation, there was a guard of honour of a hundred men in the little station at Byculla; a band stood ready to play; and the Chief Political Secretary to the Government, Mr. Ravenscroft, was on the platform. Presently the train bearing Mysorean royalty puffed into the station. Eyes were strained, necks craned forward, the band struck up, the Secretary advanced, and from the mountain thus in labour there came forth, not exactly a mouse, but a little boy of some twelve years of age, so enveloped in gold and purple as to be all but hidden from view. Nor were his attendants the bold *militaires* that we looked for. Some were dressed in blue and some in white, some were not attired in very much of anything; while as to their arms, they were as much the representatives of almost antediluvian days as they could well be. Some had match-locks, others pistols—these being the descendants of the men who, in days gone by, defeated Major Lawrence at the head of a British force, and very nearly prevented our grasping the South of India at all. Twenty-one guns were fired, the troops presented arms, the band played, and the Royal boy was hurried into a carriage and taken from the station to Cumballa Hill.

As we returned to Byculla we looked over a gaol—the House of Correction at Byculla—temporarily placed under the superintendence of Major Prendegast Walsh. The sepoys who stood at the gates, the white sergeant warders who walked up and down the garden, the coloured gentlemen who, with leg irons clanking, were tending the plants and trees, and the bars, bolts, grated windows and guarded doors, with notice to the effect that no admittance is allowed "except on business"—what *business* has a man in gaol?—were scarcely suggestive of merry-making and rejoicing. You would be puzzled to connect this establishment with the Prince's visit in any way, and yet it had something to do with it after all.

Received at the doorway by Major Walsh, who is the most courteous of officials, we mounted to what is called the European Hospital. Not to see the sick, however, for, fortunately there were no white men sick in the place, but to see how greatly even prisoners can contribute to the general mirth; for, in this admirably-managed prison the motto is to make each inmate earn as much money as he can for the paternal Legislature which finds him a hiding-place, and, turning every opportunity to excellent account, Major Walsh was employing the more deserving and clever of the people under his care in decorative work for the coming festivities. In the room were designs for the saloon in which, a day or two hence, seamen and school-children were to be feasted: and, albeit that the workshop is a prison and the workers convicts, bright pigments and skilful brushes had formed shields and banners which had merit and beauty—such, indeed, as would please the Prince and the people too. Close by were thousands of little tinfoil bannerets of gold and silver hue, specially formed to decorate the edibles on the tables when the mariners might rest and be thankful. Descending a staircase, we entered an open yard, into which a huge shed opened, and here we saw the continuation of the decorative work. Artificial flowers of every kind—for Bombay knows nothing of real blossoms in November—wreaths, festoons, and brilliant paper-hangings of intricate pattern, but admirable construction, were all before us. Thirty or forty men were working away with all their might, not at the degrading shot-drill or disintegration of oakum knots, but with tinted tissues, weaving them tastefully into all kinds of shapes, and learning from the study of art lessons of tenderness and care.

It was a humanising influence to which they were subjected, and if the Royal visit effects no more than the mental improvement of these rough, white vagabonds, it will yet have achieved much good. Of course, the whole of the criminals were not under similar training. To provide work for three hundred and fifty of society's outcasts, black and white, is no easy task, and ingenious must be the mind which can make the most of such a mass of labouring power. Major Walsh had done much, as we saw by the carpenters, who were making chairs and tables, the men who were weaving mats and making towels, and those, too, who were on the treadmill driving mills and machinery. Nevertheless, there was a goodly company engaged in shot exercise—an equally large number in cells. For some of these latter a strong bolt or lock seemed to be a very necessary provision. Those villains, for instance, were pointed out whose favourite avocation had long been of the Dick Turpin kind. Their style and title is that of Dacoit; and in their time they have seen and done much at which men usually shudder.

Their chieftain stood at his cell door and saluted the Governor as he passed. A more perfect type of what is known as the brigand universally could not be imagined. He would pass current anywhere for a robber. His moustache and curiously curled beard, his fierce eyes and gashed face, the great sabre cut on his left arm, which he exhibited with some pride—a cut, by the way, given him a short time since when he was captured by a cavalryman, and cut down in the midst of his villany—his dress and his very style of turban, all proclaimed him to be an energetic scoundrel, who would as soon cut a throat and commit a robbery as eat the food which was just being brought him. His followers were fair imitations, but far behind their accomplished master. Ruffianism such as his was an accomplishment only to be gained after diligent labours for many years, not an accidental art quickly learnt and easily assumed. It had been the life-long study of this estimable person, and he had gained perfection by perseverance only. He and his two promising pupils had each at various times attempted to escape, and were in consequence the unwilling bearers of heavy irons for the rest of their sojourn in Major Walsh's establishment. Were it not for this, they would probably quit the uncongenial scene without due warning, and recommence their misdeeds in the hills and vales of the Presidency—a very undesirable arrangement for the present.

Leaving them to their fate, we entered the hospital for natives in gaol, and found two or three dying opium-eaters, a man who was shamming illness because he had to receive twenty-five lashes with the cat-o'-nine-tails and did not like the prospect, and one or two who were suffering from low fever. Then to the cooking-house, and so out into the gardens once more, having passed through one of the best-managed prison establishments in the Empire.

CHAPTER II.

SOCIAL LIFE IN BOMBAY.

Early in the evening a few days afterwards I found myself a guest of one of the most influential Mohammedans in Bombay. The invited were not numerous, for the notice was short; but, in place of great formality, there was hearty hospitality. It was my first introduction to the private house of a Mohammedan in India, and it was with no small amount of curiosity that I regarded all about me.

The carriage-drive through the grounds was simply superb; such foliage as we have no conception of in Europe made a thick green arch, down which the light streamed from the windows of the mansion. Sounds of music, too, fell upon the ear; and at the far end of the avenue, close to the door, stood a crowd of servitors gaily dressed, holding lamps in their hands, and receiving the guests with low salaams.

Once arrived in the reception-hall, the spectacle was even more novel. All round the apartment were velvet couches, with comfortable pillows, on which guests were comfortably reclining. Servants were moving swiftly about, handing iced water, sherbets, cheroots, and hookahs: at one end of the apartment was a mellow-toned, mechanical organ, which played English airs very prettily and very softly, while through a doorway, partially covered with a curtain, we could see into the interior of another saloon, and there descry a party of singing girls and instrumentalists. Just then our host, followed by the males of his household, entered the reception-hall, and gave to everybody a welcome; then, taking one of our party by the hand, he led him through the curtain, and so into the inner room of which we had just had a glimpse, while the rest were led in like manner by the members of his family. In this apartment, we now found, two girls were seated on cushions placed on the floor, accompanied by four male musicians, one of whom played a small description of kettledrum attached to his waistband, two having instruments somewhat similar to a hurdy-gurdy in their hands, while the fourth had a tambourine. I do not trouble you with the native names of these instruments, as the mere concurrence of letters would convey no idea to the mind.

So soon as everybody was seated, some on couches and some on cushions, a signal was given by the host, the girls and musicians stood up, and at once began. I had been previously told that these were two of the best singing girls in Bombay, and that, in fact, they sang almost as well as the best male singers, which it appeared was a tremendous compliment to pay them. Imagine my astonishment, then, when I found that in singing they absolutely closed the nose from all participation in the sound, thus giving to the music what we very erroneously call a "nasal" sound of the most extraordinary description. Yet when the ear once became accustomed to the strange thumping of the drum, the harsh noises drawn by the bows of the players from the hurdy-gurdies, the shaking of the tambourine, and the jingling of little bells which the girls wore on their ankles and wrists, it was, after all, by no means an unpleasant sound. Indeed, the song was plaintive, pitched in a minor key, and often sung very softly; the instruments, albeit that they were apparently somewhat rudely constructed, maintaining all the while a weird, moving sound, which harmonised with the singing and sustained the voices. Every now and then the girls, who were very richly dressed in scarlet and gold, whose heads were covered with gauze of gold thread, and whose long dresses were of plaid, also heavily trimmed with golden lace, would dance slowly, continuing their singing meanwhile. Then one would leave off, and the other would begin a slow movement, which, though very graceful, doubtless was somewhat monotonous. Occasionally one of the men behind—a very accomplished singer, I believe, but certainly the owner of one of the most hideous faces I had ever seen—would catch up the refrain, and shout out, in the same nasal tone, a verse or two of the song, whereupon the girls would both shuffle about a little—I can scarcely call their movements dancing—and the man with the drum would thump away with increased energy.

This, then, was the terrible nautch dance of which we had heard so much in England. But perhaps the reader will say that the songs were objectionable. To this I can reply that the most uproarious and most mirthful one that we heard that evening was the Persian song, "Tazah ba tazah, nu ba nu" (Fresh and fresh, new and new), a pleasant chant, in which the hearer is recommended to apply the principles of fresh and new to all he does, whether in drinking wine, making friends, or making love. Rather did the singing incline one to melancholia, particularly when the possessor of the objectionable countenance shouted out, and the drum was beaten more violently than usual. Still, there was no doubt that the Mohammedans—staid old gentlemen, smoking their pipes and cheroots, and occasionally sipping coffee or iced water—enjoyed it thoroughly, and that the entertainment was looked upon as exceptionally lively, and, indeed, as almost a gala performance. And when, now and then, the girls lifted up the ends of their veils, and disclosed fully to view their by no means handsome faces, this digression from ordinary usage was evidently regarded as a mark of great complacency, and was appreciated accordingly.

At length we intimated our desire to depart; whereupon our host, after some little remonstrance at our inconsiderate haste—we had only listened to the monotonous dirge for two hours—made a sign to the bearer of atter and pan; whereupon two men came up, one carrying a basket of flowers in his hand and the other a tray of betel-nuts and pan-leaves, and in a few moments we were sitting with garlands of richly-perfumed blossoms around our necks, and huge bouquets in our hands; while the host sprinkled us with scent, presented us with two bottles of otto of roses apiece, a leaf of pan and betel-nut, and the customary spoonful of scented liquid called attar. Then, with many bows, we were led to the door, and so dismissed.

Next morning, at a very early hour, I started, in company with Mr. Arthur Crawford, several years the Municipal Commissioner of Bombay, and now political agent, collector, and magistrate with the Hubshee, to look at the Grand Bombay Markets, which were erected by him, and are still called by his name. To see them in their full swing it was necessary to go there betimes; for, as in Covent Garden the produce is received at a very early hour, so here, as well as there, it is sold quickly, and the dealers disappear. A somewhat lengthy drive brought us to the outside of the building, a large and stately edifice, covering a wide expanse of ground, and boasting a verdant quadrangle and a fountain such as we have not anywhere in England. On the outside was the name of Arthur Crawford, "writ large;" and no sooner did the good people of the market descry their benefactor, than, with great show of respect and even affection, they made a path for him through the hundreds of buyers who were already at the stalls. I have called Mr. Crawford a benefactor, not because he spent his own money, but because in six or seven years he disbursed more than three millions sterling of the public funds in sanitary and public works, and because, as a result, Bombay possesses a finer market than London, is cleaner than any Eastern city I have yet seen, has its abattoirs far from inhabited places, and is one of the best administered under our rule in the East.

Would that I could present these "bazaars" to your eyes as they appeared a few mornings since! A magnificent, double, iron roof, covering fifty-six thousand square feet of space, supported on tastefully-designed, iron columns, and pleasantly decorated; beneath it hundreds of stalls, displaying everything edible that Bombay can boast for sale. Four thoroughfares were apportioned to the sale of fruit alone; and as we passed between these lines of admirably-arranged stalls, we found Mussulman and Hindoo salesmen squatting upon cushions in the centre of oranges, plantains, pummelos, melons, nectarines, guavas, and apples. I never saw half such a supply of rich, juicy fruit heaped together before. Piles of rosy pomegranates, luscious apples, shaddocks, peaches, and pistachio nuts, all were there. They were displayed in pyramids, in circles, in squares, with rich, green leaves between them, so that it would be well nigh impossible to pass on and buy nothing. And then, leaving these, we came upon the flower market, with its jessamines, verbenas, roses, and tropical blossoms of a hundred kinds. Flowers had been precious lately in Bombay—doubly so because of the demand consequent on the fêtes and their scarcity in the Presidency itself at this time of the year—and round the women and men who made the garlands stood a clamouring, heated crowd. Yet, as we went along, bouquets of exquisite loveliness were offered us, and were pressed upon our acceptance. The air was laden with the delicious perfume of these Eastern flowers, and the seven thousand square feet of blossoms presented a sight to which our European eyes were wholly unused. But, if these were delightful to the vision, the vegetables and spices which covered thirty-five thousand square feet of stalls were more practical. All kinds of "herbs for the use of man," all sorts of pleasant accompaniments for meat or ingredients for soup, every variety of tuber or edible grass were here. These, also, were stacked with marvellously good taste; round them the natives swarmed with baskets and cloths, while in charge of them were merchants in most picturesque costume, who laboured hard to be rid of their wares, and to quit the market. Then there were stalls for the sale of tobacco, for the vending of spices, for the serving of butter—on green leaves again—and the distribution of flour and bread. Round the sides of the market were shops, moreover, in which were retailed European goods and Chinese produce, so that in this great hive of commerce all, save meat and fish, could be procured, even to articles of clothing and ornamentation. Indeed, had we been devotionally inclined, a gentleman was ready to sell us for three-halfpence an offering of incense to the gods, a present, and four kinds of paint wherewith to decorate our foreheads, and give ourselves a very religious appearance.

Crossing the square in the centre of the market-place, we now came upon the stalls in which beef is sold—the abomination of the Hindoo, but the delight of Englishman and Mussulman. And as to see a slaughtered ox is an offence to the Hindoo, we found screens put up at the doorways, so that passing religionists should not be troubled by the sight of a piece of beef. Only Mussulmans kept the stalls in this market, and they were surrounded only by Mussulmans or Europeans, while over every stall was the name of its owner in English and Hindustani characters. So, too, mainly in the market where mutton is sold, there were nearly all followers of the Prophet, it being a tenet of Brahminism that the destruction of life is a sin.

But, if the inspection of the market was instructive as showing what individual effort and energy could realize, the sights which followed were not less amusing. I have said the day was yet young when we started on our tour; those who know India will be aware that this was just the time for visiting a Hindoo temple. Thus it was that on our turning through a somewhat narrow doorway we found ourselves in a huge court-yard, crowded with people. On the immediate right was a tree, under the shade of which sat a number of "holy men." With the Hindoos holiness and dirtiness are almost synonymous, and certainly these were the worst-washed men I ever saw. With the contents of a great pot of ashes they had besmeared not only their countenances, but the whole of their bodies; with big pieces of rope they had tied their already matted hair into knots, and thus heightened their natural ugliness. They had used red and yellow paint wherever those pigments would serve to render them less attractive in appearance, and they had squatted down in a puddle of very holy mud, and were just then eating the offerings of the faithful. Yet they were apparently greatly revered and beloved. There was a tender-hearted, old gentleman, with a great basket of sweetmeats and cakes, giving them all a good breakfast when we entered. The copper cans which lay about on the ground near the puddle were full of annas and pice; they even had a good supply of pan and betel-nut; and, as though holiness with contentment were great gain, they were as stout as they were godly. I gave the most sacred among them two annas, whereupon he rolled a leaf of pan and offered it to me, and, when I declined the tempting morsel, placed it in his own mouth, tinkled a little bell, put his hands to his face and uttered a prayerful groan, and then sat down in the mud once more and looked happy. I should say, at a rough guess, that the holiness on that man was a quarter of an inch thick.

I have mentioned the tinkling of a bell; there were a good many bells tinkling just then; for on the side of the entrance opposite that in which the holy men sat was the Temple of Mombadevi. In front of the temple doors were a large number of pigeons—some hundreds I should suppose—as fat, as well cared for, and quite as tame as the pigeons of the Piazza di San Marco in Venice, and as sacred as the gentlemen in the mud puddle; also five or six sacred buffaloes, a dozen sacred goats, two very sacred but apparently very mischievous monkeys, and a sacred donkey. On the steps of the temple the people congregated, going in, first to one shrine and praying, and then to another. When they had prayed satisfactorily and given an offering to a deity, they rang a bell which hung suspended in front of the shrine, and went away quite pleased.

I noticed two things of interest, the first being that at one shrine they were worshipping a picture—without at all knowing what it represented—of the Madonna and Child; the second that some of the shrines were more fashionable than others. There was a lovely idol, with a head like an ourang-outang, ears nearly a yard long, four arms, eight legs, and a couple of mouths, which was quite deserted, and only got two bundles of pan and a banana during the morning; while a rival, who looked like a tipsy lion, with a moustache resembling Victor Emmanuel's, slightly turned up at the ends, a long Dundreary pair of whiskers gracefully curled, six eyes placed in good and useful positions, three tails, and only two legs, was "making a mint of money." The fates were unkind and unjust. There were plenty of bells in front of the ourang-outang-like god, yet nobody rang them; a very holy man sat at the shrine, yet nobody went there. There was even a bench on which the faithful could rest while they prepared their offerings, yet nobody sat on it; while the lion that possessed the moustache and whiskers received the fat of the land, was accosted by devotional ladies and gentlemen every minute, and had enough offerings in front of him to warrant the belief that the priest who attended to his shrine must live happily the day through, and altogether enjoy what the Americans call "a very good time of it."

This was not all, however, that this religious spot afforded. Past the tree, and still in front of the temple, was a huge tank, three hundred yards square, or thereabouts, and in it hundreds of Hindoo women were bathing in honour of their religion. There they were, painting and washing, washing and painting, fulfilling a religious duty and performing a very sanitary act at the same time. A profane person might have perchance wished that the holy men under the tree might have been pitched into the water too. But that would have probably shocked those holy men's nerves, and so rendered them less good and admirable than now. Mr. Crawford said that he should like to pull down the wretched shanties which surround the tank, and make in their stead a fine public garden. But at present this will not be done, and Mombadevi Tank must be let alone.

Needless is it to describe two other temples that we visited; but a word should not be omitted respecting a religious institution through which we passed. I have mentioned that a large number of Hindoos believe in the sanctity of life of every kind, and it was to visit an establishment belonging to this sect that we now entered a gateway not far from the Mombadevi Temple. A curious sight at once presented itself. Hundreds of cows and buffaloes were enclosed within one set of rails, hundreds of goats within another. All kinds of animals had pens appointed them and people to tend them. We have in London a Home for Dogs, about which a good deal the reverse of complimentary has at different times been written, and not without cause. Stray dogs, unruly dogs, sick dogs, are all received, yet somehow or other they disappear, are sold, strangled, or poisoned in this "Home" of theirs. Here, however, is a real home for the maimed, the blind, the starving, and the old. When a Hindoo has a horse which he finds too ill or too old for work, it is sent here, and thence to pastures in the country; cows that will give milk no longer, goats that are useless, dogs that are toothless, and even monkeys that are too old to chatter or to climb, are placed here, too, and all carefully tended till they die. So sacred is the charge that voluntarily do Hindoos support it by a self-imposed tax; so good is it considered to feed these poor animals that carts of hay are continually coming in for their sustenance, and pious old men attend and distribute the provender. When we were in the place, cows that had recovered from their illness were eating the sweet hay which lay near them in profusion, with the greatest satisfaction; the goats that were pronounced well were feasting and gambolling; sick dogs had savoury messes, dogs that were not sick were equally well fed, and the monkeys were evidently as happy as their cramps and cranks would allow. "I doctor, sar," said a dusky gentleman with a walking-cane, who came up to us while we were looking at his horses; "and I keep loving animals very much." "Keep loving them as much as you can," was the reply of my companion, "and then you'll go straight to heaven some day." "Yes, sar," said the doctor, and forthwith evinced his "love" for animals by stroking a huge buffalo that stood close by, and giving it a great handful of grass."

CHAPTER III.

RECEPTIONS OF RAJAHS.

"Chairs for the Guicowar and the Maharajah! Make way there, please!" An official, a very courteous, but very energetic one, Mr. Lee Warner, Under-Secretary of the Presidency of Bombay, dressed in full Court uniform, is directing the movements of a slender Hindoo who, besides bearing a huge, red turban, in shape and size very like a lady's sunshade, is struggling along under two cane-seated chairs on the outskirts of a most brilliant throng. The *locale* is the Boree Bunder railway station; the occasion, Lord Northbrook's arrival in Bombay. To meet the Viceroy are gathered together in that little terminus all the rank and power of North-Western India. Should I give you a list of their names and titles you would have a lengthy collection of extraordinary words. I could tell from an official list, which has been published, the exact number of followers each one has, and the number of "guns" to which each is entitled. But for many reasons I forbear. Mingled with the chieftains and sirdars are a large number of officers from the fleet, all in full-dress uniform, military officers in scarlet, clergymen in their robes, and Political Residents in Court dress.

A picturesque crowd is that which is thus shut in from the front of the platform by a cord of blue, fit subject for the minutest of painters; yet, so far as I can see, no painter is present. I am alone on the red carpet on which the Viceroy is presently to stand when he reaches Bombay, without even so much as a railway official to keep me in countenance. Railway policemen are here, it is true, but they are on the lines.

Long lines of soldiery hold the way to the station, but they are in the road. Other spectators are looking on beside the fashionable crowd behind the rope, but they are on the tops of goods; others on the walls round about, chattering, gesticulating, fighting, wondering—these natives of India waiting for their ruler.

It was for no idle purpose that the chairs were brought for which Mr. Lee Warner begged a way. In the centre of yon brilliant gathering stand two little boys, each dressed in black velvet, grandly ornamented with diamonds, and attended by a large number of followers. In point of age they seem to be respectively thirteen and nine years old. They are clearly princes in rank, and, indeed, the greatest here. The taller one is as dignified a little ruler as was ever seen. He holds his head erect, and stands in front of his followers and by the side of Mr. Dalyel, the Commissioner, with all the conscious pride that the greatest potentate in the world could command. And not altogether without reason, for he is the Maharajah of Mysore, has a wide tract of country, and a huge revenue, and succeeds to a stately home and princely inheritance. In facial expression he is almost the very image of Madame Adelina Patti—handsome, sharp-eyed, and graceful. Round his neck are strings of pearls and diamonds of immense value; his wrists are encircled by bracelets, even his ankles are enveloped in jewels, and from the little turban which has been placed in coquettish style upon his head there shoots an aigrette of precious stones such as Nasr-Ed-Din of Persia would gaze at with amazement. His Royal brother is the smallest specimen of sovereignty I have ever seen, yet he is even more important in vice-regal eyes, for this is the Guicowar of Baroda. If he of Mysore is radiant with jewels, this royal seedling from Baroda is more magnificent still. On his neck and breast, his turban, and his very shoes, everywhere glisten diamonds, emeralds, rubies, and pearls. He is well aware of his own importance;

and, though not so old as his Mysore rival, acts his part well. And when the chairs are brought and the two sit down, each eyes the other with great curiosity—perhaps also mentally placing a valuation on the other's jewels—and then each turns his head away with an expression very like contempt.

At length the Rajahs, chieftains and sirdars are all in the station, and have taken their places; and the Governor of Bombay steps on to the red carpet, followed by his son, who is his private secretary. The naval officers are also asked to step on to the carpet, and some of the principal authorities of the town are likewise invited to this place of distinction. There they all stand for a few minutes, during which the Viceroy's train is signalled from Byculla. That there should be late arrivals was, of course, to be expected. And I grieve to say that one of them was a judge—not a judge such as we see in England, clad in scarlet, and wearing a long wig, or even dressed in ermine, with a short wig; but a funny, old gentleman of olive colour, with a red turban on his head, and his nether limbs encased in a starched, white petticoat. Very stout, very brown, this funny, old man shuffles into the roped space, and, clasping his hands together, awaits the Governor-General. Then a ridiculous, old person, with a Mahratta turban, puts in an appearance. One wonders why such grotesque, old people should be allowed to spoil the general harmony of the scene. Yet they turn up everywhere—at durbars, at ceremonies of all kinds—just when one is most admiring everything, and thinking how much more picturesque it all is than any sight in England; and with their ugly faces and uglier head-dresses, their extraordinary petticoats, yellow stockings, and bootless feet, lower the scene from the sublime to the ridiculous, and make the beholder almost mad with disappointment. These turbans of theirs are as large as an ordinary umbrella, and contain eighty yards of thin riband; they are generally pink or scarlet, have a little eminence in the centre, which looks like an intoxicated cone, and then bulge out over the ear and shoulder in the strangest possible style. Why does not somebody seize this latest arrival at the station and bundle him out! He spoils the whole scene, and troubles the spectator exceedingly.

By this time, however, the viceregal engine is in sight, and there is no time to turn anybody out. Besides which it is an engine to regard with awe and admiration. I remember once at Sheffield seeing an official with a white wand, who had deputed himself to receive the Prince of Wales, make a profound obeisance to a goods engine. Onlookers laughed, but excused the blunder on the ground that the gentleman meant well. Here, however, is an engine he might bow to without being laughed at. It is immense in size; it is brilliantly painted; round the funnel are garlands of flowers, and on its front, in golden colours, is the royal coat of arms. Nobody does bow to it; but that is because the Viceroy's carriage is just behind, and his Excellency is stepping out, so that everybody is making a bow to Lord Northbrook, and thinking nothing about the engine at all. And as there is no one with a white wand here, no officious person, no meddler or muddler, everything goes easily and pleasantly. The Viceroy goes at once to the two Princes, who have been favoured with the chairs, and shakes hands with them. Then he grasps the hand of the Maharana of Oodeypore, who is close by, and then that of the Rajah of Kholapore, and so passes all down the station, while the band outside plays "God save the Queen," and the troops present arms. Carriages drive up and drive away, and in half an hour the station platform, which just now contained so brilliant a throng, is deserted.

And now let me describe another scene, more imposing and more important, more interesting also, as being exactly similar to one in which the Prince of Wales himself took part a few days later on. It was late on the Tuesday night before the Prince landed, when I received an invitation from the secretary of the Viceroy, Captain Evelyn Baring, to breakfast at Malabar Point, the temporary residence of Lord Northbrook, on the following morning. There was, however, in the note even more than this, for it contained a postscript with the information that his Excellency would receive the principal chieftains at present in Bombay in the audience room of Government House, at seven A.M. Such a summons could not be lightly valued, and I hastened to acknowledge the missive, and prepared to obey.

The daylight had not appeared when I found myself in a gharry, driven by an ill-tempered Mohammedan—ill-tempered because awakened early—towards the beautiful bay which fronts Malabar Hill. Now and then a streak of sunshine would dart across the sky and the sea, telling of the close proximity of day. The surf was breaking on the land with a sullen roar, but not a breath of air could be felt on that sultry morning. On went the grumbling driver, until at length long lines of troops were descried, native infantry with arms at the "present," native cavalry with lances held aloft, pennons dangling in the air, and English constables, clad in white clothes, all drawn up in regular order, waiting the arrival of the great personages who were presently to come to visit his Excellency. A few moments more, when the sun was up, scorching everybody, I was hastening up the steps of Malabar House. On seeing a place for a first time, the eye naturally wanders all round. Let us glance at the building before us. On the broad staircase on either side are soldiers of the Viceroy's body-guard. Some bear halberds, some lances, some swords; they are broad, strong men—few of them less than six feet in height, and look magnificent in their small, striped turbans, their long, scarlet coats, and golden waistbands. Better soldiers than these cannot be found. In the mutiny Lord Canning held to his native body-guard, and refused the guard of English troops; and Lord Northbrook still refuses to believe that anything can be safer than the watch that is kept by his stalwart Punjabees. On arriving at the top we are at once on a broad, covered verandah, extending all round the house—a delightful retreat from the rays of the sun, and just now full of a welcome breeze which has suddenly sprung up, and is coming in from the sea. Here, again, are soldiers of the body-guard, marking the entrance to the State room which opens on to the verandah. A few steps bring us into the very centre of the viceregal Court, all ready as that Court is for the reception of the Rajah of Kholapore, who is momentarily expected.

The scene is extremely impressive. A lofty audience-chamber, with two marble pillars at one end, cutting off, say, a fourth of the space, and thus forming a kind of recess for the throne; this throne, just now occupied by Lord Northbrook, is constructed of silver and gold, having a golden lion for one arm and a golden bull for another, bearing a purple and golden crown about a foot above the back, and altogether forming one of the finest State chairs ever designed. This also is placed upon a daïs one step high. On the right hand is a long row of empty arm-chairs, running down half the length of the room; on the left an equal number of chairs, not empty, but filled by officers in brilliant uniforms—Captain Baring, mentioned before; Colonel Earle, the admirable Military Secretary; Mr. C. U. Aitchison, the Foreign Secretary; Major Henderson, acting as Assistant Foreign Secretary—the Viceroy's personal staff. Behind the throne are gathered an array of servants picturesquely attired in bright, red uniforms and gold and white turbans, holding up scarlet fans, golden umbrellas, and other insignia of Eastern royalty. Round the room at regular intervals are more of these attendants, bearing maces with crowns, and elephants' heads in silver, and halberds. But by far the most important item in the whole room, next to the Viceroy himself, has as yet been unnoticed, although upon it depends more than would be conveyed in the strongest letter of approval or dissatisfaction that was ever penned at Calcutta and sent to a native prince.

At first glance there is nothing very extraordinary about it either. It is a long, oval piece of crimson with a golden border, the Royal arms being in the centre. Yet how far the Viceroy may advance on that carpet when about to meet a guest is matter for serious deliberation and special notice in the "Gazette." Beyond the line "Dieu et mon droit," in presence of a Nawab, and his Excellency would raise a thousand jealousies, make said Nawab insane with delight, and lay the foundation for a series of troubles, the end of which could not be predicted. Stop but six inches from the edge when a Guicowar or a Maharana enters, and a rebuke would be conveyed and received of profound importance and meaning. Even the number of steps the Viceroy may take on that wonderful rug-work are defined by a decree in council, and he must no more take five when three are ordered than the officer in charge of yonder artillery battery just preparing to fire may let off twenty-one guns in honour of the Chief of Jamkhundee. He may let off two less than that number in honour of the Rajah of Kholapore, and, indeed, is now preparing to do so, for his Highness, attended by nine of his principal sirdars and an escort of cavalry, is just now being driven at a great rate along the pathway to the house. The troops are presenting arms, and the band is playing. Bang go the guns, with a deafening sound. Two officers run down the steps, and the ruler of Kholapore is assisted from his carriage and conducted to the audience-chamber without delay. As the sound of approaching footsteps is heard, the Viceroy rises and stands upon the daïs, till the faces of his guests are seen in the ante-room. The "Gazette" order for the day states that Lord Northbrook will receive his Highness "at the edge of the carpet, and conduct him to a seat on his right hand," and no one knows all this better than the Lilliputian highness now entering the doorway. Perhaps it is the experienced government of Mr. Aitchison, perhaps the jealous eye of the boy-Prince, which regulates the steps of the Kholapore party. Anyhow, the youth only arrives at the outer edge of the carpet at the precise moment when the Viceroy's toe touches the inner edge, and the Viceroy's extended hand reaches into uncarpeted space. With a rapid bow the little Rajah grasps his Excellency's fingers, and is then led to the chair covered with golden cloth—which stands next the daïs on the right, and is to be used for all princes who come—followed by the English officer resident at his Court, and his sirdars, all of them portly men, in singular costumes.

As soon as the Rajah is seated, we are at liberty to criticise his dress. I think there are, if possible, more diamonds round that little neck than on the previous day—larger pearls for bracelets and finer rubies as earrings. The diamond aigrette in the gold turban is, moreover, supplemented by another tuft of brilliants, and the finger-rings on the Royal hands are more costly than before. The pale-faced child can scarcely weigh five stone—diamonds, clothes, sword, and all; yet there he sits, coolly chatting with the Viceroy, and now and then sending a glance of ineffable contempt round the room, as though it was not a bit more ornate than it should be, considering that so important a personage as himself is in it as a guest. So a few minutes pass, and then Major Henderson rises, and with a bow, introduces the sirdars to the Viceroy. One by one these portly chieftains rise, and, advancing to the throne, make a low obeisance, and hold out a bag of gold to his Excellency. In times gone by the gold would scarcely have been held out with safety. An emperor of Delhi in the olden time would probably have not only taken that, but demanded a good deal more. In these enlightened times the Viceroy only touches the money, the sirdar shuffles back into his place, and, as coin-carrying is not pleasant to an indolent person, and one bag of money, which is only to be touched and not used, is as good as twenty, he simply transfers the bag from his own, yellow handkerchief to the red one of his successor in homage, and so the money goes round.

"Attar and pan will then be given to the Rajah by the Viceroy himself," runs the circular. Attar and pan are given in consequence. Two bearers, clad in scarlet, enter the room from a side door, the one carrying a glass bottle on a silver stand, the other some gold and silver leaved packets on a salver. Slowly advancing in Indian file, they stand at length before the Viceroy, who rises, and, taking from the bottle a silver stick, conveys a drop of attar of roses to the extended handkerchief of his chief guest. Next a gilded packet—it contains the leaf called pan, some betel-nut, a clove, and a little quicklime, all admirably adapted for chewing, says the Hindoo—is transferred by Lord Northbrook to the right hand of the Rajah, who, after making a profound bow, hands both handkerchief and packet to an attendant. The sirdars are now treated in similar fashion by the Foreign Secretary and his assistant, according to heir rank, and then, at a signal, all rise, the Viceroy extends his hand to the Rajah, and, leading him to the very edge of the carpet, once more shakes hands with him, and bids him adieu.

But a greater than he is close at hand. In a few minutes fresh artillery salutes announce the new comer, and the guard of honour has scarcely stacked its arms, before it has to present them once more. And the promptitude is not without reason. Chamrajendra Hadiar Bahadoor, Maharajah of Mysore, is driving up the pathway—a prince entitled to a salute of twenty-one guns, to be met on the edge of the carpet, to receive attar and pan from his Excellency's own hands, and to be treated with profoundest respect as one of the principal rulers of India. Strange to say, out of all the armed retainers who accompany his carriages only one ascends the broad staircase with the Prince and his guardian (Colonel Malleson), and this, a fat, old gentleman in a starched petticoat and stockings, wearing a curious turban of yellow calico, and carrying a big bag of money as "nuzzar" for the Viceroy. His Highness is dressed just as he was on the previous day—in black velvet, with the same turban and aigrette of brilliants, the same splendid necklace and the same rings; on his left arm, however, a sparkling armlet of diamonds, and on his ankles more pearls than before. He is a stately, little fellow, this Maharajah, only thirteen years old though he may be; and he stops at the edge of the carpet till the Viceroy reaches it with all the dignity of a great sovereign, takes his place in the chair of honour as though it were the throne of Southern India, and converses with the Viceroy with all the affability and ease of an accomplished man of the world. His reception is of the same kind as that of his predecessor; he takes the attar and pan, and is gone.

The next guest is the Maharana of Oodeypore. I do not know how many books have been written to prove that this gentleman is the greatest prince in India. He claims to rank above the Guicowar of Baroda and Prince of Mysore, and to receive like them, a Royal salute instead of only a welcome of nineteen guns. He is the head of the Rajpoots—the purest race of Hindoos—a sacred person in his own right, and the representative of the only dynasty that successfully withstood the victorious emperors of Delhi and lesser warriors for eight hundred years. For the rest, he is a stately, young man of about twenty-three summers, somewhat badly marked by small-pox, but, for all that, kingly in demeanour and not unpleasing in countenance. He, too, is received at the edge of the carpet, and led by the right hand to the place of honour by Lord Northbrook. His followers, indeed, hold their heads as high and stride along as proudly as though they were all kings in their own right, instead of tributary princes. Their wonderful costumes of bright green and gold, their white turbans, and their jewels, as they follow their master—who wears nothing but white linen, and boasts only two or three large diamonds—are extremely picturesque; and when they come forward one after another, and are presented to Lord Northbrook, bowing to the earth and kissing the tips of the fingers just touched by his lordship, their appearance is not less effective. They thought, it appears, that the Viceroy would rise to receive them; but England's power has grown while theirs has decreased, and since they last saw the Queen's representative, times have changed, and they now only obtain a gracious nod, and have to be satisfied.

The same ceremony which dismissed the brethren of Kholapore sends them away, and the Rana of Oodeypore is succeeded by the Rao of Kutch. This good gentleman, despite his brigand-like appearance, is a very estimable person, rules a large State wisely, and generally steers clear of difficulties with the Government. At first glance he gives one the impression of a very lordly individual indeed—one, in fact, who might be met at the edge of any carpet in the world, with great propriety. But not so. The line in the middle which says "Dieu et mon droit," might so far as he is concerned, read 'Kutch et mon droit,' for it is just there that the Viceroy awaits him, and not an inch nearer. Moreover, the guns outside are only firing seventeen rounds, and one almost imagines that the band left off playing a little sooner than before. But never mind, Rao Pragmul,* you are bravely attired in your dark green velvet habit and light blue riband over the heart; your red and gold turban is exceedingly becoming, and your step is very creditable. It is a pity that you are only allowed five attendants, however, for more of such dresses might easily be seen with an untired eye. The hundred and one gold mohurs which the Rao presents being touched, and a short conversation over, his Highness is led down to the centre of the carpet once more, and thence to the doorway, by the Foreign Secretary.

He is not long gone before an unusual stir is noticeable. Arms! Present arms! Make way for the Guicowar's horsemen and carriages, for, to the sound of a Royal salute and a Royal march, the *protégé* of Sir Richard Meade is coming along

* He died soon after the Prince left Bombay.

the pathway. Men of the body-guard stiffen in position, the viceregal suite is in its place, and the Viceroy is already past the middle of the carpet ere the little Prince is through the doorway. Led by his guardian, he steps cautiously forward, so as to time his footsteps to those of the Governor-General; and just as his Excellency's feet are at the edge, this Royal waif and stray, this little King by accident, stretches out his hand, and with complete calmness thus salutes the Viceroy. His stride along the carpet to his chair of state is as remarkable as his dress, which is indeed striking. More jewels than ever glittered round that little neck. Nearly four hundred thousand pounds' worth of diamonds, pearls, rubies, and emeralds adorn the person of this little boy; such an aigrette was never seen in any other turban. Some English ladies whom I know, and who take delight in jewellery and find pleasure in brilliants, would have been beside themselves with joy at such a spectacle; even amongst men accustomed to such sights there was a perceptible murmur of applause. I need scarcely say that twenty-one guns saluted this important item of sovereign humanity, that attar and pan were handed him by the Viceroy with all respect, and then at length he was led to the very edge of the carpet, before being handed over to the Foreign Secretary, and taken to his carriage.

Next came Sir Salar Jung, the guardian of the Nizam of Hyderabad. So remarkable is this man that, although he is only an "Excellency" and by no means Royal, he is honoured with twenty-one guns, and received in the centre of the carpet. His business here is to represent the Nizam, who is actually too ill to come. The resident English physician has declared against the young Prince's journey, a prolonged illness supports the plea, and Sir Salar Jung is here to render homage for him. Take a good look at his Excellency as he sits by the side of the Viceroy, clad in simple white with only a light blue riband across his breast. In appearance, closely cut hair and short moustache, he is very like Prince Bismarck ; he has the broad forehead and quick eye of the German Chancellor, and is apparently as frank as he. Men who know him well speak in admiring tones of his grasp of European politics ; his administration of the wild population of Hyderabad shows his force of character and strength of will. If Madava Rao is the first of Hindoos, Salar Jung is the premier Mohammedan, and as such is esteemed by the Government.

But, if the reception given to the chiefs by the Viceroy was grand, their reception of him on his paying return visits to them was no less striking. I do not refer to the "no-gun men." They were asked to go to the Government Secretariat, and receive the Viceroy there. But I allude to the Guicowar, the Maharajah of Mysore, the Maharana of Oodeypore, and such dignitaries. It was at the house of the last-named that, by the courteous request of the Viceroy, I found myself an invited guest a few minutes before his Excellency arrived. It was while looking round on this extraordinary assemblage of chiefs that Colonel Herbert—the Political Resident at Oodeypore—touched me on the arm and introduced me to his Highness, who was pleased to converse in very good English, till the arrival of the Viceroy was announced at the gate. Then the chiefs stood round the hall, the Maharana advanced to the Viceroy's carriage, and, taking his Excellency by the right hand, led him to a couch at the head of the saloon, and gave him the seat of honour as to a superior monarch. Of course the English officers were on the right hand of the Viceroy, this time they being the guests. Colonel Herbert now came forward and introduced each chief present by name to the Governor-General, each one advancing as his name was called out, and offering a "nuzzar," or present, which the Viceroy formally touched. Next appeared two attendants with wreaths of flowers for the neck of the Viceroy and his suite, bouquets, moreover, of red flowers for their hands, attar for their handkerchiefs, and pan for their mouths in case it should please them to eat it. And all these being presented in due form, the whole party rose, the Viceroy was again led to the door by the Maharana, the band played, the troops presented arms, and the visit was over. This was exactly similar to all the other return visits of the Viceroy; and I am particular in thus detailing the incidents, as they were the same as those which befel the Prince afterwards.

Having on the following Saturday received an invitation to visit the Maharajah of Mysore, an hour's drive brought me to Altamont, the house which has been engaged for his Highness during his stay in Bombay, and in a very few minutes I was in company with the highly esteemed Colonel Malleson, political agent in Mysore, and author of a valuable work on the Native States of India, and Mr. Dalyel, administrator of the kingdom, waiting the coming of the Maharajah in the reception saloon. A more happily chosen spot for the court of a powerful prince could scarcely have been selected. At one end of the hall, which would comfortably seat some hundreds of people, was a magnificently carved screen; in front of this a yellow satin and gilded couch was placed; on either hand were chairs of state, running down half the length of the room, placed in such a manner as to accommodate all the chiefs of Mysore when in council assembled. It was here that the Viceroy was received, and it was here that the Prince of Wales would make his call early the next week.

On a table to the right of the couch were ranged in tempting array the presents which the Maharajah was about to make to the Prince. A magnificently embossed cup of gold, called "Alexandra," and made many years ago in honour of the marriage of the Prince and Princess of Wales, stands in the centre. The history of this cup is somewhat singular. A short time ago, before the Prince's visit was talked of, the Maharajah determined on giving it as a prize to the best race-horse in his dominions, in honour of the Princess of Wales. The race was run amid great excitement, but, curiously enough, his Highness' own horse won the cup, and so here it was, ready to be given to the Prince for the Princess herself. It is engraved with her name, is beautifully worked, as such work can be done only in Mysore, and has for handle to the lid a massive, gold elephant. The value is about £3,000.

Round this cup is ranged a gold service for attar and pan. There are a gold receptacle for attar of roses, a golden casket for the pan and betel-nut, a golden stand for incense, a rose-spouted cup of gold, for scented water, and other beautifully designed cups and salvers for the completion of the set. But the most beautiful present of all is a belt of gold which is placed on a little table by itself. For long years it has been in the treasury of Mysore, highly valued, much admired, and now it sees light only to leave Mysore forever. In size it is too big for any lady, being intended for a very stout king, but in point of beauty it is fit for the most queenly waist in the world. All over its front flash diamonds, emeralds, rubies and pearls—in fact, it contains every kind of precious stone found in Mysore, and is on that account alone a most valuable and interesting jewel. In the centre of the back it has a hinge, in front a diamond clasp, and altogether it is one of the most resplendent ornaments that could be designed. Its intrinsic cost was many thousands of pounds, but as a work of art it is still more valuable.

While looking at these a messenger announced the approach of the Maharajah, and a moment afterwards his Highness came into the saloon, and, holding out his hand, bid me welcome to his house. He was glad, he said, to see Englishmen; for he hoped some day to go to England himself and learn all about the great country from which they came. Then, turning round, he introduced a bright-eyed, intelligent youth of nineteen or thereabouts—who, his Highness said, was hereditary commander-in-chief of the army in Mysore. With excellent accent and admirable good taste, he spoke English perfectly, and in a very few minutes showed that he looked forward to no sinecure, although his army might never be large. He knew all about the Franco-German war, was intimately acquainted with Russian movements, understood even the principle of summer drills in England, and expressed a desire to see the troops of all these nations himself. "You Europeans," he said, "are so well disciplined that I could but learn much by travel, and I shall go to Europe on the very first opportunity." As for the Maharajah, he chatted pleasantly about the sights of Bombay and its relative beauty when compared with his own capital. He was just going to see the caves of Elephanta, and he intended to learn all he could while in the Presidency. He dwelt upon the pleasure of cricket, of which game he is very fond, and the advantages of underhand twist bowling, which he finds bothers the Mysorian cricketers exceedingly, and then upon the pleasures of sport. Thus fifteen minutes or so passed pleasantly, and concluded with a kindly invitation to visit him at his capital and see his people. A more intelligent young gentleman I have never seen; and if such is the result of English training and instruction, the system promises well, and Colonel Malleson and Mr. Dalyel have good reason to be proud of their charge.

CHAPTER IV.

THE ARRIVAL OF THE PRINCE.

On the 8th of November, 1875, "His Honour of High Title, the Star of the Sky of Wealth and Fortune, the Great Star of the Firmament of Glory and Prosperity, the Generous One of the Age, the First One of the Time, the Essence of the Family of Honour and Loftiness, the Prop of the Dynasty of Might and Pomp, possessing the dignity and rank of Saturn, of exalted honour, the Cream of the Princes of the Age, the Glory of the Nobles of England, Albert Edward, Prince of Wales," landed in Bombay. That is the statement of a Persian writer who was good enough to read me the beginning of his admirable article, and to give me an English translation. Of the fact of the Prince's landing I was a faithful witness; of the titles which the Persian has conferred upon the Prince, I say nothing. Yet surely, if banging of artillery and cheering can impress the mind with an idea of the grandeur of the Prince who landed, the Persian may be pardoned for his selection of compliments.

Never was a heartier or more loyal reception accorded to anyone anywhere. For weeks past Bombay had been in a ferment. In the excess of their loyalty the powers that be, actually quarrelled. Sir Philip Wodehouse got to loggerheads with Rear-Admiral Macdonald, the result of which was that the Admiral requested his officers not to attend the Governor's levee; then the Rear-Admiral, reading his instructions from the Admiralty with great exactitude, informed the ancient representative of British government in Bombay that his orders would not allow of a salute being given to the Viceroy on the occasion of the Prince's landing. "No flag can be saluted in presence of the Royal Standard," wrote Admiral Macdonald; whereupon the Governor very nearly went into hysterics, and the local newspapers wrote columns of rubbish. At length the knotty point was settled; Admiral Macdonald telegraphed to England for instructions, and received permission to salute the Viceroy and the Prince as well; the Governor received the intelligence with bewildered gratitude, and has remained in a state of amazement ever since.

Then, of course, the decorations were matter for serious consideration and endless disagreement. Had everybody's suggestions been adopted, and each suggester set to work with plenary powers, Bombay would have presented in a short time a very singular spectacle indeed. But somehow or other the authorities contrived to repress some and quicken others, so that in the end the place looked fairy-like in its beauty. Bombay is less of an Indian and more of a Levantine city than any other. Within its environs people from every part of the world find a home. There are seventy-two different sects of Mohammedans alone. No one knows how many different kinds of Hindoos there are. Chinamen are numerous, too. There are representatives of every European country and people who are able to judge, say, of Asia also. Every now and then you come across a Nubian or Abyssinian. Egyptians are here in scores; Arabs stalk about in the bazaars; and I believe I espied a Kaffir in a shop near Byculla. With such a variety of nationalities there would very naturally be a diversity of colour, and hence the picturesque appearance of the crowd which assembled to welcome or to gaze at the Prince of Wales.

To most of the inhabitants the Royal visit was very agreeable. The cabdrivers quadrupled their fees; the tradesmen in the bazaars had the most delightful opportunity for fleecing Rajahs—"young men from the country"—that ever presented itself; and as for the Europeans, they were all placed on some committee or other, saw their names figuring everywhere, and their speeches reported with unwonted regularity. All this being the case, no wonder Bombay turned out to witness the Royal entry. Great preparations had been made. The genealogy of the Prince had been carefully traced and copied into the native papers. Poetry such as has been seldom read was written and published. All along the line of route—it is needless for me to attempt to give the names of the streets—masts called, for want of a better name, Venetian, had been erected; flags were flying therefrom; festoons connected mast with mast; coloured lamps, shortly to be lighted, were placed in position; and triumphal arches, more or less pretty, appeared at every cross road. Then the people came out *en masse*, and crowded every road, street, and lane. Let it be remembered that in a city like Bombay this is less difficult than it would be in London. Here the inhabitants, as a general rule, perform their toilettes by the side of the road. Gentlemen are shaved while sitting on a kerbstone, ladies clean their teeth in the centre of the thoroughfare, friends adjust each other's top-knots on their doorsteps, and in the street ablutions go on merrily. Witnessing the procession forms nearly the sum total of what the natives did on that—to them—memorable day.

Visitors to the Dockyard and to the Club windows were requested to appear in full dress. But no dress of the white population, "full" though it may be, comes up to the costumes which the natives donned that morning. And when I drove from Parell and saw the gaily-painted houses, the brilliantly green trees hung with coloured Chinese lanterns and long lines of flags, the trophies of banners, the triumphal arches, and the busy road, all teeming with natives attired in bright costumes, I felt that the Prince could have never looked on such a scene elsewhere. I cannot say so much for the mottoes which figured over the gateways of the Rajahs and chieftains on the route.

Perhaps allowance should be made for the fact that almost all the ingenuity that Bombay possessed had been exhausted on the illumination designs for the next night. To make the place resplendent with light in honour of the Prince's birthday, every possible design had been adopted. From every tree hung lanterns; over every gateway were archways of lamps; on each lamp-post designs of crosses, stars, triangles, and circles, glittered—for even in the daytime the glasses glittered in the sun like diamonds—loops, made of bent twigs, supporting transparent cups full of oil, lined the roads, and great gas jets, such as we sometimes see at home, completed the arrangement. But if this was satisfactory—and I fancy that a drive round the town the next evening reminded the Prince of Wales of the fairy tales of his youth rather than of anything else—the mottoes were decidedly poor. You saw a fine archway with letters in gilt and plenty of blue paint. You naturally expected something very appropriate to the visit, and set yourself to decipher the printing, when you found that it runs "God bless your Royal Mother," or, turning in another direction, "Long Live the Royal Family," or in another the single word "Victoria." Here and there in front of a Parsee house was some such remark as "Very glad to see the Prince of Wales," or on a Mohammedan bungalow the letters "A. E.;" but, for the rest, "Welcome to India," or "Welcome to Bombay," occurred very frequently, and then the ingenuity in this branch of display came to an end, with one exception—namely at the Dockyard gates, of which I will speak presently.

It was quite early in the morning when the "Serapis" was sighted from Malabar Point and introduced to Bombay by two guns, and nine o'clock had scarcely struck ere she entered the harbour. Instantly the yards of the men-of-war, which lay in two long lines, were manned, and so deafening a salute poured out from the ships and the battery on shore that for many minutes' space the very windows rattled. To attempt to see anything of the "Serapis" at such a time was simply foolish, for the smoke in a dense cloud hid not only the coast, the islands, and the distant hills, but enveloped the ships so completely that for nearly a quarter of an hour no part of them could be discerned. When the smoke had gone and the air was clear once more, it was seen that the "Serapis" had taken up a position close by the "Osborne," which had arrived the night before, and that she was not decorated with flags, as were all the ships in the harbour, but simply displayed the Royal Standard from her masthead.

I have already mentioned the native part of the town; I will now describe what was going on in the Fort, which was more particularly the English quarter, so far as shops, offices, and public buildings are concerned. Very soon after seven o'clock, well appointed broughams were driven into the Fort all full of ladies and gentlemen bent on enjoyment. Happy were the people whose offices or shops lay on the line of route, for they could and did invite their friends to luncheon—called "tiffin" here—and to a seat in their windows. Happier still were the bachelors who belonged to the Bombay Club, and whose right to windows there and to invite friends was undisputed. But there was a happier class yet—the people who had space available for the erection of a tasteful stand whereon to place those whom they delighted to honour. All made the best of their opportunity; all did their utmost to celebrate the event; and the result was that the Fort presented a pleasant picture from the earliest hour in the morning. I have, in a previous letter, mentioned the Esplanade. On this morning it looked more beautiful than ever, a broad expanse of green grass, well covered with trees, intersected by a fine road, and approached by a magnificent street, shaded by wide-spreading banians. In the centre of the Esplanade is a tasteful statue of the Queen, and, for a wonder, the Decorating Committee had the good judgment not to improve it in any way. By night it would be lit up brilliantly; but by day it was neither bedecked with rosettes nor flags. The statue of the Queen, a splendid piece of sculpture in marble, was left alone, and, as a consequence, was an ornament, and not an eyesore. At the moment of our entering the Dockyard in order to take the places which were assigned us, the pathways were full of people, the seats in front of the houses were full, the windows were crammed, the space on the Esplanade was occupied, and that part of Bombay which is not aristocratic or official enough to be asked to the Dockyard, or to have a seat at club or office windows, sat down to see the Prince pass on the way to Parell.

As an artistic structure the Dockyard shed had undoubted merits; it was capacious, light, and airy. A great temporary building, thickly roofed, so that the rays of the sun cannot penetrate it, open at the sides so far as is compatible with excluding said rays in those directions also, and of course open at both ends, it was the very model of an Indian shelter. One end looked out upon the sea, where the "Serapis" lay at anchor, and several of the men-of-war were in position also; the other terminated in an archway of exceptional beauty. I have, in regard to the rest of Bombay, complained of a certain lack of ingenuity in respect of the triumphal arches and their mottoes. Here, however, was no ground for any such complaint. In broad, English, golden characters on crimson ground, was the word "Welcome;" on either side of this was an inscription in Persian and Hindostanee. And a pleasant thought it was which, in characters unintelligible to the English eye, but well understood by the natives, was thus portrayed. "Worlds of Welcome and Long Life," said the writer in gold upon crimson on this pretty arch, while on another a little way off he varied the phrase, and drew the characters which mean "A Thousand Welcomes to the Prince!" The interior of the shed was in keeping with this idea. Banners were hung everywhere, the seats were tastefully decorated with red cloth, banks of flowers rose in what would otherwise be vacant spaces, and the air was laden with perfume. Nor was there any scramble for place or precedence. Maharajah and Maharana, Guicowar and Hubshee, all had their seats. Councilmen and Councillors, Consuls and newspaper correspondents, had all their appointed positions, and sat quietly awaiting the advent of the Prince. On the right-hand side of the passage facing the town, sat the Guicowar of Baroda, covered with jewels and surrounded by attendants. In the next corner, half reclining, half leaning on his sword, was the Maharana of Oodeypore. Opposite His Highness Prince of Baroda, sat the Maharajah of Mysore, and separated by a tall flower-bush from him, was the Rajah of Kholapore. The other and less important chieftains, all clad in marvellous dresses, all glittering with jewels, and all accompanied by vast numbers of retainers, were in seats appointed for them, and waited with curiosity the arrival of the Prince.

They had not long to wait, for it was now 4 o'clock, and already a gun is fired. Let me draw the remarkable scene which follows as it actually appeared to me. The Viceroy and Governor of Bombay have severally boarded the "Serapis" and bid the Prince welcome; the yard-arms have been manned and the guns of the fleet discharged in honour of Lord Northbrook; and the cannonade will soon begin again, for His Royal Highness is about to land. Steadily looking through a glass, we can see the boats of the navy getting into line; we notice close by the "Serapis" a larger boat than the rest, with the Royal Standard at the stern, getting into position at the Royal gangway, and immediately afterwards, figures in red descending the steps. Still there is no firing, no noise, when the boats all start off in line, their oars dropping into the water and then glistening in the sun. As they come towards land, considerable excitement prevails in the shed. Political officers in their gold lace coats, Maharajahs and Rajahs in dresses of velvet and diamonds, Thakoors, sahebs, and chiefs are all standing up; the ladies, brilliantly dressed, are leaning forward; Parsees—one old gentleman has a most portentous-looking address under his arm—are gathering together; the troops for the last time have their arms at the "present." On the landing-stage the municipal corporation has gathered, and the Governor of Bombay, with his staff, is at the extreme end of the little pier. Onward come the boats, the oars flashing and dipping. As yet it is too early to see who are in them, and attention is once more directed to the interior of the shed. Then we notice that the Maharana of Oodeypore has a shield; that the Maharajah of Mysore has left all his diamonds at home, and only wears strings of pearls; that the Guicowar has brought all his brilliants with him; and that after all, Sir Salar Jung, in a black velvet dress, trimmed handsomely with gold lace, is by far the most important native present, so far as appearances go. Let it not be forgotten that there are notable Englishmen here also. See Sir Richard Meade in his full-dress uniform, as he stands holding the Guicowar's right-hand; notice Mr. Dalyel and Colonel Malleson, on either side of the Maharajah of Mysore; look at Colonel Herbert, with the Maharana of Oodeypore, and Mr. Crawford—he who built Bombay market, and made himself a name—with the Hubshee. These are all remarkable men, worthy of admiration, seeing that on such as these our Empire in the East depends. Nor should a curious row of native journalists be overlooked—gentlemen in turbans or Parsees' hats, starched, white petticoats or red dresses, some with boots, and some with no boots at all—the representatives of native opinion in India, all of them literary persons of merit, in their own estimation at least.

But, while you are looking at these, the Prince's boat is approaching the shore, and the band, which erewhile was playing a march, now ceases; for the cannonade has begun, and a tremendous din is being made, which would drown ten bands, or, indeed, a hundred. For a few minutes this thunder continues, and then, as it is silenced, "God save the Queen" is heard; the foremost boat touches the pier, the Prince springs to land, and a loud cheer arises—a cheer which is taken up on the sea, carried to the men who are on the yardarms of the vessels, and by them sent back again to the shore. It is a welcome fit for a Prince and worthy of a great Empire. Followed by Lord Alfred Paget, the Duke of Sutherland, Lord Carington, Canon Duckworth, Lord Aylesford, Colonel Owen Williams, and the less important members of his suite, accompained, moreover, by the Viceroy and the Governor of Bombay, the Prince passes the guard of honour, dressed in white, and only stops when he comes to the Parsee with the address. Then he makes signs of readiness; without delay the address is unfolded, and the Parsee begins. It is not so portentous as it looks, but is well written, being the handiwork work of W. Maclean, the editor of the "Bombay Gazette"; and it is short, which is, indeed, another undoubted merit. In general terms, it was an expression of welcome and an assurance of loyalty to the Crown. The Prince's reply follows, and is as short as the address. His Royal Highness acknowledges the loyalty of the people, and thanks them on behalf of the Queen. He notes what they say of religious and political freedom, and congratulates them and himself on the establishment of this freedom in England. Then, in reply to some kindly words, about the Princess of Wales, he remarks that she, too, would gladly have visited India, and concludes by expressing his determination to convey to the Queen the assurance of their good-will. This ends the speaking; the Prince at once moves forward, followed by his suite, and, as he passes along, shakes hands with each Maharajah and Rajah. Of course Sir Salar Jung is the first thus complimented, for he has the post of honour; the rest follow in order of precedence. And thus the door is reached, when his Royal Highness enters his carriage and drives away. Thus the streets are reached, and the crowds of people are treated to the sight of the Heir Apparent of England—a sight they acknowledge with loud and continued cheering.

CHAPTER V.

ROYAL FETES.

I shall always associate the illumination of Bombay with a singular sight which was witnessed in the very centre of the Mohammedan quarter on the following night. The Prince, having gone on board the "Serapis" to cut his birthday cake, was expected to land a little after six o'clock and drive round the town. In honour of the event the inhabitants, Mohammedan, Parsee, and Hindoo, had done their utmost to outvie each other. I have already stated that a characteristic trait of the native mind here is the intense love of glass and light. When in doubt as to the ornamentation of a room, the Hindoo hangs up a huge chandelier; if still in doubt, he adds another, till sometimes he gets eight or ten in an apartment which would be admirably lighted by a single gas jet. By this time he is perfectly happy. He may have no chairs and no table; the floor can take care of itself—a mat and a pillow are quite sufficient for that, but he is well satisfied if plenty of glass hides the ceiling. If he is very wealthy and very reckless, he makes another addition, which adds to the beauty of the apartment from his own point of view. From a dealer in the bazaar he purchases a large number of the cheap German portraits, some eighteen inches square, highly coloured and heavily framed and glazed, and at a distance of half a foot from the ceiling he hangs thirty or forty pictures of ladies with green hair and yellow lips, gentlemen with blue cheeks and pink eyes, with pride and satisfaction. He has no prejudice in the matter. He admires the portrait of the Pope as much as he does a likeness of the Emperor William, and he will put Napoleon III., Henri

Rochefort, and the Crown Prince of Prussia in a line without the slightest care. As a rule he does not know for whom the pictures are intended. That is not at all necessary. Like some of us at home, who have in our rooms "A Portrait of a Gentleman," he values them simply because they are plentifully painted, and because, when he lights up his chandeliers and sits on the floor, he can see the gas glittering in the glass.

Nor must it be assumed that he will rest here. If he chances to have a verandah—and most likely he has—he will hang a few chandeliers out there as well, with a dozen pictures or so of the Napoleon and Rochefort sort, so that his friends and acquaintances may admire his taste for art, and envy his possessions. And, besides all this, he will hang a lamp outside nearly every window, so that on festivals he can light them up too, and thus be happier than ever. Possessing such a taste, then, there is no need for wonder if he can illuminate when requested to do so. It is a labour of love—a pleasurable task, which he understands much better than hanging out bunting; and the way in which he proved this on the night of the illuminations has placed the matter beyond a doubt for the future. Bombay, however, is peculiarly fitted for such a display. Long, picturesque streets, composed of quaint, Oriental houses, with over-hanging gables, and gaudily-painted fronts of mosques, Hindoo temples ornamented with all kinds of images, shrines, churches, and noble public buildings abound—the genius of the people did the rest.

I question whether such a sight as that which met the Prince when he landed at the Mazagon pier and joined in the procession was ever seen before. It was not that he was in a gold and silver chariot of immense value. Nor was it that the troops drawn up in the fitful flashing glare appeared like giants. The real spectacle was the town and its inhabitants. The people thought the reverse, and gathered to gaze at the Prince; and the most wonderful sight of all was the populace. Wherever they could stand or sit they occupied a place. Wherever they could put a light they fixed one. Not garish stars, crowns, or flames of gas, but hundreds of thousands of tinted oil-lamps, burning with a subdued light, yet marking out every line of architecture in this extraordinary place. From the pavement, starting out from the people who sat thickly on the paths, rose pyramids and clouds of fire; the steps of public buildings were covered with myriads of glasses, all full of burning oil, fed by women, who with cans in their hands flitted hither and thither, and kept up the blaze. The great Government buildings were marked out in the same fashion along the roofs and the lines of windows, over the doors, and even to the tops of the roofs, without regard to trouble or cost; and if public places were thus radiant, the private dwelling-houses of the natives rivalled them with their chandeliers, lamps, and transparent devices.

It was one of these that I specially noticed, and it told more about the native character than volumes specially written could have said. Under a glittering canopy, closely packed together, with their best turbans on their heads and their finest linen robes, sat a cluster of Mohammedan patriarchs. Their childish glee was immense, and they waited with pardonable pride for the advent of the Prince. But it was not their delight or dress, nor, indeed, was it the arch under which they sat. High overhead, in great, square letters brilliantly lighted from behind and plain to view for nearly a quarter of a mile, was the inscription on which they had set their hearts. It was a quaint expression, one probably that will be read with a smile by the educated and refined people at home: but it was the heartfelt exclamation of these simple folk, and ran thus: "Tell mamma we're happy." No one that looked for a moment at the collection of ugly but contented faces under that archway could have had the slightest doubt that their transparency told the truth, and that in view of the visit of the Prince, the Mohammedans of Bombay are happy.

In Bombay the native is not only acknowledged as "a man and a brother," but he is a constant companion. You meet him at receptions; you tread on his shoeless toes at levées; you sit next to him in the councils; and if you chance to be an evil-doer, you may make his acquaintance, first of all, in the garb of a policeman, and, secondly, in the robe of a judge. He takes the chair at meetings, regulates your gas and water supply, probably stands toward you in the relation of a landlord, and occasionally in that of a creditor—in which latter case, I am told, he is a little less relenting than Portia, who, it will be remembered, first recited an ode to Mercy, and then pursued the misguided Shylock. But at the Byculla Club you only see him in the guise of a servant; he eats no dinner in the grand saloon; his residence is not in the chambers which skirt the racecourse; the American chairs in the reading-room are not for him; and if he were to venture to come there, he would probably meet with much such a reception as a stranger in the London Stock Exchange. Thus at the ball which the Byculla Club gave to the Prince of Wales next evening, the Parsee's ineffably ugly head-dress as well as the hideous turban of the Mahratta were alike absent.

A great many uncomfortable prognostications had been hazarded about that ball. The Prince would not come, there would be only seventy ladies to seven hundred gentlemen, nobody of any importance would be there; it would be a failure, and nothing else. But, to the confusion of the croakers and the delight of the club, all this was reversed. The Prince not only came, but danced nearly every time the band played; the ladies were very nearly equal in number to the gentlemen, the night was one of the merriest on record, and the whole thing was a grand success. The club deserved it. To make a supper-room they had erected a huge booth with palm leaves and canvas, and decorated it so beautifully with flowers that it resembled the garden which Aladdin saw when he found the lamp more than a temporary structure of a day's growth; and for the dancers the dining-hall of the club had been beautified without any regard to cost. Artificial fountains had been placed in adjoining rooms, leafy bowers constructed, and even a wall of ice blocks fixed behind these bowers, so that, when sitting in them, the heat of Bombay was forgotten, and the climate found to be that of the temperate zone.

I remember once hearing a lecture on dancing. The speaker was a melancholy man, whose chief objection to the diversion was that its votaries unconsciously waste a great amount of time in pursuit of what, after all, was an evanescent and unsatisfactory pleasure. What that unhappy person would have said of the Byculla ball, it is impossible to conceive. Whether it was the effect of a good, European, military band, or the novel fact of a large gathering of ladies, or the presence of the Prince, or the determination to maintain the character of the club, it is impossible to say. But, whatever was the cause, the hours were made to fly by with such extraordinary rapidity that when six o'clock came, they were still waltzing, regardless of daylight and the clock-hands alike. Did the Prince dance? Ask any lady in the room. Without favour of any kind, and determined only to give happiness to everybody present, his Royal Highness led first one and then another into the space reserved for himself and suite, till at last he ordered that even this restriction should be done away with, and to the amusement of poor old Sir Philip Wodehouse, who looked on with undisguised astonishment, galloped round the room as though he had lived in Bombay all his life, and was not the observed of all observers. How the various sets were formed it boots not to say. English readers would not recognise many names, and, indeed, would gain but little information if they did. Suffice it to say that all went off satisfactorily, that the supper was a great success, and that, when at length the dancing was over, the Byculla Club had to congratulate itself on having given one of the most admirable fêtes in Bombay.

But if the Byculla ball was a success, the Masons of Bombay can boast of having achieved something exactly the reverse. The first thought which strikes a stranger on arriving at this gate of India is one of amazement at the butter they offer you at table. How it can be made so nasty, by what ingenuity cream can be so terribly spoiled, and who first found out the way of producing such an unsavoury mess, are questions that occur to the mind in succession. So with the ceremony attendant on laying the foundation stone of the Elphinstone Dock, an incident on which the inhabitants of Bombay had set great expectations, one marvels how such a strange jumble could have been contrived. It was certainly not the result of lackadaisical managers. Everything was arranged with the precision of company drill. How the Europeans were to dress, what would be required of Parsee brothers, what Hindoos might not wear, and what was expected of Mahammedans, were all detailed with marvellous minuteness.

As to the programme, it was a document quite a yard in length, and explicit in every particular. Not only did it regulate the procession, but it provided for everything that it should do. Who were to carry drawn swords, and who wands; who should have the plans in his pocket, and who should carry the coins; where the visitors "of distinction" should walk, and where those who were not "of distinction" should come; who should bear the trowel, and who should mix the mortar, were all specified by name, with long strings of letters after their cognomens, and the designation of their lodges. Even the lowering of the stone was to be achieved, not to the lively tune of a waltz, not to some unconsidered air from Lecocq, nor even to a "song without words," though a Mendelssohn might have written it, but "to slow music." The very movements of the "brethren" who guarded the banners and the brethren who had no banners to guard, but wore aprons and sashes, were to be regulated by brethren who had long white wands, whose discretion might be relied upon. The prayer was ready, the address was written, the corn, wine, and oil were in their places, to be poured upon the stone at a certain stated moment, and even the "brethren" drawn up on either side of the carpet, upon which the Prince in entering would walk, had their toes in the exact position indicated, and their banners in the places signified by the instructions "in such case made and provided."

I will not trouble my readers with an account of the position occupied by the Grand Pursuivant, the Grand Zend-Avesta Bearer, the Grand District Chaplain, and the Ionic light. It is of more importance to know where the specially invited spectators were. Under a beautiful canopy, tastefully decorated and pleasantly ornamented with green foliage, tiers of seats were placed on either side the central avenue, all numbered and ticketed. Where the Rajah of Kholapore and where the Chief of Jumkundi should sit, how many followers the Khan of Jinjeera might bring with him—the gentleman who wears a gilt European chimney-pot head-dress upside down—and what was to be done with them, had all been arranged. When they came in, therefore—those of them that did come—they were taken to the seats apportioned to them, and placed there—not allowed to go nearer to the foundation stone or further from it, but fixed in the numbered seats, as though in the stalls at a theatre. At length a drum-and-fife band outside announced, by the nearest imitation to "God save the Queen" that it could devise on the spur of the moment, that the Prince had arrived, and then the regulations began to work. His Royal Highness was met at the door by what a local paper calls a "brilliant throng." It was a throng, certainly; of its brilliancy I am by no means so sure. If, however, sashes of an uncertain blue and collars of a dingy red constitute brilliancy, the gathering was what the newspaper called it, without doubt. Along the avenue formed by the brethren whose backs we had been contemplating, moved the procession—grand stewards, grand deacons, grand organists, grand bible-bearers, some scores of grand officers with sticks and banners, and all the implements of architecture on cushions. And behind all came the Prince of Wales, preceded by grand sword-bearers and a gentleman, who, whatever his technical name, should be called grand candle-bearer.

Proceeding to the throne, which was close to the foundation stone, the Prince sat down, and was immediately surrounded by the "brilliant throng" and the brethren who had kept the line. From that time we saw no more, except a long row of badly matched, and in many cases indifferently clothed, backs. The Rajahs are usually patient men when they come into contact with English officials. They will wait almost any length of time, walk almost any distance, and go in almost any order. But they could not stand the slight put upon them at the docks, and they quickly rose in a body and moved off. The backs of Parsee hats and European coats were, after all, not sufficiently interesting to detain them any longer. I am told that speeches were made; that an address was delivered to the Prince; and that his Royal Highness replied in the following terms:

"Right Worshipful, Worshipful, and other Brethren,—I thank you for your address. I have learnt with great pleasure the flourishing condition of the Craft in this part of India, and the efficiency with which lodges annually increasing in number fulfil the objects of their institution by uniting together men of various races and creeds in the bonds of fraternal brotherhood, by giving them common objects of exertion for extending the knowledge of our ancient Craft, and for promoting the good of all mankind. It is a great pleasure to me to join the brethren in Bombay in a work which will tend to the protection of life and property, to the extension of trade, and to add to the prosperity and happiness of large bodies of our fellow-men."

I was also informed that at length the stone was declared well and truly laid, but I cannot vouch for this. The continued view of five hundred and fifty-two backs was, after all, somewhat tedious.

I wish that those who would deprive our mariners of beer could have seen the sailors of the fleet at the entertainment which began before the Masonic festival, and lasted long after it was over. With that hospitality which is so characteristic of the Anglo-Indian, the people of Bombay had determined to feast the men of the fleet; and accordingly invited them—two thousand in number—to a great banquet in the booth where, on the day before, the children were fêted. I have already told you how the decorations of the booth were made in prison; how goldfoil and tinfoil flags were manufactured by the detained ones; how wreaths and garlands of artificial flowers were contrived, and how even great efforts in the way of painting were made. Would that the reader could have seen the berth when finished, with its avenues of palm leaves and its coloured festoons; the table spread with roast sucking-pigs, plum-puddings, ducks, fowls, great pieces of beef, and all the rest that the sailor loves. I have hinted that there was beer on the table, and so there was. By each plate stood a bottle of Bass' ale and a bottle of Guinness' stout—not tiny pint bottles, containing only a draught, but the large vessels of delight known as quarts. Besides this, there were pipes—clean, white clays—and cakes of tobacco, lemonade and seltzer water for the teetotallers, and an illuminated card as a souvenir of the festival. No wonder that as the bands played "Unita" the sailors and marines marched bravely in; no marvel that, to the tune of "The Roast Beef of Old England," they grasped their knives and forks with the air of determined men. I never saw food disappear with half the rapidity before. Sucking-pigs divided into quarters, fowls into halves, great heaps of salad filled every plate, and very soon every mouth too; and for a time there was a silence, only broken by the clatter of knives and forks. It was a moment of action, not talking, and the sailors knew it. Little need was there for their officers to walk up and down to encourage them to make themselves at home. They were quite at home, and for half an hour ate continually, unabashed by the crowd of ladies who looked on and envied their appetites.

But even sailors cannot eat forever, and at length the knives and forks were heard no more, although more pigs were on the table, and reinforcements of ducks were being brought up; the mariners were obliged to fall back upon their pipes and beer. This they did, and it was just in the midst of all this hilarity that the band played "God Save the Queen" and the Prince of Wales entered. Down went the pipes, up jumped the sailors, and out went such a cheer as was surely never heard in Bombay before. And then they ran for a form on which the Prince might stand and look at them, whereupon his Royal Highness jumped up in the most good-natured fashion possible, and, with a glass of lemonade in his hand, shouted out in a clear, strong voice: "My lads, I am very glad to see you. I hope you are all enjoying yourselves. I drink to the health and prosperity of the Indian and Flying Squadrons." It is superfluous to say that the sailors were excited. They cheered again and again, and would by no means sit down till his Royal Highness had gone the round of the tent and taken his departure in a carriage. Then the noise somewhat subsided; there was more smoking, and after that came singing.

One song almost deserves to be given, for it was the composition of a Jack Tar. It was sung by a Mr. Spry, the captain of the forecastle of the "Serapis," and capitally did he sing it. The tune was the well-known air of "God bless the Prince of Wales," and the men joined in the chorus, as though it were their very last opportunity.

"Look at your noble vessels in bunting dressed so gay;
The sight is grand, their yards well manned—yes, 'tis a glorious day.
And skimming o'er the water, like birds upon the wing,
Are boats, brave hearts containing, to greet their future king."

CHORUS: "Come, all ye British seamen; with shouts the air shall ring;
Three loud huzzas, my hearty tars, for England's future king."

"Long may such cries of welcome be heard from India's shore!
May Heaven pour down on England's crown its blessings evermore!
Our tars upon the ocean, long may their pennant wave,
Our troops maintain their glorious name—the bravest of the brave."

Chorus, &c.

When this was done, the band played polkas, and the sailors danced on the green, with the tinfoil flags in their caps and green leaves in their button-holes; and in this way the festivities were kept up long after the moon had replaced the sun, and lit up the scene with silvery in place of golden rays.

As a country noted for struggles and battles, India may, I think, fairly claim to hold its own from time immemorial, and it has now another battle to add to its abnormally lengthy roll. It had been announced that "the first Royal levée ever held in this country" would take place at the Secretariat. Those who wished to be presented to the Prince were to send in their names; those who were selected went, of course, in full dress. Of the three thousand or so who desired to come a third received tickets, and prepared to go. Now, full dress meant a singular variety of costumes. To the Parsee it signified wide-spreading starched petticoats; to the Hindoo a white dress with less starch; to the military man full uniform, sword and spurs; to the civilian Court dress or the claw-hammer coat. I am particular in specifying the swords and spurs, as they were destined to play an important part in the day's proceedings. I have mentioned the dress of the Parsees and Hindoos for a similar reason. The Secretariat is outwardly a fine, handsome building. Inside, too, it has a vast number of rooms, in which native clerks and European officials transact the business of the Presidency with more or less despatch. But it is not fitted for a levée, especially when a thousand persons are invited to "assist" thereat. The afternoon was terribly hot; scarcely the faintest breeze came from the sea, when the crowd in "full dress" arrived at the Secretariat.

To make the position clear to the English reader, it is necessary to say that a daïs had been erected at the side of one room, and that it had been arranged that the Prince, accompanied by his suite, should occupy this, while the happy holders of cards marched by and bowed. To prevent anything like a rush into the Royal presence, the room immediately leading into the reception-saloon had been very judiciously divided into several compartments by stout barriers, over which policemen kept guard. But similar precautions were not taken with regard to the library which preceded this—the room into which the card-holders were shown. Here was an apartment capable of holding a hundred people without serious discomfort on a moderately cool day, say for ten minutes. In such a case no particular discomfiture need have been experienced. But here was a broiling day, the hottest to which Bombay has been treated for some time, and by way of making amends for this additional inconvenience the crowd, as it arrived, was allowed to press into the room without let or hindrance. It is almost needless to say, that in a very few minutes the place was so full that not another individual could gain foothold, and that the result was a very pretty and instructive scene. I omitted to mention that special directions had been given to the invited to be at the Secretariat very early. Let me now add that by some misunderstanding or other the Prince came very late, and the situation will be understood.

In that heated room four hundred persons were crushed together with all the force that as many more coming up the staircase could employ; and for half-an-hour this state of things continued without relief. But it was when the first barrier at length opened, and a dozen or so of the perspiring courtiers were admitted, that the fun began. No sooner did the barrier rise for an instant than a rush took place from all sides of the room, the converging force of the crowd bearing upon the unfortunate ones in the centre. For a few minutes Parsees, Hindoos, and Englishmen were pushing alike with all their might. But presently there was a movement for which I could not account. The natives appeared to be directing their efforts to getting away from the military men, of whom there were scores in the crowd, rather than to reaching the barrier. There was a stout Parsee with his hat on the very back of his head, making a series of grimaces for which no mere pressure could account; there was a grim smile on the faces of officers which could scarcely be caused by the crush and the fray. Was it the full dress that had done it? Yes; those military men wore spurs, and the Parsee dress was thin. Need I say more? What the hard sword-handle failed to effect—and that was a powerful agent in persuading neighbouring natives to move a little further off—the spur achieved with ease. No Parsee would venture to place his unprotected ankle against the uncomfortable appanage of the soldiers' full-dress, but struggled hard to place a trousered European between himself and the warriors; so the crowd swayed backward and forward; coat-tails were torn off; cravats and collars became limp; starched gowns were tangled and rent; and in the end the steaming, rumpled crowd passed by the Prince in a dishevelled, disreputable condition, such as might be expected of men, who, for nearly an hour, had been mangled in such a throng on such a day.

Once in the reception-hall, however, everything was well arranged. To the right of the Prince stood Sir Philip Wodehouse; on the left of his Royal Highness were the Duke of Sutherland, Lord Alfred Paget, and Lord Charles Beresford, all in uniform. Behind them were ranged the Government servants, attired in scarlet coats, and wearing turbans of white and gold. These took it by turns to wave the huge gilt punkahs, or fans attached to the ceiling, and so stirred the air, and rendered the heat less oppressive than it would otherwise have been. As for the Prince, it is almost needless to say that he received those who were presented, pleasantly, bowing gracefully to them as they went by, and now and then bestowing some particular mark of approbation upon well-known and honoured members of the community.

Immediately after the levée the Prince was conducted to a wide-stretching piece of grass-land near the Esplanade, where some thousands of the children of Bombay were being feasted and amused. It is impossible to imagine a prettier sight than that which these little ones presented. A huge bower of leaves and coloured bunting, divided into compartments in such a manner as to resemble a miniature forest, had been erected for them, and inside this the children had been treated to tea, ices, fruit, and cakes. By the time the Prince arrived, however, they had all left the booth and taken up their position in long lines opposite a kind of stand erected for the reception of his Royal Highness, and here they patiently waited the coming of the Prince. The great characteristic of a Bombay crowd is the variety of colour which is massed together, and in the case of the children this was especially noticeable. Nearly all the Parsee boys wore gold or silver caps, black velvet jackets trimmed with gold lace, and little silken knickerbockers of various hues. The girls had light shawls over their heads—cerise, light blue, bright green, yellow, pink, purple, and white being the most common. The effect was exceedingly striking, and could not have been produced in any other country. Suddenly a signal was given, and all the little ones jumped up and began to cheer. Simultaneously the carriage of the Prince, escorted by a body-guard of Dragoons, entered the enclosure, and hastened up to the stand. Without any delay his Royal Highness alighted, mounted to the place assigned to him, and bowed repeatedly to his tiny admirers, who testified in every possible way their delight at thus seeing the Prince. But, if they cheered when he thus bowed to them and smiled, their voices rose to the shrillest pitch when a pretty Parsee girl, stepping lightly up to his Royal Highness, made him a deep curtsey, and then threw a garland of white flowers over his neck. They jumped on the forms and waved their hands; they shouted, and stamped, and clapped their hands together, and danced for very joy at thus seeing the distinguished stranger accepting their gift, and actually standing in front of them with the garland on. A moment later, another little girl ran up the steps of the stage and presented the Prince with a bouquet of flowers; whereat the children cheered again.

But the ceremony of the evening, so far as the little ones were concerned, was yet to come. A lane was formed in front of the stand, and thither a number of pretty girls and boys were conducted. Then, amid perfect silence, these young people struck up a song in Guzerathi in honour of the Prince. First, the girls would sing, clapping their hands together now and then in a rhythmical manner; then the boys would reply, and presently all would join in a strange chorus. Sometimes their song was low, almost in a whisper; then they would shout out with all their might, and make the air ring again. Perhaps their chant was a little long, and, to those who could not understand it, a little tedious; but his Royal Highness looked graciously on, and, when it was finished, thanked his little admirers, and so drove away amidst more cheering than ever. These were the words of the song:

"All hail to thee! most noble Prince; this day
To thee in song we would our homage pay;
Though far away thy mother's splendour streams,
These distant realms are gladdened by the beams,
When thou, her empire's heir, our Prince, art found
Here, in our midst, upon the Indian ground,
While all the nation rises up to greet

> Our Royal guest. But for a welcome meet
> What can we render but our loyal love,
> And hope that all thy life may noble prove!"

As the sun was setting, fireworks were sent up for the amusement of the little singers and their companions, and then they dispersed.

Perhaps the most enjoyable fête at which his Royal Highness was present in or about Bombay was the visit to the Caves of Elephanta. It had been previously announced that the trip would take place at evening, that the caves would be illuminated, that the fleet would be lighted up, that fireworks would be let off, and that a pic-nic would take place; and to gain invitations half Bombay excited itself. They would have given up the receptions, their seats at the dock stone-laying ceremony, and even sacrificed their tickets for the Masonic ball, for the sake of the Elephanta Caves and its delights. But it was all to no purpose—only 160 were invited, and these started from the Apollo pier. It was a particularly bright afternoon when we assembled on the pier, ready to embark on board one of the three steamers which were in waiting for passengers. The ships in the harbour were gay with bunting; over the purple hills which skirt the water could be seen a dark blue sky of which you have no idea in England; the sun's rays danced merrily on the waves; while, through the crevices in the rocks, where light did not penetrate so readily, and which thus enabled the eye to overcome the glare, could be seen the round moon rising. A few more minutes and we were all on board; a very few minutes later and the sun had suddenly disappeared below the horizon.

There are certain sights which remain impressed on the mind; such a one shortly presented itself to us who were bound for the Elephanta Caves. Let me say that these caves are situated in the centre of a huge hill which rises abruptly from an island, and may be seen for miles. All over the sides of the hill is jungle—thick, impassable bush: rumour says, full of snakes—a grand spot being left here and there for those who love pick-nicking and a day in the wild parts of the island. To reach the temple or cave in which the Hindoos many years ago worshipped, it is necessary to ascend a long flight of stone steps; and here it was that the ingenuity of those whose business it was to arrange the fête had first exerted itself. All along these steps, reaching nearly to the top of the mountain, were brilliant lines of light, thousands of tiny lamps suspended from arched supports all along the line of passage, right up to the very mouth of the caves. It is needless to say that we greatly admired all this, and were not long in going up the ascent, and ranging ourselves in lines, in order that the Prince might pass through to the banqueting-hall; for the caves were arranged for a banquet of no unimportant character—not a mere "snack" of refreshment, but a substantial repast, such as people need at six in the evening who have come a considerable distance on the sea. When his Royal Highness came the band struck up merrily, the guests went to their places, and the feast began.

The native religion and the native temple may ordinarily be dark, but we certainly had light enough. From the rocky ceiling hung large chandeliers; from the floor rose pyramids of light in the shape of devices in lanterns; the daïs on which the Prince sat was glittering with wax candles, and even the smaller caves, which boasted curious histories, were illuminated in like manner. It is unnecessary to detail the banquet; and as for the speech, it was comprised in a single sentence by Sir Philip Wodehouse, who murmured: "Gentlemen, I propose the health of 'The Queen,'" and then sat down; whereupon the Prince rose, and departed to view the caves, the company following. A short inspection sufficed, and the steamers were quickly filled in anticipation of the return voyage. A few minutes effected a start, and then one of the finest pyrotechnic displays ever seen was witnessed. On the top of the hill rose a great blaze; down the steps the light of the lamps was changed successively from white to red, blue, and green; the line of fire was continued to the water's edge, and even blazed brightly on the water. It was a volcanic mountain in eruption, with the huge crater in full play and the red-hot lava running down the sides. And as for the ships in the harbour, they suddenly sprang into light, too, and from stem to stern, from yardarm to yardarm, from masthead to boom-point, blazed with illumination. As the Royal steamer and those containing the guests passed between the lines of men-of-war, blue portfires were burned, thousands of rockets went up, and altogether the energy of the sailors was so great and the supply of rockets so plentiful, that one might readily have imagined a great naval action to be taking place, or have supposed that the bombardment of Bombay was in full swing. We moved along quickly, wondering greatly at the grand display, but perhaps a little glad to be out of reach of the falling sticks, till we reached the Apollo Bunder, and there searched till after midnight for carriages that had strayed or drivers who had gone.

Of minor incidents there were many—the visits paid by the chiefs and the return visits to the chief, the receptions at Government House, Parell, and the Masonic ball on Thursday night, all aiding to fill up the time which remained after the major ceremonies had been arranged.

Up to this time the Prince had not given away any of his fire-engines or organs. Whom they were intended for remained yet to be seen; books, swords, and rifles mainly representing his Royal Highness' gifts up to this period. Of course these gifts were selected with a view of suiting the particular tastes and needs of the recipients. Thus the Rajah of Kholapore, aged fourteen, hed a gold snuff-box, with the Prince's monogram on the outside of the lid, a silver medal commemorative of the visit, a large sword, and some English books of pictures. The Maharajah of Oodeypore, aged eighteen, got a snuff-box, a book of English coronation ceremonials, a sword, a rifle, a medal, and a riding-whip. The Guicowar, aged nine, received a particularly large snuff-box, a sword longer than he is tall, an album of photographs, a book of engravings, a medal, and a watch and chain. A very irreverent person suggested that a handsome whistle, a top, and a box of the best building bricks would have been more suitable; but he was very properly suppressed. Somehow or other, the Nizam of Hyderabad's representative received no snuff-box, but in place of that got, for his Royal but youthful master, a huge silver flagon of the time of Marlborough (teetotallers mark that!), three rifles, a ring, some "valuable" books, and a scabbard belt. The Maharajah of Mysore, who has nearly reached the mature age of fourteen, found himself the proud possessor of a snuff-box, a silver flagon—also of Marlborough's time—a sword and scabbard belt, three books ("valuable," of course), a riding whip, and a pair of field-glasses—at which extraordinary miscellaneous assortment his Highness seemed somewhat amazed.

The presents made to the Prince already would fill a large museum admirably. Daggers, Cutchee guns, tea-services, rhinoceros-hide shields, swords, lances, glass, necklaces, anklets, bracelets, shawls, carpets, ancient guns, suits of armour, jewels, and cups only represented part of the things—they were almost as diversified as the selection the Prince's advisers made, and almost as useless. A white elephant, a mangoose, a box of snakes would complete the collection.

CHAPTER VI.

LIFE IN POONA.

How the Prince was received at Poona, how he listened to an address and made a suitable reply, and how he afterwards drove to the Government House, which is called Gunnesh Khind, and then gave a ball, needs no description. I propose, however, to give you some idea of what kind of place it was which his Royal Highness visited, and how the time was spent.

Poona is, without doubt, a lovely city. High up among the hills, some three thousand feet above the level of the sea, though actually situated on a wide plain or expanse of table-land, it is refreshed by brisk breezes, which greatly temper the heat of the sun. If the days are sultry the evenings are cool; even when the sun is highest there is a shade under the wide-spreading trees which fill its gardens and overhang its roads. Its houses—I refer, of course, to those occupied by Europeans —are half hidden by the foliage of plantain, mango, fig, and tamarind. Beautiful shrubs with bright scarlet leaves, roses by thousands, and myriads of convolvuli are on every hand, and even the hedges of prickly pear lend their own, wild grace to complete the scene. Such a place needed but little decoration. It was like attempting to ornament a conservatory; and this the good people of Poona saw, and very wisely noted. No festoons of artificial flowers, therefore, spanned the road, no mimic branches of palm were made into imitation bowers. Triumphal arches there were, but they were in keeping with the idea of an Eastern city, and one was especially worthy of notice. A light, semi-circular structure spanned the road. Its centre was a huge glass square, surmounted by a dome, such as you see at the top of every mosque. On either side this was supported by another glass square and four minarets. The whole was coloured a rich blue, and then further ornamented with gold and silver leaf. On the lower part of the arch itself was written in Persian, "A thousand welcomes to the Prince," also in letters of gold; flags hung from Venetian masts at its sides, the whole being flanked by large trees covered with great, green leaves.

But, if no paper roses or linen lilies decorated the road, the place had been made to assume a very holiday-like appearance; for from the branches of the trees were suspended many thousands of Chinese lanterns, like brilliantly-painted fruit; from the pathway rose pyramidal stands for the support of lamps and glasses, and wherever colour could lend its aid it was enlisted in the work. Leaving all this pleasant view behind, the cool bungalows in their luxurious retreats, the splendid trees, and the well-built arches, I drove into the native quarter, which was preparing, in its way, too, to receive the Prince. Poona European, Poona fashionable, may change every day. Wealthy Parsees from Bombay, well-paid civilians, strangers and sojourners though they may be in the land, will come up and build new houses, enclose new gardens, and decorate new bungalows, and the face of Poona where Englishmen live will alter continually. Native Poona, the city that was captured by the English half a century ago, is the same forever. If it existed in the time of Abraham, it was much in the same condition then as now—the manners of the people and their dwelling-places, their temples and their bazaar.

I thought it would be interesting to see whether these ancient streets and thoroughfares had any welcome for the Prince, or whether the inhabitants, having come out into the high road and stared their fill, had gone back to undecorated homes to forget all about the great Sahib who had just made his entry. My first glance augured badly. In the street upon which I came a temple was open, the people were pouring in, a priest was outside inviting worshippers to enter, and a band of four tomtoms and five reed-pipes was making a terrible din. The only decoration visible was a painting upon a wall representing the goddess Parbuttee with four arms and a spear, seated in a chariot mounted on five wheels, killing a tiger with seven legs, a blue head, and a red tail. As a work of art it was incomparable, but from the loyal point of view it was just then worthless. Parbuttee may have been the dread of tigers of this description, and very properly so too; but the pictorial record of her killing them had nothing to do with the entry of the Prince of Wales. My disappointment was but momentary. A corner turned, another street entered, the line of route which the Prince must take if he wished to touch upon the bazaar, and the decorations sprang up on every side.

Pray do not imagine for a moment that gilded trophies of art or massive archways of highly-decorated and well-stretched canvas were numerous, or that Defries had been called in and given unlimited instructions to decorate the place according to his latest designs. There were flags; but they were mostly of the pocket-handkerchief size, and in many cases were actually small pocket-handkerchiefs; there were triumphal arches, but they were generally composed of three very rough scaffold-poles, a couple of sheets, and a pendant portrait of his Royal Highness as sold in Germany for half a thaler. Festoons and wreaths were there; but nothing half so funny had ever been seen before. Decorations were made with ragged blankets, strips of red cloth, pieces of coloured paper, and old curtains, at which the tiniest English boy would have laughed, had he seen them; and altogether the decorations of the streets, setting aside the lamps for the illuminations, which were very numerous, could scarcely have been worth many shillings. Yet, worthless as were the materials, these simple offerings of loyalty were more valuable than many a splendid monument in the outer town. No wealthy

Parsee dependent on the continuance of British rule for very existence had supplied these decorations; no rich civilian, drawing high pay from Government, had paid for these flags. They were the freewill-offering of a well-governed, satisfied, happy people—the once conquered but now loyal Mahrattas; the once formidable but now friendly Mohammedans and Hindoos. They did not cheer a great deal when they saw the Prince; the reception they gave him was cordial, though not enthusiastic; but they went away to their homes and testified that they were glad to see him by doing what they could to make their hovels and temples, their tanks and their shops, look pleasant, in case his carriage should chance to drive that way during his stay in Poona.

It was about three o'clock on the Sunday afternoon when I drove from Poona to the hill and temple of Parbuttee. On the road some scores of pilgrims, carrying flowers, bags of rice, and in some cases little bags of money, were toiling along in the direction of the sacred staircase and the shrine of Shiva. Some were walking; a party of five had chosen camels as a means of transit; one gentleman, who, by the way, presently said one of the longest prayers on record, was going on a bullock; and three or four were moving along on their knees. These last appeared to be very holy men, for their hair was very long, their faces were very dirty, and their costume, to use the mildest term, was insufficient. At length we reached the foot of the staircase which leads to the top of the sacred hill. This celebrated temple, perched as it is on the top of an eminence overlooking a vast champain, with its towers, walls, and steps, reminded me very much of Windsor Castle.

After some toil the summit was reached, and a man whose head was clean shaven, all but a small top-knot, introduced himself as the second priest. The chief, who was eighty or thereabouts, was just then engaged in counting the rupees, annas, and pice which the faithful had brought during the day,

THE ASCENT TO THE TEMPLE OF PARBUTTEE, NEAR POONA.

and mentally apportioning the sum he had to divide. The collection of coins appeared valuable; and, when this old teacher and priest did presently condescend to speak, it was money that formed his principal topic. Not so the priest who volunteered to conduct me through the temple. "I'm a Brahmin," he remarked, "and a priest here. I dare say you wonder," he continued, "at the way I speak English. There is no need for wonder. I was educated at the Deccan College in Poona." Educated he certainly had been, for his diction was as good as that of most Englishmen. "Yes," he said, as we entered the shrine, "education is a good thing. It expands the mind. There's the god of learning, you see" (pointing to an extraordinary image with ever so many animals' heads). "And there," continued the educated man, directing his index-finger towards another indescribable figure, "is the god of light." "Do you think the Prince will come here?" enquired the priest, as we mounted another short flight of steps, and looked out of the window from which the last Peshwa watched the defeat of his troops in the battle of Khirkee; "because, if he does, I dare say he'll make us a nice present. What with illuminating the place last night and white-washing it throughout, I've spent a good deal of money. The Governor of Bombay came and gave us 80 rupees, the Viceroy sent a letter with 120 rupees in notes the day after he came, and I think his Royal Highness would behave handsomely. I certainly hope he will come."

It was a singular picture which presented itself at this moment. Over the plain, in the centre of which Poona lay, half hidden by the trees, could be seen still coming, worshippers by the hundred. At the very moment when the bells in the shrine were tinkling in honour of Shiva, the bells in the church steeples of Poona were ringing the Sunday chime; and the worshippers of the Genius of Destruction were passing on their way to their devotions, the Votaries of the Genius of Love. I enquired how many pilgrims visited the shrine, and learned about 2,000 a day was the usual number. Moreover, I found that eighty priests live on the corn, wine, and oil that the devout bring thither, and that, to enable them to eke out their religious existence, Government grants the temple an annual subsidy, which was till lately 30,000 rupees, but is now 24,000. "Everybody that comes here gives something," thoughtfully remarked the priest as I turned to go, and he held out a box, in which I deposited a rupee; whereupon a horrible crew of deformed ones followed me down the steps uttering loud cries for relief, and a score of children whose knowledge of English was confined to "Sahib, give," continued the chase for a quarter of a mile.

Next morning, a little before eight o'clock, the Prince, accompanied by his suite, rode to Parbuttee, and visited the shrine. Breakfast was provided by Sir Philip Wodehouse at the foot of the steps, and there were actually elephants ready to convey his Royal Highness up the ascent; with such aid, the Prince at length stood on the summit, and looked at the shrine. The educated Brahmin was there, and did the honours of the place with due form; and in the end he got the anticipated present from the Prince in the shape of a large bag of rupees (200, I believe), which he afterwards shared with the amiable old gentleman whose peculiar province appeared to be the care of money and valuables.

The review at Poona was a decided success. By four o'clock in the afternoon the troops were on the ground. The site chosen was the race-course, a few miles from the spot where the celebrated battle of Khirkee, which decided the fate of the Mahratta nation, was fought. Over the very ground on which the 1st Division of the Bombay Army now stood, Mahratta cavalry were wont to manœuvre daily, and, as though the intention was to show the difference between the old order of things and the new, not a single horseman, except the few who kept the ground, was placed on parade. Let us look at the picture which is presented for the Prince's inspection by the troops under that admirable soldier, Lord Mark Kerr.

In the centre of a plain, surrounded by hills, are two long lines of infantry soldiers, flanked on either side by artillery. Nearer inspection shows these foot-soldiers to comprise seven battalions of native infantry and two English battalions. The white men, belonging to the 7th Fusiliers and the 15th of the Line, comprise the right wing; the 1st Bombay Grenadiers, distinguishable by their red caps, are in the centre; while on the left are the rest of the native regiments, dressed similarly to English troops, save that in place of the helmet they wear a white puggaree. They are drawn up in close order; the guns, on the right, are ready to salute the Royal party when it shall arrive; and Lord Mark Kerr, with his suite, as general of the division, is the centre, just in front of the band.

To see the pleasant show the Mahrattas of all the country round, to say nothing of Poona itself, have come in many thousands, and, as is their wont on such occasions, are squatted on their haunches, and are chattering with all the glee of children. There is little need of the policemen with whips to keep them in order; they are far too deeply interested in the spectacle to be troublesome, as their simple faces and clasped hands clearly indicate. Besides, they have on their very best turbans, and the starchiest of white gowns they can boast—to say nothing of the fact that every papa amongst them has brought all his sons, and that hundreds of these little people are seated with their elders, munching sugar-cane and plantains, and adding their share to the general hubbub. Up in the grand stand the *élite* of the town are perched—the collectors, revenue officers, officials of all kinds, and military men, together with ladies whose brilliant dresses add to the picturesqueness of the scene. Then there is just such a long line of carriages as one sees on a fashionable race-course in England, extending to a great distance, and constituting altogether a very creditable turn-out for an Indian city.

Presently, Sir Charles Staveley, who is just now Commander-in-chief of the Bombay Army, comes upon the ground, and rides about as nervously as he used to do in the days at Aldershot, when he was trying to discover the whereabouts of Carey and Lysons. Sir Charles Staveley has very good reason to be anxious, for time is flying, and there is no sign of the Prince. At last an orderly gallops across the ground, waves his hand to the artillery, and the guns on the left begin to fire the Royal salute. A minute later the Prince arrives, followed by his suite, and, preceded by General Mark Kerr, at once gallops over to the artillery and begins an inspection of the line. All of a sudden a horse is seen to rear and throw its rider. The animal dashes across the plain, and is making for the crowd, when a native officer rushes pluckily up and stops it. He has scarcely done so before a rider is seen spurring his charger towards the grand stand, calling for a surgeon. "Somebody's hurt; who can it be?" is the question anxiously asked, and field glasses are turned towards the Royal party, whither the doctor is making his way. Then it is seen that Lord Charles Beresford is being lifted into a palanquin, and that he is insensible. The Prince must needs go on and inspect the troops; but the sufferer is left in very good hands, and is slowly brought up to the grand stand, where a carriage is procured and waits for him. Dr. Fayrer and Dr. Close lift their charge very carefully into the carriage, and, on examining him, find that, though shaken, he is after all not seriously hurt. They give him a glass of champagne, which so revives him that he forthwith takes a cigar, and is conveyed home.

Meanwhile the troops are forming up on the left, the Prince has returned to the flagstaff, and the artillery are coming past at a walk. Steadily, in half-batteries, well-trained and with admirable precision, these famous gunners go by, the spectators applauding their soldierly appearance. Following them, come the men of the 7th, the band playing a capital march and the troops stepping out admirably. They are followed by the 1st Bombay Grenadiers, whom we just now saw in line—a fine battalion, well drilled, dressing well, and going by in grand divisions almost as steadily as the European regiment which preceded it. Three more battalions of native infantry follow, also in grand divisions, and also in good order. This closes the first brigade, and the second is not far behind. But just at this moment there is a snort, and at a terrific pace, with a terrified man on his back, another horse shoots across the plain, and darting through the Prince's suite, only clearing the Prince by about a yard, dashes in amongst the crowd. To all appearance there must be great loss of life, for the people cannot get away, closed in as they are by carriages, when it is seen that a mounted officer has stopped horse and rider by a swift jerk, and prevented what threatened to be a fearful disaster. All this is done in much less time than it takes to tell, and the Australian horse is in safe keeping side by side with the animal which threw Lord Charles Beresford. The troops having gone by are now re-formed, and come past again in close column of battalions, the artillery rattling along at a quick trot and keeping good time. Just as it is getting dusk, the whole are brought into line again and advance, the bands play "God save the Queen," the troops present arms, the review is over, and the Royal party leave the ground.

Immediately Poona is in a blaze of illumination and pyrotechnic display. Rockets spring up in every direction, set pieces appear suddenly on the right hand and the left, coloured lights are burned, and all kinds of fireworks splutter and bang, while the happy Mahrattas in long strings, hand in hand, walk about incessantly, and forget all their fancied troubles. "They have been a good deal excited," said a political agent who chanced to be at Poona, "about the Mulhar Rao affair lately; but these fireworks will overcome all that." I think he was right.

CHAPTER VII.

GAMES AND SPORTS AT BARODA.

The Prince was well received at Baroda. The scene which presented itself at the railway station the morning he arrived was in keeping with his previous receptions.

The city of Baroda proper lies far from the embodiment of science which we owe to George Stephenson. The inhabitants are as singular in their costume, and I should say as objectionable in their habits, as they were when tea-kettles, to say nothing of steam engines, had yet to be invented. And as the railway has not, for manifest reasons, come to them—that is to say, to their very doors—they have declined to come in their corporate capacity to the railway. Individually they come by thousands; but they have not extended their buildings nor enlarged their borders so as to embrace the line and its belongings. Three tradesmen, more enterprising than the rest of their countrymen, have established shops at which stores to the value of about eighteenpence are regularly kept. But, beyond this, the unsoaped, semi-nude native prefers the bazaar to the open country road, and sits quite contentedly there, far from steam-whistles or the noise of railway-trucks. As a consequence, there is a fine open space in front of the station, fringed with pretty Eastern trees, amongst which figure three or four palms, plenty of banyan and plantain trees, and a goodly number of large-leaved and heavy-foliaged specimens such as can only be found in a climate like this.

With a view to watching somewhat closely the behaviour of the people on the occasion of his Royal Highness' entry, I started for Baroda on the day previous to the Prince's visit.

Through the kindness of Sir Madava Rao, the distinguished Prime Minister of Baroda, a resting-place had been prepared for me—no small boon in a district which is innocent of hostelries and knows nothing of inns. By some mischance, however, I missed the carriage that was sent to me, and as a result made my first acquaintance with the eccentric vehicle known as the Baroda bullock-gharry immediately upon my arrival. It has always been my practice to "speak well of the bridge that carries me over." But the Baroda bridge, or, rather, Baroda bullock-carriage, must be the exception, and prove the rule. I will not attempt to describe that doleful ride; yet it was in the progress of this experience that I saw first the preparations which were being made to receive the Prince. Thousands of natives were hard at work all along the line of route from the railway station to the British Residency, also outside the town. Triumphal arches—notwithstanding that Mr. Hill, the resident chief engineer, had only received a few hours' notice—were springing up as rapidly as though it had been the sole business of his life to construct ornamental spans of leaves and bunting, instead of building excellent roads and bridges. On either side of the road were miniature arches and festoons of green leaves. Flags, too, made literally on the spot—for they were being cut out on the roadside by Mahratta workmen—were being hung, and places arranged for Chinese lanterns and the little lamps with which it is the practice to illuminate here. It must be remembered, too, that if the very situation of Baroda, which is placed in a lovely grove of trees, aided in the work, no cunning contractor with tons of material was at hand to command the thousands of labourers and furnish them with carefully planned and elaborately prepared devices. On the contrary, all had to be done in a day, with whatever was ready to hand; and if the Prince congratulated Mr. Hill on arrival, and expressed surprise, as he did, it was no more than the merest justice to a most energetic and ingenious man. Suffice it to say that, when the eventful morning arrived, Baroda was fit to receive a King.

It is not of the decorations that there is need now to speak; it was the spectacle which Sir Madava Rao had, with characteristic ability, prepared for his Royal Highness. "I will show the Prince," said the amiable Premier, "a sight such as he will not see anywhere else in India," as we stood on the railway-station steps and looked upon the space in front. And certainly the picture presented was perfect. Drawn in a long line exactly in front was a regiment of the Guicowar's infantry, neatly attired in buff. Behind them, in uniforms of light blue, with light blue turbans and long, shining, pennon-supporting lances, were the Guicowar's cavalry. All round were natives by thousands, in costumes of every kind and colour. In the centre of the square were, however, the chief figures of the scene, for there fifteen magnificent elephants, splendidly housed and caparisoned, stood side by side. Every elephant was painted all over with some bright pigment—light yellow, light blue, light red, light green. On the forehead and down the front of the trunk were painted devices of most intricate description, singularly clever and curiously effective. I have said that they carried their housings and trappings. The howdah on the elephant which was to carry the Prince was of fine gold, in value worth forty thousand sovereigns. Cloth-of-gold hung down his sides, anklets of gold were round his legs—even his tail was ornamented; his ears were brilliantly painted, and his tusks were encircled with huge rings of red-coloured ivory. As for the other elephants, they, too, had valuable seats for their riders, railed cars of silver fixed on silver cloth, fastened in their places with silver buckles.

Presently the Guicowar drove up in a pretty, little carriage, made wholly of silver and gold—a work of art, indeed, such as can hardly be surpassed—and on his arrival he was received with the English National Anthem by the band, with "present arms" by the soldiers, and a vast amount of bowing from the crowd. His retainers, the chiefs and sirdars of the kingdom, in number nearly a hundred, ranged up in two lines a little lower down the road than the place where the elephants stood. Suddenly a number of fog-signals, which had been placed upon the line for the purpose of indicating the approach of the Royal train, were fired, whereupon the two companies of the 83rd regiment of English troops, drawn up on the platform, presented arms. The Resident of the Station, the Assistant Resident, the English officers, and the officials of the place, stood round the Guicowar and Sir Madava Rao, and the band struck up "God save the Queen." As the engine approached the Prince was seen standing outside the saloon carriage, looking on the platform with evident interest, and, as soon as the train stopped, his Royal Highness descended and shook hands warmly first with the Guicowar and then with the Premier.

Sitting down on a couch, the Prince conversed for some minutes with his Highness, who afterwards led him outside the station, where the elephant with the golden howdah was kneeling. Taking the Prince of Wales by the right hand, the little Guicowar asked him to ascend the ladder to the howdah, which, albeit that the elephant was kneeling, was yet six or seven feet from the ground. To this the Prince assented, and, being followed by the Guicowar and Sir Madava Rao, was hoisted into the air, and so sat high above everybody, on the right of the youthful ruler of Baroda. The staff of the Prince followed, four sitting in each howdah, till all were in their places, whereupon a procession was formed of javelin men, banner-bearers on horseback, chieftains, hussars, irregular cavalry, Royal Artillery, and the elephants, the whole being brought up in the rear by the Guicowar's soldiery. Slowly moving along, the Prince passed by the gates of the city towards the cantonments, where, under Colonel Thompson, the Brigadier of the district, and a distinguished officer, the excellent native 9th and 22nd infantry regiments were found drawn up. Receiving their salute, the Royal party made for the Residency, where a durbar was shortly afterwards held, at which the Guicowar and the Prince sat together in the sight of the principal men of the State.

It had been announced that in the afternoon there would be an elephant fight and other sports, and I made the best of my way to the arena to see the sports of which I had heard. This was a large, oblong space, strongly walled in, entered through a gateway, across which three thick bars of wood were thrown. Inside this space were three structures, which were at once noticeable — a huge grand stand of four storys; a circular structure of brickwork, about five feet high, with a tree in the centre, and two flights of steps cut in the stone; and a circular walled structure, looped with holes just large enough to allow of the ingress of a man—particularly a flying, terror-stricken, elephant-hunted man—should such a one need its hospitable shelter. Overhanging the walls were trees rich in foliage, forming a splendid background from whatever side you scanned the picture. On the tops of the walls thousands of Mahrattas, in all kinds of costumes, were perched, their faces full of glee, and their arms full of children; on hills, which overlooked the arena were thousands more of them; peering in at the various gates between the bars were hundreds again; and inside the arena, about one hundred athletic men, some with spears, others with flags, and the rest with nothing save ropes and chains, were standing about waiting to take part in the promised fun. Outside the gates were cages full of tigers, rhinoceroses, buffaloes, and rams. Two huge elephants were fastened to the walls inside, about twenty painted and decorated elephants were ranged in a line opposite the grand stand, where was assembled a brilliant gathering of English ladies and gentlemen—the former in gaily coloured silks, the latter mostly in uniform—waiting for the Prince. They had not long to wait, for, just after we entered, a blast of trumpets announced his Royal Highness'

AN ELEPHANT FIGHT IN THE ARENA AT BARODA.

approach, and a moment later showed the golden carriage of the Guicowar in full motion, with his Highness and the Prince of Wales inside.

The first entertainment on the list was a wrestling match between half a dozen couples of semi-nude muscular savages. There was a bald man, who was evidently a very old stager; a Nubian, whose chief aim was to hug his opponent and fall on him, a tall man, who every now and then lifted his rival into the air, and tried to throw him out of the square marked out for this class of the sports; and a short, stout man, who enjoys the reputation of being the best wrestler in India, and who is very proud of the title. Two particular points are worthy of notice—one that each athlete had greased his body so completely that it was next to impossible to grasp him; the other that the use of the feet in wrestling was wholly disregarded, and that the French hug round the neck was the style of competition, rather than the Cumberland mode of wrestling. Picture twelve particularly strong men attempting to throttle and throw each other; now struggling till their eyes nearly start out of their heads, and now rolling over and over in the thick dust, emerging at length from the conflict begrimed and besmeared, and only vexed to find that they must go away and make way for the elephants. Anything like remonstrance would, however, have been somewhat out of place, for a number of men were hovering round the captive elephants fastened to the wall, the tame and decorated elephants were leaving the ground, and all kinds of preparations were being made for a struggle.

I rather suspect that these elephants were sly, old fellows, who, like the gladiators in olden times, did not hurt each other a bit more than was necessary, and often "made believe" in a sadly deceptive fashion. These had clearly been in the arena before, and knew just what was expected of them. First they rushed at each other, and with their blunted tusks pushed and tugged for a few moments, and then stopped. At this juncture a Mahratta came out with a stick; whereupon one of the elephants rushed at him, chased him into one of the recesses in the wall, and pulled a lot of the brickwork down. This diversion, however, lasted but a minute. Entwining their trunks with quite as much care as the wrestlers who had preceded them in the ring had joined hands, and adjusting their tusks in such a position as would give the greatest leverage, the elephants once more began the tug of war. And a terrible tug it was. Two huge beasts, of almost fabulous size, straining, pushing, groaning, strove for the mastery. The younger of the two elephants was the better formed and the more courageous, and very soon he had worsted his opponent and driven him against the wall. No sooner had the larger but weaker elephant run to the wall for shelter than the conqueror lowered his head, gave a roar of defiance, and charged with terrific force. The tusk struck the conquered one with a fearful thud, the wall and the miserable elephant's head had a sharp collision, and a moment later the bars of the gateway close by were on the point of being forced, when two men ran out with rocket tubes, discharged the contents at the elephants, and separated them in a moment. Away ran the victor across the arena, followed by the vanquished one, and for an instant there was quiet. Immediately after another encounter took place, and was going on merrily, when hampering irons were slipped round the hind legs of the infuriated animals by the Mahrattas employed for the purpose, stout ropes attached thereto, more rockets discharged, and eventually the animals were led into captivity.

Meanwhile a very wily old elephant was being prepared for the arena. His business was to attempt to catch a horseman, who, mounted on a white Arab and armed with a spear, was already within the precincts of the arena. For a moment or so the huge beast walked slowly about, as though he were in his native woods taking a gentle stroll after dinner, and not within a hundred miles of horsemen or footmen either. But, just when he looked most unconcerned and careless, he gave a sudden rush, got his trunk in the saddle of the rider, and only missed by an inch or two unhorsing the Mahratta and making him pay for his temerity. Had that Arab steed stumbled, or had the man lost nerve, the elephant would have ended the contest in a very summary manner.

The next contest on the list was between two huge rhinoceroses, and, as the beasts were led in, all necks were craned forward and all eyes strained to look at them. One had a long, sharp horn, and was a fearful animal to behold; the other, thickly set, had a blunter horn, but, if possible, a more powerful back. So soon as they were loosed, they rushed at each other with tremendous determination. For a time they struggled hard to push their respective prows into each other's necks, but to no purpose. In vain two men on each side patted their horny sides and invited them with loud cries to continue the battle; their encouragement was useless. Still one was a little afraid of the other, for suddenly the owner of the blunted horn turned round, and, with snorts like the magnified grunts of a frightened pig, rushed from the struggle. Onlookers held their breath, for the keepers were not far from being run over, and consequently crushed. But, as luck would have it, they ran away, and "live to fight another day." More than this, men procured buckets of water, and emptied them over the backs of the gladiators, stroked and patted them, prodded them with long spears, and in other ways urged them to deeds of valour. As soon as the animals came close together again and felt each other's weapons of war, they simultaneously snorted and scampered off, and positively refused to fight. It was clearly a drawn battle, and Sir Madava Rao ordered the creatures to be led away forthwith.

Then came the turn of the buffaloes; two of them were ushered into the arena—one a young, light-coloured animal, and one a dark beast. A perfect crowd of rapscallions accompanied them to the fight, and, with spears, ropes, sticks, and fists, encouraged them very considerably. The buffaloes, however, needed very little incentive. Rushing at each other at a tremendous pace, they struggled violently for a moment; and the young one was winning fast, when one of his horns broke off short, the blood spurted out, and it was forced to retreat. Away rushed the poor brute, chased by its enemy. Fortunately the gate bars were sufficiently wide open to admit of escape, and the vanquished, bleeding bull flew through, scattering the spectators in every direction, and mingling the turbans in almost inextricable confusion. Another couple of buffaloes followed and fought, one of them being thrown by the other, which at once attempted to rip it open. Happily, its horns were blunt, and before it could do more than inflict a deep flesh-wound, the beasts were separated, and another couple introduced.

This third conflict was not, however, a severe one, and it was scarcely over before several couples of rams were introduced to the ring. Rams with peculiarly hard heads and strong horns have for long years been the especial pride of Baroda down to the uproarious days of Mulhar Rao, the man now living quietly at Madras. Some of the strongest pates ever discovered were brought to the show, for the delight of his ladies and subjects. Then the rams were allowed to fight till they killed each other, the sight of blood being by no means distasteful to the gentleman who was accused of having attempted to kill Col. Phayre. But more human days have dawned, and in the presence of the Prince, at least, no very desperate encounter was allowed. The plan of action was simply this: Two animals were brought within about ten feet of each other and then let slip: instantly with tremendous force they rushed at each other, and their skulls met with a tremendous crash. If by this first thud either ram was knocked down, it was at once declared beaten and led away. Sometimes, however, victory was not so easily decided, and it was not till after a dozen sharp blows at

A CAPTIVE TIGER LED BEFORE THE PRINCE AFTER THE SPORTS IN THE ARENA AT BARODA.

the least that one of the rams gave in; while in one case a sleepy fellow, who clearly saw no fun in the whole proceeding, allowed himself to be knocked over without making the slightest resistance. Another, as though perfectly aware of the rules of the game, looked round for somebody to take him away.

In this way several battles were decided, and then a long string of men, in all kinds of singular costumes, entered—eight leading a huge tiger, which was so encumbered with chains as to be helpless; one riding in a little carriage drawn by two of the black bucks for which Baroda was so celebrated; another leading two white does of surpassing beauty; a third with a tame sloth; and the rest, some twenty or thirty in all, carrying birds' cages all filled with feathered curiosities of the rarest descriptions. This spectacle concluded the entertainment. In a few minutes the Prince and suite drove away, highly delighted, and the huge crowd dispersed.

It was announced that the Prince would go out hunting with the cheetahs next morning, and that a vast quantity of deer had been beaten up for the sport, and that those who desired to see the sport must be astir before even the lark would dream of rising. The stars were, consequently, the only light which such huntsmen as did not quite belong to the Prince's party had as they drove through the sleeping city of Baroda, its deserted bazaars and empty streets, and along the road which leads to a country palace of the Guicowar, boasting the euphonious name of Muckinpoora. If the huntsmen were thus early, the cheetahs and their keepers were even earlier, for when the rendezvous was reached, some two miles on the other side of the palace, away from the city, they were found; the cheetahs, five in number, sitting hood-winked and tied on the top of flat, open carts, while their keepers stood around them and stroked them. Close by were a number of bullock carts, each drawn by two animals, each intended to hold three people, albeit that they had no seats whatever, but simply a cushion on which we were expected to sit cross-legged. The Prince had a bullock cart of silver and gold, with seats in it, and even a spring, which, considering everything, was an immense concession for the Barodians to make, even to royalty. All was thus ready very early; but, unfortunately, the Prince was not very punctual, and the sun had risen some height in the heavens—a condition almost fatal to the skill of the cheetah—when he arrived. Once there, a start was quickly made; and then, behold the following procession: A pilot cart with three enthusiastic sportsmen in it, kneeling; the Prince's wagon, containing his Royal Highness and the Duke of Sutherland, each in Indian hunting costume, namely, the huge sun hat, tweed coat, and white trousers, each person carrying a rifle and a hunting knife; five carts with cheetahs, each animal attended by three keepers; and about twenty small wagons, their occupants in almost every conceivable position compatible with the arrangement of three stout men on a square yard of cushion in a springless vehicle passing over rough ground.

Presently, as we came into some very English-like scenery, we espied in a wide field, not a quarter of a mile distant, several hundred deer quietly feeding. Now was our time, and the hearts of all beat high. As quietly as might be, we approached the herd, and soon came within a hundred and fifty yards of them, when a cheetah was unhooded and let slip. Stealthily creeping along through the grass, this terrible beast bounded into the very centre of the deer, and for a moment it seemed as though he must certainly capture one of the terror-stricken, beautiful creatures, with such tremendous springs did he urge the chase. But this time the deer were too fleet, and bounded along with such wonderful rapidity that, after a chase of two hundred yards, the savage beast sat down and waited for the keepers to come up and hoodwink him again. Almost immediately afterwards another herd was descried in an op posite direction, and it was then resolved that we should be divided into two parties, the one led by the Prince bearing away to the left in chase of the herd that had just escaped, and taking three cheetahs; the other, under the guidance of Lord Aylesford and Lord Charles Beresford, going to the right.

That this arrangement was a good one was proved very shortly. A mile had scarcely been traversed by either party, when each came within easy reach of herds. Of the two, the Prince's party was just then the more fortunate, for in the very centre of the deer they chased were two large bucks with remarkably fine horns, fighting with great vigour. To let the cheetah go at these two rivals was the work of an instant; to catch the largest one by the neck and drag him to the ground after a short struggle was an act which involved no great expenditure of time. On the other side a beautiful doe had been chased by a cheetah, caught by the neck, and after a sharp struggle been brought to the ground. The sport had now begun in earnest, and for the next two hours we were taken over ruts as deep as ordinary ditches, over hillocks and through hedges, sometimes almost shaken out, and in the case of one cart turned out with a veritable capsize, letting the cheetahs slip frequently, sometimes getting game and sometimes not. To those who had never before seen the action of these savage animals the sight was undoubtedly full of interest; but, from an economical point of view, I should say that cheetah hunting is not a success. In two hours and a half five cheetahs killed four bucks and four does. Two rifles in experienced hands would have killed forty in a like time. So, indeed, the Prince appeared to think, for he presently left the cheetahs altogether, and went shooting on his own account, and succeeded in getting a fine pair of deer, the buck having horns of very satisfactory size. After this there was breakfast at Muckinpoora, and at night the Prince dined at the mess of the 22nd Regiment, commanded by the gallant and amiable Colonel Nuttall.

There were many interesting things to be noted about Baroda. The palace in which Mulhar Rao perpetrated untold wickedness; the narrow streets, with open sewers running on both sides, and open troughs of bad drinking water—made still worse by crowds of naked children who paddled therein, and mixed mud paste with the liquid intended as the drink of their excellent parents—not a foot from the sewers; the strangely built mud houses, boasting no doors, and very frequently no roof either; the hideous paintings on the outsides of the temples, the shrines in the streets, the gates, and the celebrated clock-tower, built in the form of a Chinese joss-house, and painted light blue, were all worthy of a prolonged inspection.

It was worth the journey to Baroda to see the holy men who lived there. For Baroda, you must know, is a peculiarly religious place, and possesses more deformities and burlesques on human nature, more unwashed fakirs, and more objectionable devotees, than any other city of its size. It was there that, not long since, a very pious person roasted the calf of his leg, in the presence of a number of admiring Hindoos. On the road leading to the Motee Bagh I had pointed out to me another religious gentleman who, in addition to wearing for many years a thick coating of mud, carefully renewed every morning, and only relieved in its monotony by two or three streaks of brick-red paint on the forehead, had lately cut off a couple of his toes and a finger or two, in honour of a god that looked exactly like the representation of a frantic monkey with two tails and four arms. But there was no necessity for seeking these superlatively good people. They turned up in every direction and every moment. They were as numerous as the dogs in the street, and that is saying a great deal, when it is remembered that Baroda has more and uglier specimens of the canine breed than even Constantinople. The sanctified tribe marched along, with their shrivelled arms, earless heads, mud-begrimed faces, and long, matted hair; they appeared at the corners of the streets and in front of the shrines, and just when you were hoping that the last of them had gone, you found them at your elbow. Not that they wished to beg; on the contrary, I did not in any instance see a fakir condescend to do anything but scowl. Blind men might ask for alms—and there were many blind people in Baroda; beggars might clamour for money at the gates of the arena; but these holy men simply regarded us, from the Prince downwards, with profound contempt; for, in addition to the luxury of being allowed to wear as little clothing as they pleased and as much mud as they liked, they had many of them the assured right, in consideration of their sufferings and virtues, to have at any moment and forever, twenty times as much enjoyment as anybody else—the gods willed it, and the priests declared it. Ask for alms? If, in admiration of their inherent and singular goodness, you felt constrained to press half a rupee upon their acceptance, they would doubtless take it, for they live upon such tokens of esteem and affection. But they would certainly not implore a gift, and if it were offered, would return no thanks. I doubt whether a more impudent set of scoundrels exists on the face of the globe. They even escape the policeman's whip, an instrument which is applied pretty unsparingly to the rest of the populace, and which works wonders in a crowded street, when authority and power want to pass quickly.

But it was not of the fakirs, nor the streets, that I just now intended to write. My intent was to speak more fully of the palaces of Baroda and their occupants—not the old building in which Luxmabae's baby was enthroned and dethroned, all in the space of ten minutes, the residence of the last Guicowar, and his agreeable circle of male and female acquaintances; but the two suburban palaces of Motee Bagh and Mukinpoora, and Sir Madava Rao, the Prime Minister of Baroda.

It was at the first named mansion that I called on my arrival in the State. A courteous note from the Premier demanded personal answer, and it was with no reluctance I faced even the mid-day sun. It so chanced that the moment was an exceptionally favourable one. The place was *en fête* for the Prince's reception; his Royal Highness was expected to drive thither from the Residency very shortly, and not only the hall of state, but all the apartments were prepared. I have already spoken of the golden howdah, the golden carriage, and the golden bullock-gharry of Baroda. You have heard of the diamond aigrette which adorns the Guicowar's turban, and the diamond necklace which encircles his neck. Be prepared, then, for plenty of magnificence on entering Motee Bagh. Yet look at the same time for the tawdry and tinsel. You will not be disappointed in either. India everywhere presents the same spectacle, and Motee Bagh is no exception to the rule.

As you pass through the streets an unclad imp is playing in the dust. You look closely at the unkempt hair, and behold a cap that is worth half a sovereign at the very least. The coolie who brings or carries messages two miles for sixpence, probably wears a rich, purple silk jacket, fit for a prince. That and an excessively dirty rag complete his clothing. You enter the house of a native, and find on the rough, earthen floor a carpet of surpassing beauty. Wares of great value are exposed for sale in shops compared with which a barn is a mansion; and if you want to find a palace, your quickest and best plan is to proceed in the direction where hovels are most numerous and streets are narrowest. So at Motee Bagh. The troops drawn up in the garden are well dressed and well armed, yet the sentry in the corridor is in rags and tatters, and carries an old flint fowling-piece in his left hand. The fountains, too, are of white marble, very beautiful basins, altogether admirable, till you see that the jets are crooked, and will not throw more than a cupful of water a foot high.

On your first entry into the palace itself you find in almost every room chandeliers enough to stock a warehouse. At Muckinpoora there were in one verandah alone, 70ft. long by 24 wide, eighteen large chandeliers with thirty-two lights apiece, seventy-two bouquets of light with three jets to each, besides other receptacles for lamps and candles. Here the lighting arrangements have been made in the same proportions. You would think you were in a shop of chandeliers and looking glasses, and that the dark gentleman who comes up the room to meet you intended to inveigle you into buying one at the very least. But he has no such intention. I do not suppose he would part with a single burner on any consideration. There would be a vacant space in the ceiling if he did, and no Hindoo with any pretence to taste could tolerate that. He would probably be happier than he now is, and would possibly smile still more, if he knew how to hang a few more chandeliers up in the saloon where the Prince will be presently received, and into which we have just entered. Facing the door, and with its back turned to a large window from which a magnificent view of the surrounding country can be obtained, is a sofa of solid silver—legs, arms, back, all pure silver; and on each side of this a silver chair. You do not look at the other chairs in the room, as these wholly engross your attention; and thus it is that, without in the least intending to be rude, you involuntarily notice that the seats of these splendid chairs and couch are very shabby. The same story over again. You turn round, look at the pictures on the wall, and find that, with the exception of their frames, which are very thick and costly, they are not worth a pound, even to a German printseller. Portraits of celebrated chiefs, and pictures of the Madonna and child, three prints of "a lady," and German-produced "likenesses" of the English Royal family complete the collection. Close by, in a cabinet carefully locked and guarded, were a tin engine and two little trucks, such as you may purchase in the Lowther Arcade, and in an ante-room, on a handsome marble table and a silver stand, was a toy donkey which wagged its head when touched, and which, in any London repository, is valued at exactly ninepence.

Still it must not be imagined that the man whom we had come to see was in any way like the palace in which we found him. Nothing but the severest simplicity was noticeable about him. Excepting only the huge medal which the Prince gives to every native of distinction, and which is about as ugly and unmeaning a decoration as it is possible to conceive, Sir Madava Rao wore no ornament of any kind. Like Sir Salar Jung, the great Mahommedan Minister, he dresses in plain black or white. On this particular occasion he wore white garments. At the first glance I was greatly impressed by this celebrated Hindoo. His English was perfect, lacking anything like a foreign accent. His manner was that of a man who had seen the world rather than of one who had never left India. And when he sat down and began to talk, his conversation was in harmony with all that has been said of him. The uppermost thought in his mind appeared to be the possibility of war and the consequent speedy return of the Prince, and he proceeded at once to discuss the situation. The position of England, the relative strength of the great Powers, the aims and ambitions of Russia—all seemed to be familiar to him, and for some minutes he chatted away with all the easy flow of thought of a European statesman. From what I have since heard, Sir Madava Rao's theories about good government are being carried into effect in Baroda; and there is, therefore reason to believe that before long the city will lose its open sewers, and possibly some of its holy men, and become more like a fit residence for a civilized prince.

CHAPTER VIII.

THE VOYAGE TO CEYLON.

As is well known, a painful uncertainty as to the route likely to be followed attended the first part of the Prince's trip in India. For nearly a fortnight not one of the Royal suite, save only Sir Bartle Frere, had any idea of what their future movements would be. Would the Prince go to Mysore? No one knew. Would he reach Madras? No one could tell. Would he go to the North-West? Perhaps. Would he go home? Possibly. There were rumours of cholera in the south, and fears of war at home; and these, coupled with the intense love of Sir Bartle Frere for mystery, were sufficient for all parties. So it resulted in the Prince going off to Baroda, after twenty-four hours' notice, and next setting sail in an equally hurried and secret fashion for Southern India, without anybody knowing where he was going, except one or two favoured ones.

In this way we all set sail, and were at sea fully a day before we were told where we were going to; and when the intelligence that possibly we should touch at Trivanderam was at length imparted to us, the majority of us were about as wise as ever; for, although in guide-books and gazetteers, Trivanderam was stated to be the capital of Travancore, all that we could learn besides was that it possessed no harbour, that ships had to anchor in an open roadstead, and that the beach boasted a surf such as European boats would never resist for a moment —with whieh pleasant and comfortable knowledge we beguiled the time while the voyage lasted. It now appears that had we been learned in astronomical lore we should have known that at Trivanderam there was erected, forty years ago, an observatory of no mean importance, with transit clocks and instruments, telescopes, refractors, and reflectors, and that it had since then been allowed to fall into disuse and dilapidation. But we were not astronomically inclined, and, with the exception of now and then straining our eyes in search of the Southern Cross, which, after all, never appeared, cared no more for observatories and telescopes than the present Rajah of Travancore does. Beyond this, too, it seems that had we been well instructed in heraldry, and knowing in things pertaining to ceremonies and chapters, we should have been aware that the Rajah who built the observatory was the same sensible and liberal-minded potentate who, in 1851, presented to the Queen the ivory chair in which she would sit were she to hold a Chapter of the Garter at Windsor. This knowledge, however, came too late; all that could be gathered was that game of all kinds abounded in the Rajah's territory; that the Prince wanted a little shooting, and that it was to be got in the neighbourhood of Trivanderam.

It was early on a Saturday morning when, by nautical calculation, an inspection of the shore, and consideration of the charts, we were judged to be opposite the long-looked for place. Now, naval men are far from averse to going on shore. Their ship is undoubtedly their home; they take great pride in her, from masthead to keelson; but give a jungle-full of tigers, and a plain full of bison, the prospect of a good day's sport, and a good dinner, and the most ardent sailor will begin to burnish his express rifle, fill up the cartridge-case, and prepare to land. Gradually Trivanderam was approached, and then was seen the beauty of this southern part of India. Our glasses made out that the inhabitants of this favoured land were actually enjoying a shower of rain. What would we not have given for a shower just then, with the thermometer in the shade at 94 deg., and no breeze? Pleasant, doubtless, is the bright Indian sun, pleasant the clear, blue sky and the grand expanse of purple-coloured sea; pleasant also an escape from the November fogs of

London, the chilly, wintry blasts, and the all-pervading mud; but, oh, for one hour of pelting, soaking rain! I don't believe a man would have raised an umbrella. To be drenched to the skin would have been a positive luxury. However, we did not land at Trivanderam, and we consequently got none of the rain. How provokingly near we came to the land! Cables were ready, the town could be distinctly made out, the observatory with its sightless old telescope and the residence of a Rajah, long groves of palm-trees, little fishing boats, and, at the back of all, towering mountains, round the heads of which clouds whirled madly, as though the wind, rushing through the crevices in the rock, was throwing them at each other for the sheer fun of the thing. There was clearly a pleasant breeze ashore, whatever we lacked at sea. Still, it must not be supposed that the water was still. We could see the surf beating madly on the strand, and our ships rolled about on the swell, till we had to hold on by both hands to avoid being capsized. It was a warning what to expect if we cast anchor, and apparently the Admiral took it, for, with a good deal of sail on, to catch what little wind there might be, we steamed away south, and presently left Trivanderam behind us.

On we went, hugging the shore and marvelling at its beauty. Rich, tropical vegetation covered the plain right down to the seashore. Palm, plantain, mango, and banian crowded together in one vast jungle. Nor was this splendid foliage confined to the plain. Far up the sides of the towering mountains, it formed a rich, green covering, under which game of all kinds might repose, and the natives of the place be happy. If the peaks of the hills were bare rocks, showing terrible precipices, the lower portions of the eminences were, at any rate, covered by a grateful shade. And every now and then some pretty, little village or lonely Portuguese church would peep out from the trees, or a little fleet of fishing boats would come from the shore. Then we would come in view of a red coral reef, or some well-marked place on the chart, such as Moottam Point, with its sandy face and bleak, bare top, till at length we were off Cape Comorin, the Land's-end of India, and by the declining light of the fast disappearing sun, gazed with awe upon the huge, white rock and the far-stretching shoal. We had not landed at Trivanderam, but such an excursion to the extreme point of Southern India had well-nigh made up for all our disappointment.

Meanwhile, the Prince had landed at Goa, the Portuguese settlement, and the place whence come all the Portuguese servants who make life a burden to the traveller. You heartily wish them at Goa, or indeed anywhere else, a hundred times a day; yet they are indispensable. In such a climate, and with such a system as prevails in India, you must, wherever you go, take your own servants, or you will get nothing to eat, nothing to drink, and will lose your luggage. Then comes the question, What kind of servant is best? The native of Madras is a proverbial rascal, and I am able to say, without prejudice, that he deserves his character. The Hindoo is a perpetual bother in travelling, for he can only eat in a certain way, at a certain time, and cannot go to sea. As for the Mohammedan, the experience of an Englishman out here speaks volumes. Temper-provoking, crafty, troublesome, full of excuses for laziness, and frequently dishonest, you are in constant danger of being provoked to use your cane upon them, in which case the chances are that you will be fined by a local magistrate, and have your name published in the newspapers. Such being the case, you are driven to employ the inhabitant of Goa, partly because he speaks English fairly, partly for the reason that he washes himself occasionally, and can upon a pinch present an appearance bordering upon respectability, though that is not often; and partly also because he distinctly understands the inadvisableness of stealing your clothes, and confines his operations to cheating you out of small sums in paying your bills—an achievement which affords him infinite satisfaction, and is possibly less annoying to the victim than are the vagaries of the native servant.

There are many ways of decorating a place, but the most original method I ever witnessed was adopted at Baroda. It was getting dark in the evening on which the Prince was to drive through the native town when I passed over the bridge that led to the railway station. Across the bridge was a triumphal arch of palm leaves; on both parapets oil lamps had been placed in such a fashion as to illuminate the road very grandly. But it was neither the arch nor the lamps that surprised me. There was nothing very extraordinary in the arrangement of the foliage or the situation of the lamps. Nor was the bridge itself worthy of any great attention. On that bridge, however, was a sight to be witnessed which I had not seen before. The decorators were manufacturing angels. It has probably not been the fortune of many among the British public to see the youths of Baroda. They are mostly Hindoos, who never wander from home; and just as they do not go to the outer world, so the outer world very seldom goes to them. I may therefore mention, by way of information, that a Baroda boy is one of the most ill-favoured in the land. He has a face like a Hottentot, arms like a chimpanzee, a dark-brown skin, and bloodshot eyes. Anything less angelic it is impossible to conceive. Yet it was out of material like this that the Guicowar's decorators were making angels.

Two ideas were prominent in the mind of Sir Madava Rao's decorators; first, that his angels must be white; next, that they must have wings. Whether he had read of Pope Gregory and the Saxon slaves, or had borrowed his ideas from Milton, I do not know. There was a society that Hood wrote about, which, finding that it was impossible to rub negroes white, determined to gild them; but the Baroda artist was far cleverer. With a huge pot of whitewash and a collection of properties which would have done credit to the store-room of a London theatre, he set to work furiously. Ten boys were fixed at different points of the bridge, and the position known in the army as "eyes right" once obtained, the angel-maker proceeded. With a great brush, such as is used by bill-stickers in London, this ingenious man whitened each young Barodian from top to toe. Then to white cords passed round their breasts he attached golden wings of the most approved pattern. On their half-shaven crowns he fixed long, flowing, auburn wigs, and surmounted this piece of decoration with gilt coronets; in each hand he placed a long white wand, and the picture was complete. You need not be told the result; how in the flickering glare of the lamps these angels more closely resembled white-washed imps than seraphim; how now and then some urchin more mischievous than the rest would take off his locks and expose a bald, black pate; or how, as he passed by, the Prince was thrown into convulsions of laughter. I only mention the incident to give you an idea of the pitfalls into which native decorators are apt to stumble when to their care is confided the beautifying of a place.

Mr. Gregory, the excellent Governor of Ceylon, had fortunately no such helpers, and in spite of the extraordinary difficulties he experienced, fast turned the beautiful city of Colombo into fairyland. I believe it was Bishop Heber who remarked that in Ceylon "Every prospect pleases, and only man is vile." About the villainy of Cingalese man I cannot say much. He is not good-looking; he wears long hair done up in a chignon at the back, with a tortoise-shell comb to keep it off his forehead; he chews more betel nut than the Hindoo of the mainland; he delights in a long, bright-coloured petticoat, and, unless he is a Mohammedan, wears no turban; but whether he is vile or not, I cannot say. The Cingalese cabman knows well that you must ride when the thermometer is 100 deg. in the shade, and he is a trifle exorbitant, almost as much so as his London cousin would be under similar circumstances; but that is not villainy, it is human nature. Yet I will not quarrel with the writer of the hymn. He is right as to the prospect; the men may take care of themselves.

Ceylon is certainly a lovely island. We descried—when a long way at sea—a land of orange and cinnamon groves; a land of the date and the bread-fruit; where plantains have the largest leaves, the banyan tree most foliage, where the palm spreads widest, and lovely singing-birds are most numerous. For, doubly-favoured isle, it has the rain of the Temperate Zone intermingled with the heat of the Tropics. The ground is continually fertilised, the plants and trees see the sun always; the spice-laden air is full of richness, and the surrounding sea makes night cool and refreshing. Colombo from the sea is a fine picture of architectural beauty in a deep setting of green. Vistas of pleasant retreats and leafy shades, of a wide beach and handsome buildings, meet us at every turn. And when we landed we found the view from the distance excelled by the sight which a closer inspection gave us. Truly it was a wonderful place to which we had come.

With such natural advantages and so energetic and loyal a Governor as Mr. Gregory, what might not have been made of Ceylon on the occasion of the Prince's visit? I am afraid to say what orders were given by the Decoration Committee, and what arrangements were made for utilizing the natural beauty of Ceylon. All that was wanted was that the time should be specified, or, failing that, sufficient notice to allow of an alteration in the plans. Yet, strange to say, the gentlemen who managed, or rather mismanaged, the Prince's tour, although they knew perfectly well more than a fortnight ago that the Neilgherry trip was impossible in consequence of cholera, failed to make the fact known to the Council at Ceylon, and, indeed, only mentioned that the visit of the Prince would take place earlier than at first arranged. Fortunately, His Excellency the

Governor did not resent this cavalier treatment, as less amiable and sensible men might have done, but addressed himself to the task of preparing to receive the Prince. The result was magnificent. Triumphal arches—one of which, close by the landing-place, is a marvell of skill, erected in the form of a castle and pavilion—sprang up as though by magic. The Queen's House—for so the Governor's residence is called—was ready for the Prince; the fleet was in the offing; and all that was wanting was the "Serapis," with her Royal traveller.

Within an hour of landing at Ceylon I learned from the Governor that England had practically become owner of the Suez Canal; and as the notes of one who but lately passed to the East by way of this wonderful route may be of interest, I venture to give my own experiences of the canal. I do not propose to set down a single figure; my talk shall be of the manners and customs of the people who inhabit the region and the canal itself.

I do not think that at Port Said, the point where the canal begins, the ordinary Englishman would find much to please him. I have been told that after a soldier has passed the regulation year at Perim, he looks upon Aden as the Garden of Eden. A man would have to live a long while in a very bad place before he regarded Port Said in any such light. There is a railway which somebody began a long time ago; but which nobody, apparently, proposes to finish. There is a dockyard which is a model of disorder. I believe that the Arab population, which fortunately lives by itself, is the most rascally in the world, and I am sure that the streets in the native quarter more than vie, in point of uncleanliness, with the worst parts of Alexandria. I was in charge of a guide, and as I traversed the lanes and alleys of the town, took his opinion of his fellow-citizens. "The people," he remarked, "very great blackguards indeed. Best you not come ashore, sar, night-time. Arabs like to see gentlemen with watch and chain in streets at night-time very much. Plenty murders here, sar." "But," I rejoined, "are the thieves not punished?" "Oh yes, sar," was the reply; "they beaten on the feet every day, but they not care a bit." My informant was not far wrong, for we had hardly gone a hundred yards when we came upon one of the residents of Port Said undergoing at that moment the penalty of the bastinado for some malpractice or other. Temporarily, I should judge, from the grimaces he made, that he objected to the punishment most seriously, but, practically, I expect, he did not "care a bit," as his loquacious countryman said. Why should he, forsooth? The pain of the bamboo cane once over, but little inducement to good influences the native. Everything runs riot in Port Said. The Government roads, as distinct from the Canal Company's roads, are almost impassable. The streets are full of dogs, donkeys, pigs—why do Mohammedans keep pigs?—and children. The heat is fierce; the sand is blinding; crime is rife, and punishment is irregular. What can an Arab gain by being good at Port Said?

Leaving, then, this delectable spot, let us go on board the steamer, and, passing through a gate-like entrance, begin our voyage down the canal. Several ideas strike you at once. First, that the canal is very narrow; secondly, that the distance is measured by English miles and not French mêtres; thirdly, that there is a continual succession of mirages, so that phantom lakes of delicious aspect surround you, and thickly foliaged trees, to your mistaken vision, cover the desolate plane. I say nothing of the sandfly, which exceeds the mosquito in power of jaw and activity of wing, or of the melting sun. The latter you find everywhere in the East; the former is absolutely welcome in place of the pestering fly of Alexandria and Port Said. You move along very slowly, making not more than about five miles an hour, and this gives you the opportunity to notice several curious facts. One is that the construction of the canal has brought with it here and there something akin to what we are accustomed to call vegetation. There are occasional patches of green on the banks, and at some of the stations or landing places on the canal, out of which trimly-dressed French officials emerge as you pass by, there are little groves of trees. These are but of recent growth, and some one near tells you that they are fostered by heavy dews, which now fall frequently, and rain which before was not known in Egypt. We have good proof of this at nightfall, when we anchor off Ismailia. There we see a grand expanse of water, a large, natural lake, and you are wondering whether the pilot cannot be induced to take you on by moonlight, when a thick fog falls, and all hope of moving on is stopped, not only for the night, but for the greater part of the next day too.

Nothing more is needed to prove that the climate is rapidly altering, and that in the process of time the desert may, literally as well as figuratively, "rejoice and blossom as the rose." Indeed, at Ismailia there is already much rejoicing and much blossoming too. There are public gardens of no ordinary beauty, long groves of young trees, luxuriant hedges, and fruitful fields. Ismailia is by no means a town to be despised, as its well-built houses and grand summer palace testify. And if anything were wanting to prove its great respectability, it is the fact that all its donkeys are named after the statesmen and military celebrities of Europe. Napoleon, Alfonso, King William, Moltke, Francis Joseph, and Garibaldi, were all waiting at the jetty ready saddled when we landed. I chose Bismark—a grizzled donkey of great strength, and, looking back on that moonlight ride, I am bound to say that he outstripped all competitors, and carried off honours both as a racer and as a kicker Let the great of Europe know that their highest honour in Ismailia is to have a donkey named after them.

Ismailia is about halfway down the canal, and supposing the fog to clear away before midday, you ought to arrive at Suez by night. This is, however, by no means certain, even in these days of steam. Every now and again some slight turning occurs, and then the chances are that, unless directed by a very skilful pilot and a good crew, the ship will run aground. A variety of entertaining incidents follow. You may be asked to leave the vessel in company with the rest of the passengers, and so lighten the ship—a diversion by no means to be desired, as it involves the chance of your having to sit upon the hot sand for some hours, while the sailors are exerting themselves to move their unwieldy vessel. Or you may be allowed to stop on board, but required to dispense with the awning which alone makes life bearable in the desert; and, worse than all, be deafened for hours by a badly-working, clattering donkey engine and windlass, which almost invariably for the first fifty attempts to grasp the cable—which is attached to a post ashore, and which, if properly gripped, would pull the vessel round,—lets it slip at the very moment when a well-sustained pull would put everything right. If you get through the Canal with less than a couple of such experiences, you will be very fortunate. The "Serapis" went aground for a short time, and so has almost every vessel of considerable tonnage that I have heard of. Occasionally the blades of the screw are lost in the attempt to move the ship, as was the case with the "Sumatra" some time back; or perhaps the ship has to stop for twelve hours till the tide lifts her, so that it is by no means certain that if you leave Ismailia in the morning you will see Suez before night. Still, if you have good fortune, and can avoid the bad places in the Canal, you may go along quicker even than that, especially through what are called the Bitter Lakes, where ten knots an hour, or even more, may be made. In this wa you go along, through some of the most uninviting scenery in the world—arid desert, only now and then relieved by the little patches of vegetation which have recently sprung up, an occasional mirage, a flock of birds, and now and then a party of Arabs with their camels, their wives, and their chidren, sometimes with merchandise and sometimes not, but always ineffably dirty and excessively wild. They are more frequently to be seen at the little boat bridges, which are placed at certain points at one spot. They claim absolute right of way, having enjoyed the proprietorship of a road to the East from Egypt ever since Abraham roamed about with his camels and goods.

I will not attempt to describe at length the landing of the Prince in Ceylon. One or two pictures presented themselves, and these I will give you.

I have before remarked on the adaptability of the palm leaf for purposes of ornamentation. Perhaps it may be argued that in a place so full of foliage as Colombo floral decoration was needless. But given that triumphal arches are an orthodox expression of loyalty, Colombo outvied Bombay itself. It is the home of fruits, as well as flowers. The mango is richer, the pine-apple finer, and the cocoanut more plentiful here than anywhere besides. It was therefore with little astonishment that I saw pyramids of fruit eight feet high surrounding the bases of arches, fruit hanging in great clusters all along the line of route, and fruit on the arches themselves. Pray do not imagine that what we in England know as a triumphal arch was to be seen in Ceylon. Here were lightness and strength, but nothing solid or heavy. Thin bamboos strongly tied together till an arch not three inches thick, but fully seventy feet high and as many feet broad, was raised, might well excite wonder in a mind unused to such sights. Then, when all kinds of fruit were hung from the supports in rich clusters—the bright yellow and red of the young cocoanuts contrasting with the green plantains and mangoes, the bread fruit, and the areca nut—an arch was made which needed no inscription to tell its meaning, though the native Christians of Colombo had made it, and thought fit to say so.

Yet, lest there should be sameness, the ingenious gentleman to whom the decorations of Colombo were confided bethought him of something new, and as Ceylon is not only a great fruit store and conservatory of grandly painted flowers, but also the home of the elephant, he made arches of effigies of these magnificent creatures, arches of elephants composed of canvas and rich Oriental blossoms, arches representing the king of Ceylon beasts entwining trunks and tusks, and upraising their heads in order to let the Prince pass under. You never lost sight of the elephant in Ceylon. True that he was not in the streets, as in Baroda, or even in the suburbs, as in Hyderabad, but the effigy was everywhere. We saw ebony elephants on drawing-room tables, golden elephants on the collars of officials, painted elephants on banners, brass elephants on Government stamps, and the first thing that the Prince set eyes on when he landed at Colombo were two black images of elephants with eyes like tea-saucers, and long, black trunks grasping cocoanuts firmly. There were other classes of arches, however. Towers were light—so light, indeed, that a man might almost have walked away with a whole archway easily—semi-circular arches, square arches, and arches of a pattern which I have never seen before, sprang up everywhere. The materials were certainly close at hand; it was but the transfer of the branches and leaves from the trees on the roadside to the arches; but for all that the artistic beauty of the structures was greatly to be admired, and Mr. Gregory's island looked its very best.

I will not trouble you with the addresses of the Executive Council, or the Municipal Council, nor even with the reply of the Prince. First of all, because from the place in which I stood I heard nothing; secondly, because they are stereotyped; you have had their purport already, and their only merit was that they were very short. I believe the good gentleman who compiled the Cingalese eloquence was thrown from his carriage and severely bruised an hour afterwards. He has, however, for consolation the knowledge that a grateful people praise his skill in condensing the local welcome into a few very choice words.

The great feature of the Colombo arrival, however, was the

display on the water. Royal processions, on entering fresh places, are pretty much the same everywhere. The aides-de-camp of the Resident Governor walk first, three abreast, and very upright indeed. The Prince follows by the side of the Governor, bowing first on this side and then on that, and smiling very graciously. The suite come next, in something very like disorderly array, and a number of local magnates bring up the rear of the procession. It is the same at every capital, and needs no special description. Perhaps the fact that the native gentlemen wore chignons and semicircular combs in their hair, long petticoats, and low shoes, might add something to the interest of the scene; perhaps also the appearance of sundry old gentlemen, who were adorned with great discs of gold, given them as rewards for good behaviour, by successive Governors, broad bands of gold lace, and golden daggers, should be described. The readiness with which one of them, a very high functionary indeed, with an excessively ugly face, and an exceedingly pretty coat, stood to be sketched, showed that he, at any rate, thought himself worthy of especial notice, and the admiring nods of his friends testified to their approval.

But, after all, triumphal arches, curiously attired natives, and even the Royal procession itself, were by no means the things to be most carefully noticed. The scene on the water was the most extraordinary sight. There were funny old people who had engaged drum-and-fife bands, to play in their barges, loyal tunes in various keys. There were young ladies who dressed like old men, and old men, who dressed like young ladies, seated under the canopies of foliage, and placidly waiting for the Prince, who kept them for five hours, owing to unforeseen accidents, and to the foolish miscalculations of his suite. Yet there was nothing but goodwill and loyalty. The cheers which accompanied the salute from the fleet and the fort were full of hearty good-humour, and it is a question whether anywhere else the Prince met more gladsome people, or people saw a more gratified Prince.

CHAPTER IX.

CINGALESE FAIRY LAND.

On the journey to Kandy, I saw what I believe to be the prettiest spectacle in the world. Before the vivid impression it has made upon my mind dies away let me strive to depict it.

"You have seen nothing till you have been to Kandy," said the Governor of Ceylon—hospitable Mr. Gregory—as we sat and discussed the visit of the Prince. "It is the loveliest place in creation, and when you have seen it you will say so," added his Excellency. It was, therefore, with no little expectation that I looked forward to my trip to Kandy. Everything tended to make that expectation greater. Coffee-planters praised the decoration of Colombo, but recommended Kandy as a place needing neither ornamentation nor beautifying. Inhabitants of the port themselves, while proud of the city, yet point to Kandy as the *summum bonum* of civic excellence Kandy must be a pretty place, or no more faith could be placed in the word of man. Seven o'clock in the morning was fixed for the hour of our departure into the interior, so that we had the best part of the day before us. A shady sky, too, favoured the travellers, who would otherwise have been half-roasted, crowded together as we were, before the six hours' journey was a thing of the past. At length we started, and then a panorama of surpassing beauty, which never closed for a moment till we reached our destination, and still surrounds us whichever way we look, opened before us. It is vain for me to attempt to describe the landscape of Ceylon. Bring together the grandeur of Alpine lands, the mellow beauty of Swiss scenery where the lake of Lucerne looks prettiest; add to the sketch admirably cultivated fields of grain, and fill the picture with the luxuriant foliage of the tropics, and you have a faint idea of the lovely scene through which we passed.

It is a great privilege to see Adam's Peak. When first I looked at it we were fifty miles from Ceylon, in half a gale, on our beam-ends. Still, trying as was the tossing of the ship, and doleful as looked the inky sky, with its afterwards fulfilled promise of storm and lightning, there was the summit bearing the footprint of Buddha, to look upon which is as meritorious an act for a Buddhist as a journey to Mecca is for a follower of the Prophet. For aught we could tell to the contrary, the print of that wonderful foot might be on the very side of the mountain upon which we were gazing. All Oriental persuasions revere the phenomenon. Ask a Mohammedan, and he will tell you that the huge mark was the footprint of Adam; enquire of a Chinese, and he will award the honour of possessing the largest pedal appanage in the world—it is five feet long—to Fo. Portuguese writers have quarrelled from time immemorial over the conflicting claims of St. Thomas and the Eunuch of Candace to this mark on the rock; the Brahmins have every reason to be perfectly sure that Shiva's toes effected the imprint; while Moses of Chorene—a very sad man, who ought to be remembered with much reprobation—said the footprint was that of Satan himself, and not of a saint at all.

While on the journey to Kandy we had plenty of time to consider all this. Adam's Peak stood out against the sky ever so many miles away, and formed the centrepiece in the background of the picture. Round its elevated head the clouds played, yet ever and anon the summit would be lit up by the sun's rays, the sharp peak glittered as brightly as though it were incandescent. Among the things we had been told to expect was a thrill of excitement at what is most appropriately known as Sensation Rock. Have you ever looked into the interior of the crater of Vesuvius, sat in the train as it passes on the edge of the precipice which overhangs the light green lake Neuchatel; walked on the ledge which joins the Capel Curig and the Beddgellert ascent of Snowdon; passed along the line which leads to the Mont Cénis tunnel; looked down the Righi ascent; gone to the edge of any one of the chasms which abound on Mount Pilatus, or looked down the precipices over which you pass when you go over the Bhore Ghauts on the road from Bombay to Poona? If so, you can estimate the grandeur of the sight from Sensation Rock when you learn that it far exceeds in terrible magnificence any and all of these.

Moreover, you are not looking down upon a flinty surface of barren rock. On the contrary, nowhere else is vegetation so abundant. You are full of wonder as you see the myriads of trees and flowers which cover the ground. Scarcely a fruit or a leaf that belongs to tropical climes is missing. Were you to fall over the edge into the abyss below, you would never reach the earth. Palms, mangoes, plantains, banyans, bread-fruit trees, areca-nut plants, the interlacing arms of convolvuli, trumpet-flowers, huge ferns, and a hundred other exuberant members of the vegetable world would catch you. You would be killed, for a fall of five hundred feet upon the softest of couches would be deadly. But you expire upon a bed of unequalled beauty, with roses for your pillow and palms for your coverlet. Every moment the scene changed, too, in this wonderful trip. Coffee plantations climbing the hills would be seen, then the striated surface of land cultivated for rice, next thick jungle with scarcely an open space of a foot wide to be distinguished, then the mountain scenery, with its precipices, and afterwards a flower-producing district of surpassing beauty. In this way the six hours flew pleasantly by, till at length we reached Kandy and found it all we expected.

Kandy railway station presented altogether a novel sight to the Prince and those who accompanied him. All at once we found ourselves in a new land. The people belong to a different type and race; the scenery was different—everything was strange except the palm-leaf decorations, which I have admired so much before. I will not stay to speak of the flags and the other matters—suffice it to say that the station, without a single person in it, would still have looked very pretty. But the great sight was the assemblage. Away outside, on the sides of the high hills which shut the town in like a little amphitheatre, were small knots of gaily dressed people under the shade of trees, the bright red and white dresses pleasantly contrasting with the varied hues of light and deep, dark green, and on a slope inside the town, close to the station, thousands of sight-seers had taken up a position. All along the road on both sides were very extraordinary persons; they were called "headmen," and wore something peculiar, greatly resembling a square pin cushion, on their heads. Note that it was not this gear from which they derive their title. Their business is to control districts under the management of superior officers. If you chanced to be a Cingalese—and you could not find a lovelier home—you would be registered by a headman directly you were born; your arrival at the age of fifteen—a date which renders you liable for military service—would be chronicled by the headman; to a headman you would go when you wished to be married, and to a headman your relatives would go when they wanted to bury you. Such were the men who lined the road by which the Prince was to travel when he left the station. They led the way to the pretty triumphal arches circled by the town; they pointed to the beautiful trophy with a revolving minaret erected by a Mussulman grandee, which, when the Prince arrived, sent out a golden canopy resting upon wires fixed high in the air, in such fashion that it overshadowed the canopy of the Prince till he came in front of Government House.

But to return to the inside of the station. The most prominent object for the Prince's inspection, was a party of Veddahs advantageously placed on the top of a cattle truck. Here were the veritable, wild men of the jungle—eight in number—with their equally veritable, wild women. The Cingalese looked at them in mute astonishment. Even they had never seen such savages before. Miserable skeletons with long matted hair—one of them, an elderly and toothless person, resembled a ship's mop more nearly than anything else I can think of—with great, rolling eyes, almost naked bodies, grasping their bows and arrows and looking round nervously as though they would jump off the truck and dart away, these Veddahs crouched together and glared like wild beasts. They had been brought down from the hills in the Eastern province for the Prince to see, and they were a strange company to behold. Next day I saw them once more, and the result of my observation you shall presently have. Just below them stood the 57th Regiment, under the command of Colonel Logan, all in white dresses, and wearing white helmets. Then a number of gentlemen with doubtfully fitting dress coats, stood grouped together, the Municipal Council of the city of Kandy. But these were by no means the conspicuous portion of the gathering. Have you ever heard of the old Kandyan Chiefs, the grand old men who still hold the drums captured from Major Davie's force when they beat the English down to the gates of Colombo, and extended their independence for twelve years? If so, let me say that they are now the most loyal subjects of the Queen, that one of them has conferred great favours upon Kandy, and that they are now as contented as they were once troublesome. Still, had they been dressed in the costume of Europeans, they might not have attracted so much attention, certainly they would not have added so greatly to the interest of the scene. They came down in their most resplendent robes, with the pincushion cap, richly embroidered and crowned in the centre by an aigrette of emeralds, pearls, sapphires, and rubies, long white dresses and drawers, marvellously worked, and gilded jackets, and broad gold lace bands round their waists. And there they stood, in two groups, on each side of the carpet along which the Prince would pass, ready to give him a Kandyan welcome. Behind them again were some Buddhist priests, with dirty shaven heads and long yellow robes ; the people, the horses and carriages did the rest. The Prince was enthusiastically received, he spoke to the chiefs, entered the carriage, and drove away up to the town to the music of bands and the shouts of the people.

CHAPTER X.

KANDYAN CURIOSITIES.

From the day when I first read "Mangnall's Questions," and trembled lest I should forget their answers when I stood before my tutor and the desk in which I knew a particularly thick cane was hidden, I have understood that the Buddhists had eccentric ideas. But until the day I visited Kandy I did not know that they could be half so eccentric as I now find them to be.

It had been announced that a Perahera would be held in the evening in front of the Pavilion or Government House, in which the Prince temporarily stays. What a Perahera was it was not easy to learn. That it was a religious procession, and had something to do with very religious elephants was well-known, but, for the rest, my own very imperfect knowledge of the elegant language called Tamil, and the ignorance of English displayed by my informant, conveyed very little information. It was, therefore, with some slight degree of curiosity that I took my place in the garden of the Government House, and waited for the fête. I had seen sacred—very sacred—bulls, monkeys, and goats at Bombay, but as yet it had not fallen to my lot to see sacred elephants. The gardens of the Pavilion are equally beautiful with the rest of Kandy. Leaves of all shades, flowers of all sorts, surround a very pretty mansion. A fine portico with very wide steps and grandly-designed pillars opens upon a broad pathway. It was in this pathway, close by the portico, where, about ten o'clock in the evening, the seats for the few privileged spectators of the Peraheran sacred procession were placed. A somewhat similar spectacle was promised to the people for the morrow. This was to be a very select and private performance. Looking down the pathway, which was purposely very dimly lighted by a few Chinese lanterns, you saw at the far extremity a great blaze of torches and lamps. An inordinately inquisitive person would probably have gone at once to the gate, and dissolved the spell of mystery which overhung the proceedings. But those who were wise took the Governor's advice and waited on either side of the Prince till a signal was given and the glare and flare of the torches came nearer. It was then clear that an extraordinary spectacle had been prepared by the Buddhist priests as a token of extreme favour to the Prince of Wales. For there were the chiefs of the temples, the custodians of the sacred tooth of Buddha, with their elephants, banners, and insignia of priestcraft, attended by their dancers and tom-tom beaters, and accompanied by the Kandyan chieftains whom we saw at the station.

To those who have not heard religious tom-toms played by religious men, it is difficult to convey the sensation which we, who were not used to such a noise, experienced. Twenty very large tom-toms, beaten with very large sticks by very strong fists, made the attack. In advancing upon us the players had considerable advantages. They wore very little clothing, so that their sinewy arms were quite unencumbered; they were celebrated for the clatter they could make, and had been incited to excel themselves on this occasion; then they had to aid them a beautiful echo, which vastly increased the din; and, lastly, they were allowed to come as close as they pleased. I do not complain that my ear-drums tingled—I do not think anybody dreamt of mentioning the ear in connection with that terrible noise. Long before the tom-toms and their beaters had taken up a good position the sound had penetrated far beyond the ear, and was preying upon the vitals of the half-stunned Englishmen; it struck upon the cavity of the chest, it descended to the pit of the stomach, the ear gave up resistance as useless, and let the sound fly all over the body till we absolutely quivered.

While this noise was going on, there emerged from the procession about a dozen of the ugliest young men we had yet seen. They were plentifully ornamented with strings of pearls and spangles; on their ankles, wrists and necks were little cymbals, which made a rattling, clinking sound, which, therefore, would introduce a new element of misery to listeneirs, had not the tom-tom players been by this time exhausted and obliged to play with considerably less vigour. The twelve men began to dance, while the torches were held round in order that they might see where to jump. For jumping would be a better description of their exercises than any other word. First they would spring forward and then they would fly back, then twirl round on their heels, shake their cymbals, strike the little tom-toms which they carried under their arms, and utter a yell. As a savage performance it, no doubt, had its merits, but when it had been repeated a dozen times the Prince had had enough of it, and they were ordered to move on.

Next to them came a long string of elephants, ridden by priests, and very gaudily dressed. I had good reason to know that the first rider was chief of a temple, for during the afternoon I had wandered into the interior of a shrine on the assurance that my presence would not be objected to, when that old gentleman rushed in, threw off his long yellow robe, and performed a dance round me very similar to that which the jumping twelve had favoured the Prince with. A dignified retreat became advisable, as the priest was being imitated by some of his assistants, and their rage was rapidly increasing. I had, therefore, as I backed out of the temple, keeping my face towards my assailants, good opportunity for noticing the lineaments of that fierce priest's face, and hence my recognition of him when the elephants went by. Somehow or other, to his evident chagrin, nobody else seemed to know him, however, and the three first elephants were allowed to pass by almost unnoticed. The fourth was a particularly fine animal, and as he approached, the Prince held out a tempting piece of sugar-cane, upon which the loyal creature dutifully knelt, conveyed the cane to his mouth, and then, thoughtfully, held out his trunk for more. He got more cane, but not quite of the kind he hoped for; it was a stroke from a malacca, admonishing him to get up and make room for another. That other was not far behind; indeed, he was down on his knees, holding out his trunk, before the Prince could give him a handful of plantain. But his energy was rewarded—he received the fruit, and made off with it as rapidly as possible. After this fashion about a dozen elephants were treated, and then the Kandyan chiefs whom we had seen in the afternoon came up in a body, preceded by their banners and sword-bearers, made a low obeisance to the Prince and passed on.

In this way the procession continued without flagging. The dancers varied in costume, and in manner of performance; the elephants had their own idiosyncrasies: some preferred sugar-cane, some chose plantains, some refused to move till they received both. Then the dancers, as they sprang out of the surrounding gloom into the glare of light, had their eccentricities. There was one who insisted on turning somersaults till he got too giddy to turn any more, and had to be led away. There were a dozen with conical caps made of strips of brass, who danced till they had to be removed. There were tom-tom beaters, too, who played and jumped and jumped and played till Mr. Gregory could bear with them no longer, and they were chased away; and there were even dancing torch-bearers, whose gyrations were both fearful and wonderful. Little need for wonder was there that a tiny elephant, unused to such a clatter, made a shrill, trumpeting noise with his trunk, rushed at the gateway, and vainly attempted to dance too—in this instance, a fandango on the body of a native. For two hours the din continued, the enormous procession having apparently no end. But at last it was over. The Prince retired, and Kandy went to sleep.

The knighting of Mr. Gregory, now Sir William Gregory, K.C.M.G., and the exhibition of the sacred tooth of Buddha, are two events which will long be remembered in Kandy. To a Buddhist the description of the tooth and its surroundings would be most important, for great advantages come to the fortunate man who looks upon that sacred relic and lives. To a loyal Englishman the investiture ceremony would be of paramount importance. Let us be loyal, and look into the audience-chamber of the old palace, where already, an hour before the announced time, all society in Kandy is assembled.

No insignificant building is that in which we find ourselves. A large oblong apartment, with a richly-carved ceiling, supported by magnificent columns of teak, having a broad space in the centre, colonnades on each side, and at one end a raised daïs. On the daïs are a throne of crimson velvet for the Prince, and an armchair for the Governor. Flags hang from the walls; floral decorations are plentiful; the English ladies and gentlemen who are ranged in tiers inside the colonnades are brilliantly attired in evening dress and uniforms. A guard of honour holds the approaches to the daïs; the apartment is resplendently lighted; only one fault is noticeable—the Prince will face the south when presently he sits in Dunbar, the saddest omen of danger that the Cingalese know. Why did not some well-instructed person tell his Royal Highness that a King of Kandy, or an Heir Apparent to this mountainous realm, should always face the north when on the throne? Inside the centre space, to the right of the daïs, was a scene which has seldom before been witnessed. A number of Kandy ladies, dressed in white, and beautifully decorated with jewels, are seated in a long row, ready to welcome the Prince. You look at them, and see at once that they are high-caste ladies of no mean birth. The conclusion is right; these grand-looking dames are no less than the wives of the chiefs of Kandy, come for the especial purpose of seeing their lords wait upon his

Royal Highness. While we are regarding all this a stir is noticeable outside. A band, which is stationed between two lines of artificial elephants, strike up the National Anthem, and instantly the Prince, loudly cheered, enters the hall, accompanied by the Governor and suite, and ascends the daïs. The officers group themselves behind, the audience settles down, and nothing is heard but the faint cheering of the crowds outside. It is a marvel that that is heard. For a tropical storm has burst over Kandy. The lightning is flashing, the rain is descending in torrents, the illuminations which but a few moments before made Kandy brilliant, from the tops of the mountains, where bonfires blazed, to the island in the lake which occupies the centre of the city, and was resplendent with Chinese lamps, are fast going out. But we must leave the people outside, for the chiefs are passing along the hall, not on all fours, but erect and proud, conscious of their dignity, and fully equal to the exigencies of the occasion. Five abreast, with those extraordinary hats of theirs on their heads, they approach slowly, and then, as their names are severally announced, bow, and retire. Not for long, however. A few minutes later, they return, bearing in their hands a huge, silver casket, of exquisite workmanship, containing all kinds of silver instruments, for the enjoyment of the betel nut. With great grace they present this, and with equal grace it is received. Then they file off once more, and leave the space in front of the daïs vacant.

Just now the Governor is seen to leave his place, at the left of the Prince, and, in a mysterious fashion, pass down the hall by one of the corridors. There is, simultaneously with this movement, a procession forming at the far end of the room. It advances slowly, and then we see that Mr. Gregory is advancing towards the daïs, followed by Mr. Douglas, the Auditor-General; Mr. Birtch, the Colonial Secretary; and the rest of his Excellency's suite. Everybody stands up, Mr. Gregory makes a profound bow to the Prince, who at once begins a short address, which is to the purport that the Queen, recognizing the many merits of her right, trusty councillor, the Governor, has resolved on making him a Knight Commander of the Most Illustrious Order of St. Michael and St. George; that he (the Prince) has been commanded to confer the honour, and that it was with peculiar pleasure that he did so. Then a gentleman, with a roll of paper in his hand, steps forward and reads a patent, which tells how that, on the 3rd of December, the Queen was pleased to direct that William Gregory should be distinguished; and next, a document directing the Prince to carry out the patent; whereupon Lord Charles Beresford unsheathes a sword and hands it to his Royal Highness. Mr. Gregory kneels down, and the Prince, touching him on both shoulders, says, "Rise, Sir William Gregory!" and, as the newly-made knight gets up, shakes hands with him. I need not give the exact text of the address the Prince delivered. It was complimentary to the Knight, to his suite, to his province. Nor need I trouble you with the words in which Mr. Gregory expressed his thanks. Suffice it to say, that they were few, well chosen, and loyal. Sir William will always value the Order, but most of all because it has been presented him by the Prince. Then the Governor has to read the time-honoured document, which promises, in case of promotion, degradation, or death, Sir William, his heirs, or assigns, will duly return the glittering star, which the Prince has just clasped round his neck, and then, with another shake of the Royal hand, and another bow to the Royal throne, he reascends the daïs, and takes his seat once more by the side of the Prince. Without much loss of time, the Prince now decorates two members of the Council with the dignity of C.M.G., leaves the platform, advances to the wives of the chieftains, shakes hands with them all, and then, followed by his suite, makes for the Buddhist Temple, and Buddha's tooth.

It was fortunate that the temple was within the precincts of the palace, for the storm continued, and the rain fell fast. We, however, were happily able to pass by a covered way into the sacred building through the serried ranks of hundreds of Buddhist priests, all clad in yellow silk robes, a fine array of proud men, with their closely shaven beards and their bared right arms. They did not bow, for a Buddhist priest knows of none greater than himself save Buddha; but their welcome seemed none the less hearty. On we went through the sacred corridor, up the sacred steps, into the sacred shrine itself, where the high priest stood ready to welcome the Prince. There were eight priests and twenty Englishmen crowded into a little room about eight feet square, which, brightly lighted and heavily hung with drapery, combined to form a very "warm corner" indeed. However, his Royal Highness with great good humour accommodated himself to circumstances, and, refusing to listen to the suggestion of one of his underlings that all save one or two should quit the apartment, waited for the production of the sacred tooth.

It was not to be exhibited in a hurry, however, without due ceremony, or indeed, without some respect for our nerves. So he first of all produced some pretty jewellery, next some chains, a great quantity of precious stones, and then a large bell-shaped casket of silver, richly ornamented with gems and chains. Raising this very slowly, he exposed another carandua, similarly wrought and similarly ornamented, then another and another, each enclosed within the preceding. We looked with some surprise at our Buddhist friends, and wondered whether after all the tooth was there. But, at last a little gold casket was reached, beautifully ornamented with rubies, sapphires, and diamonds, and then it became evident that the last box had been reached. Besides, too, the priest had now taken the box in his hands, and was slowly raising the lid. How necks were craned forward and eyes strained to catch the first glimpse of this relic of Gotama Buddha. At last it burst into view, and

BUDDHIST PRIESTS EXHIBITING BUDDHA'S TOOTH TO THE PRINCE AT KANDY.

we were in possession of all the good which those gain who are fortunate to see the mortal remains of a god. I am bound to admit that it was large enough to satisfy anybody, and, more than that, to say that if Gotama Buddha ever did have such a tooth as that in his head, he might fairly claim to be excused from all responsibility for anything he said or did. What we saw was a huge piece of ivory, about two inches and a half long, and about half an inch in diameter, rising slowly to a smoothly rounded cone, reposing on a gold lotus leaf.

After this we were shown the largest emerald in the world, a huge gem three or four inches long and nearly two inches deep, in the form of a likeness of Buddha. Of its value the priests could say nothing; but there was little doubt that it was real, the Prince very shrewdly remarking that the Buddhists were too good judges to be deceived in such a matter; then an anklet which used to be worn by the Kings of Kandy, and a number of other jewels, amongst them a great sapphire as large as a walnut, very richly set. This concluded the exhibition, whereupon the Prince presented the priests with two handsomely-bound dictionaries, promised to hear a part of their scriptures read presently, and also to receive as a present a copy of their sacred books. This done, his Royal Highness quitted the shrine, which was once more closed and jealously guarded. So much for the tooth for which one of the Kings of Siam offered a million sterling. Next day, when I visited the temple, hundreds of eager Buddhists were crowding into the sacred room. They had brought offerings of money, of cloth, of beeds and ornaments; one carried a great bottle of eau-de-Cologne as a gift, another had brought a picture. In the corridors of the temple were some dozens of men and women with plates full of beautiful flowers, which they sold as offerings to Buddah; and altogether a strange scene of chaffering, bargaining, crowding, giving, and worshipping was witnessed.

The ceremony of hearing the words of Buddha was to take

place in the Octagon, a tower also belonging to the palace where the Kings of Kandy were wont to view their subjects. It is an eight-sided room, with an open verandah. Seated here, the Prince could look down upon the Esplanade, a green square near the centre of the town, and see the people massed in thousands waiting to see his Royal Highness, and waiting to see, moreover, the public Perahera, or Procession of Elephants, a private rehearsal of which we had attended on the previous evening. It was not long in taking place. Some priests entered, bearing two rolls of manuscript, which were presented to the Prince in return for the dictionaries, a selected reading was gone through, there were smiles, congratulations, and a parting. Then looking out of the verandah upon the Esplanade, through the heavy rain which still fell, the Prince waited the procession of elephants. There is no doubt that the sight would have been as pretty and as effective as was the rehearsal, had not the rain spoilt everything. Down it came, putting out torches and lamps and Chinese lanterns alike, making the very elephants so miserable that some of them refused to trumpet with their trunks when they went past the Octagon, a breach of manners which would otherwise never have entered the head of a well-bred elephant. Still the people stood patiently till the procession had passed and the Prince had gone, when they slowly separated, though drenched to the skin by the dismal rain. Next morning the Prince went away to the far interior to shoot elephants.

Here it was that his Royal Highness met with the only accident of his trip; and after this fashion. It is universally conceded that no human being can by any possibility be in two places at once. Let me, therefore, while delaying to chronicle the adventures of the Prince in the forests of Ceylon, recount first of all what befell the Duke of Sutherland, Lord Alfred Paget, Lord Carington, and one or two others of the Prince's suite who left Colombo for Neuralia, and so parted company with his Royal Highness for a day or two. To do this it must first of all be understood that Neuralia is a hill station, blessed with a climate very similar to that of England, producing all the fruits and flowers that we love best at home, while at the same time it has many blossoms and trees of which we in England see nothing. More than that, its woods abound with game of all kinds; the elk is plentiful, bison and buffalo abound, cheetahs, too, and panthers, to say nothing of the great guana —a lizard of gigantic proportions, which runs at you, opens its great mouth, and if report be true, bites like a young alligator —snakes, and leeches. Then there are floods which swamp the country; so that perils wait the huntsman by water as well as by land. You may be strangled by a boa, eaten by a panther, or drowned by a stream at any moment—excitement enough for anybody. It was to this pleasant district that part of the Prince's suite went.

I wish I could picture to you the country through which they passed; high hills covered with coffee-plants, plains of paddy (or rice) fields, thick jungle in which the lentana, the palm, plantain, and other plants are found—a vegetable thicket only to be found in the zone of the tropics. It must not be supposed that the Prince's party travelled thither on foot. On the contrary, an appointed carriage—an omnibus in size—conveyed them to the place where Sir William Gregory spends a fourth of the year, as Governor of the island. Thence the trip was of a more sportsmanlike character. Quitting Neuralia early in the morning, the party proceeded, partly on horseback and partly on foot, to the place where sport was expected. At length an estate belonging to an hospitable planter named Denning was reached, and here a pack of deer-hounds was found. Without more ado these were soon taken out, and as quickly were in full cry. Through the jungle, round by paths marked by travellers, over hills and across valleys, the elk was pursued, till at length it was caught by one of the foot-hunters who pursued the game armed with long knives for the purpose of killing it should the dogs fail. They had been exceedingly useful in this instance. The elk was found to be stabbed and dead, and with this, as rain was falling heavily, the party returned to Neuralia, and next day rejoined his Royal Highness.

The news that the Prince had met with an accident created some consternation in Colombo. Intelligence of that kind looses nothing by travelling, and it was soon stated most positively that the Prince had had a very narrow escape, that the carriage in which he rode had been broken to pieces on the very edge of a precipice, that he was picked up out of the relics of the vehicle in much the same manner as a cask of flour is removed from a wreck; and that altogether the "catastrophe" was one of the most serious description. I at once telegraphed home to the effect that all this was an exaggeration. The facts were these: the Prince having spent a Sunday at Ruanwella, advanced on the Monday morning to a kind of platform in the jungle, close to which it was reported a party of seven elephants were hidden. Amongst them was a "rogue"—that is, a peculiarly vicious tusker—whose charging propensities were already well known to hunters in Ceylon; and it was hoped that the savage animal would fall a victim to the Prince's rifle. To ensure this, if possible, a number of beaters were sent out to drive the elephants past the crow's-nest on which the Prince was stationed. But it was all to no purpose; the elephants refused to take part in the fun, and, after waiting for three or four hours, the Prince was as far from shooting the "tusker" as ever. At last wiser counsels prevailed, and the Prince, descending from his waiting place, entered the jungle, accompanied by two good shots of colonial celebrity. Presently the Prince got sight of an elephant, fired, and brought him down; the beast was, however, only wounded, for he got up, and went off almost immediately afterwards, with great ease. Another chance of sport offered itself, however, almost directly, and this time it was successful; a fine large elephant was shot, and his tail secured as a trophy for his Royal Highness. One or two more were wounded later on, and then the party prepared to return. Returning, however, from a shooting expedition in Ceylon, is not always an easy, or, indeed, practicable feat, and the Prince, in the return journey from Ruanwella was unfortunate. The night was dark, fireflies and the torches of natives, stationed at various intervals, were the only lights to be seen, when at a sharp corner about five miles from the scene of the shooting a piece of bad ground was found. It is not an easy thing to drive "Cæsar and all his fortunes." The Governor's coachman lost his head, and upset the vehicle. Over it went with a crash, but so complete was the somersault that no one in the carriage was hurt. The Prince was safe, though covered with *débris.* Lord Charles Beresford, the hero of the Poona accident, crawled out unhurt, and an aide-de-camp who was one of the party was not inconvenienced. By the light of torches the elephant's tail, the Prince's trophy, was discovered amid much merriment. His Royal Highness took his seat in a spare carriage, and proceeded at once on his journey to Colombo, being so little incommoded by his misadventure as to hold a levée in the afternoon, visit the Horticultural Gardens later in the day, and attend a State dinner and State ball in the evening.

CHAPTER XI.

THE VEDDAHS OF CEYLON.

Who is it that says a Veddah cannot smile? If it be Mr. Hartshorne, as an indignant and personal friend of the Veddahs told me, let him hear of the following incident.

The Prince had hardly left the railway station, and his followers had scarcely done struggling for carriages, when a Cingalese clergyman, by name the Rev. D. Somanader, courteously enquired if I would like to make the acquaintance of the savages on the top of the railway trucks? I had read Mr. Hartshorne's story with too much interest to hesitate for one moment, and I at once invited the whole of the Veddahs to a breakfast in the garden adjoining my apartments. Seven o'clock was the hour appointed, and, true to the minute, the eight gentlemen and three ladies composing the party, attended by Mr. Somanader and a clergyman of the district, named Coles, entered the garden.

The breakfast of a Veddah is not a serious business. Very often it consists of plenty of fresh air, a drink of water, and a long walk. Our cuisine was an improvement on this. We had green cocoa-nuts, plantains, some rice, and a little curry. You must know that the Veddah likes meat as well as fruit. In his native home he enjoys a roasted monkey or a toasted lizard (the guana) exceedingly, and would not mind at any time eating a piece of venison, if fortune chances so to favour him. When the fickle goddess is not kind, he goes without flesh meat, or, like the flying ant of the island, eats anything he can get short of iron. The appearance of the cocoa-nuts delighted our guests, and they proceeded to partake of this first course with as much gusto as a London gourmand tastes his turtle and punch. It is always a joy to a Veddah to get a good meal. If in talking to him—always supposing, on the principle of the old cookery books, that you can first catch your Veddah, and next, that when you have caught him, you can understand his pleasant language—you suggest exertion of any kind, he is courteous but firm upon one subject. Before he works he must eat, and he will point to an empty stomach at once to indicate this to you. This peculiarity was accordingly met by the provision we had made, and it was the business of the Veddahs to make the most of the opportunity. Taking the hatchet kind of hammers they carry in their waist-cloth, they knelt down and cut through the fibrous covering of the nut, through the hard shell also, and so reached the kernel, which they pushed into their mouths as rapidly as possible. I thought I detected a smile on the face of one shock-headed old gentleman, without teeth, when he found that his nut was one of undoubted goodness. But it was needless to look just then—he laughed heartily presently, as you shall know. As for the young ladies, a very tender nut, some plantains, and bread were handed to each of them. They consumed nearly the whole at once, and handed over the fragments to a thoughtful-looking male friend, who, without regard for anybody who might chance to be hear, took off his waist-cloth, and, wrapping up the surplus eatables therein, replaced it in such a fashion that, had he been a European lady instead of a Veddah savage, the articles in question would have constituted an excellent dress-improver. Then the party adjourned into a corner to cook the rice we had given them, which enabled me to make enquiries of their guardian, and Mr. Coles, as to their manners and customs.

The party in Kandy were taken purposely from a very savage hill tribe, and only persuaded to come down by very considerable gifts of money, and ornaments for the women. Each of the girls had from twenty to thirty silver rings on her fingers, besides rings on her ankles, and arms, given her before she started: and of these treasures they were all very proud. I have spoken of their food; let me tell of their marriage customs. Living in huts, which can be built in an hour, and making their cooking utensils mainly from the leaves of trees, the household arrangements of the Veddahs are not such as to call for any serious preparation. When a young man falls in love with a maiden, he first of all obtains her consent, and then waits upon her parents, who only demand that he shall present their daughter with a piece of cloth. He assents, the cloth is produced, the lovers become husband and wife at once, and remain so. There is no religious ceremony, for of religion the Veddah has no idea. The only supernatural being of which he has any notion is a devil, which, by the way, is a very respectable sort of fiend, indeed, and not at all so implacable and bad as our Western Beelzebub. The Veddah's demon is really only a misguided person, who is fond of mischief; and when, therefore, anybody falls ill, his friends get some jaggery, or native sugar, a little piece of cocoa-nut, and any other luxury which circumstances permit of, and, placing it on a leaf, dance round it till they think the Satanic anger is appeased.

Breakfast over, the Veddahs were summoned to shoot. So much has been said about their skill with the bow and arrow, that we were careful to watch their powers very narrowly. We placed a leaf about ten inches long by six square upon a bamboo, about thirty yards from the place where they stood, and then invited them to shoot. Two arrows were sped at once; the first shot of the shock-headed old man went clean through the leaf; the second, discharged by a thin man with long hair, struck the bamboo and knocked it down. It was clear that the target was too close for such marksmen, and we removed it to nearly double the distance, when the shooting began again. In all about twenty arrows were fired; scarcely one fell six inches from the target, most of them either went through the leaf or touched it; a man at the distance would have been struck by eighteen arrows at least. When a marksman made a particularly good shot there was a shout of congratulation; when a bad shot was made the archer looked at his bow with anger and adjusted the string with great care. The thin man—why call one thin when all were skeletons?—was most successful, and won a rupee; the gentleman with the vagrant locks came next, and received threepence. As for the rupee, I am bound to say it was received as a matter of course—seized with ungrateful avidity; but the threepenny-piece was clearly a matter of surprise. A second prize evidently entered into nobody's calculation. I suspect that when a race for a plump monkey takes place, the rule is, Eclipse first, and the rest nowhere—the fortunate person who gets the monkey eats it all, and his friends look on. Anyhow, the two-anna piece was a surprise. The recipient turned it over twice—it was a new coin and glittered in his dirty palm very enticingly. In an instant he popped it into the rag encircling his waist, and then refuted Mr. Hartshorne by laughing. Yes, there could be no mistake about it—the Veddah had got something to laugh for. An unexpected threepenny-piece was all gain—he could well afford to be merry. Nor let it be thought that he was not a pure wild man. He was the typical man of the party, with more hair, fewer teeth, and less clothing than any of them—a magnificent hand at eating green cocoa-nuts, and a great lover of some bitter red bark, which he placed between his gums occasionally, and mumbled with great pleasure.

The shooting over, and this jocular Veddah having sat for his portrait, a dance was proposed and agreed to, on the exhibition of a few rupees, which were subscribed for the purpose. You must not suppose for a moment that the ladies danced. Still, the part they took in the ceremony was one that astonished me. We were under the shade of some plantains; a cool, quiet nook, covered by leaves. Five of the men formed a kind of circle; three stood at the side; the women took up a position a little way off. Till then I had not had an opportunity of looking fully at them; but now I noted that although they were very thin, their countenances were bright, their eyes bright, their carriage almost as erect as that of the Mahratta women of Bombay, and their skin several shades lighter than the men's. They were of a distinctly different type from the Cingalese, not having a single feature of resemblance; but although undoubtedly savages of a low order, they were neither repulsive nor indeed ugly. The three men struck up a song; the five began a singular dance which consisted in a hop on one leg and a bob of the head—altogether something both novel and funny. Just then I looked up, and the Veddah women were actually laughing—laughing and hiding their faces, too, as though they were bashful. What could it all mean? A bashful Veddah lady is, if I mistake not, altogether unmentioned by Mr. Hartshorne, and was quite unlooked for by me. But the secret was soon explained. Those sad dogs of Veddahs, those gay young men from the hills, were singing a love song, with some questionable passages in it, and the girls were laughing. So far as the faces of the men, dancers and singers alike, were concerned, no confirmation of this could be gained, for from the low monotonous chant and the savage dance I could learn nothing. Yet I have no doubt that the reverend guardian of these savages was right, and that Veddah humanity is very like other humanity all the world over.

CHAPTER XII.

THE SACRED TOOTH.

It was my fortune to obtain a second glance at Buddha's tooth, under somewhat singular circumstances.

Some years ago, when the funds of the temple became low, and it was necessary to raise money for the crowd of priests who live in Kandy, the tooth was exposed to the view of pilgrims for three weeks, and a good round sum was obtained. Those who gave much enjoyed a prolonged stare, smaller donors were allowed to look and move on, whilst the rest, whose offerings were insignificant, but who were admitted on the old principle that "mony a mickle maks a muckle," were hurried past. It had been expected that the tooth would be exhibited now for a similarly long period, and the faithful in the country were gathering up their skirts and girding themselves for a pilgrimage to Kandy, when suddenly the Dewee Nilemee, a kind of Dean of the Temple, issued a notice that the relic would be put away, and at the same time invited me to witness its restoration to its place. I had before imagined that the room to which the Prince of Wales had been admitted was the ordinary shrine of the relic, and at first hesitated to obey the summons; but deliberation resulted in a change of intention, and I repaired to the temple.

To reach the room to which I was told the relic had been conveyed it was necessary to go to the side of the temple, and thence by a narrow and dimly-lighted stone staircase, jealously guarded by priests, into a small square ante-room. As I entered the door of the apartment I noticed that it was covered with beaten gold, that the posts were composed of an outer strip of finely-carved wood, then a strip of ebony, next a strip of carved ivory, and after that one of embossed silver, the inner strip of all, namely, that next the door, being of gold. Passing under a curtain which was now lifted, I entered the room and found myself in the company of about twenty priests, all guarding very jealously the inner apartment of all. It was clear that I had arrived at the resting-place of the relic, else what could mean the sliding iron-barred gate, which, being drawn back, showed a golden door with ornamental posts, exactly like those I have already mentioned? A heavy curtain, however, prevented my looking through the doorway, and three or four stout Cingalese prevented my further progress. It was possible that I might have to turn back after all, for the priests gave me looks that could not be called affectionate, and muttered in their unpleasant language remarks the reverse of complimentary. I was wondering whether the purchase of a plateful of flowers which stood on a table would be of service, whether I should drop some money into an iron grating close to the door, evidently the receptacle of offerings, and so try the effect of benevolence, or whether I should retreat, when the Dewee Nilemee's face appeared in the doorway, and I was admitted into the sacred chamber.

The room I was now in was scarcely more than six feet square and nine high. The ceiling was heavily hung with what had once been yellow silk, now discoloured and almost black. The walls were bare; there were two other doors—on the right, and on the left—both fastened, and I could discover no window and no means of ventilation whatever. Facing the door, on the step of which I stood, was a square iron cage, raised three feet from the ground and reaching to the ceiling. The floor of the cage was of beaten silver. In the centre of the floor was a huge silver gilt bell-like structure, beautifully embossed, more than four feet high, and at the base nearly three feet in diameter. On a silver table in front of this cage were all the jewels we had seen exhibited on Friday night to the Prince; some half-dozen golden pagodas, the receptacles for these treasures, were there also, and nine priests were preparing, under the supervision of the Dewee Nilemee, to put all away. There lay, also, the sacred tooth on the golden lotus leaf, ready to be placed in the largest pagoda of all. Eight or ten lighted wax candles, some in stands and some in the hands of the priests, added to the almost unbearable heat of the apartment, in which thirteen or fourteen people were crowded together. With great ceremony the little golden casket containing the tooth was closed by the high priest, his brethren of the golden robe raising their hands in pious attitude the while. The largest pagoda was then opened, and all the inner cases I had previously seen were taken out and opened. One by one they received the relic, only now each was wrapped in muslin as it was placed in the next largest case There seemed occasionally to be especial care to arrange the muslin in a certain way. Everything was clearly done according to rule, and those shaven yellow-robed priests were determined to do their work well. A curious sight it was to see them bending over the relic, the guttering candles in their hand, while the Deweee Nilemee jealously watched the gradual swathing of the treasure. Case after case received it, more muslin was handed up whenever wanted, till at last it was ready for the golden pagoda. Then it finally disappeared from view, a golden key was produced, the pagoda was locked, and for the present placed on one side.

I wish I could fully describe that pagoda. It must be of great value, for it is of pure gold, is very heavy, and nearly two feet high. From the umbrella or topmost story of the pagoda, hang chains which support splendid jewels, catseyes nearly an inch in diameter, a sapphire quite as large, besides diamonds and rubies; but only an actual sketch in bright colours can convey to the eye an adequate idea of its beauty.

The next treasure to be similarly wrapped in muslin and put away was the emerald Buddha, which was also placed in a pagoda, somewhat smaller though quite as pretty. There were the anklet and one piece of open gold filagree work, heavily set with diamonds and other stones, to go into another pagoda, and then the great sapphire we saw an evening or two ago. Each was wrapped up carefully, each hidden under the closest supervision, and of each due account was taken by the Dewee Nilemee. At length the two high-priests climbed up into the cage, and proceeded to lift the top of the bell from its place. They were strong men, but the effort needed was a great one, and it was some little time before the massive piece of gilded silver was taken up. So soon as it was done, however, one of the priests knelt, and, handing out some more muslin, produced at length a silver bô-tree, a bag full of little golden images of Buddha, some chains, studs, and, in fact, about as miscellaneous a collection of jewellery as you would find in a West-end shop. Out it came by handfuls, to be counted by the Dewee Nilemee, and given into the custody of the priests, who placed the articles in the remaining pagodas. But an end will come to the production of treasures, be they never so many, and an end came to these; the pagodas were full, and it now only remained to wrap them all in thick folds of muslin. This done, the receptacle of the book was lifted up by the high priests, a deep obeisance was made, and then it was placed in the centre bell-shaped case. One after another the rest of the pagodas were placed round it, the silver bô-tree following last of all; and, when this had been achieved, and the number duly counted, the priests lifted the silver top once more, and with a supreme effort got it into position. The Dewee Nilemee, with evident pride, produced a large gold key, and locked the huge casket.

This was not all, however. A band of thin iron was now brought, and entwined round the bell in such a way that, with the aid of a small padlock which was attached to it, entrance to the bell was most effectually prevented; and, the padlock being fastened, some more muslin was brought, wrapped over the lock, and sealed with the Dewee Nilemee's seal, bearing a golden dodo, and his name in Cingalese. A gold umbrella from which chains and jewels hung was fixed on the top of the bell, ornamental pieces were added to it, till at length it stood out in the centre of the cage, a glittering pagoda, ready for the worship of all who visit the shrine and are allowed for a consideration to peer through the bars at the resting-place of the tooth. The barred gate having been drawn and fastened by a key in custody of one of the high priests, the candles were put out, and we, perspiring and faint, emerged into the outer room, saw the door locked, the second grating fastened, and a watch appointed to guard the treasure. The relic of Buddha had been safely consigned to its shrine.

CHAPTER XIII.

A WEEK IN MADRAS.

In the room where I sat to write this there was the engraved portrait of a very extraordinary old man. His face wore the most complete expression of idiotic joy that could possibly be infused into any countenance. Underneath was the following inscription: "Rajah of Rajahs, Rajah Chundoo Lal, Maharajah Bahadoor, the devoted servant of Asuf Jah; who is the Roostum of his Age, the Aristotle of his Time, the Conqueror of Countries, the Administrator of States, the Governor of Realms." Exhibited almost anywhere else, that grin depicted on Bahadoor's face would be almost incomprehensible. But, with the fair view of the wide-spreading sea shore, the pleasant champaign, and the grand city of Madras, I could understand why the "Roostum of his Age" felt very happy. If then, the ownership of the fields, the strand, and the streets of Madras made this ancient Ruler gleeful, how proud should the Duke of Buckingham, modern administrator of more than the "Governor of Realms" ever ruled over, be to-day! Since the Maharajah has departed, Madras has increased in stateliness and beauty. Palaces are everywhere, broad parks and sheltered walks have been added to what was already a grand city, till the place which the Prince of Wales entered is as proud a capital as may be wished for.

Since the mainland was reached at Tuticorin the panorama which passed before us of landscapes, cities, and people was singularly changeful. I do not refer to an extraordinary passage which it was the fate of the special correspondents of the London press to make in the Ceylon Government steamer

"Nagotna." Far be it from my purpose to excite the risibility of those who sent us to sea in a small flat-bottomed steamer, 160 tons in measurement, in one of the worst gales ever experienced in the Gulf of Manaar. How we were thrown from side to side of the creaking, helpless craft; how the captain, with a look that Dickens' ever-memorable Bunsby might have envied, admitted, on the second night, that he did not know where he was; how we arrived at Tuticorin just as his Royal Highness had left for Madura; and how, to gain a sight of his reception at Trichinopoly, we had to avail ourselves for twelve miles of such accommodation as a bullock-van whirled along by a special and very powerful engine over a very rough, because newly-made, road afforded, need not be dilated upon. Suffice it to say that we did not experience that keen enjoyment which a passage by sea and a run through one of the most delightful parts of Southern India would otherwise have afforded.

In my recollection, however, there is a curious spectacle, illustrative of the manner in which the old and the new eras come continually into contact in this strangely conservative land. Look at it for a moment, and compare it with the spectacle of the Prince of Wales' entry into Madras. The *locale* is the railway station at Trichinopoly. A great crowd of natives are on the platform; there is an English guard of soldiers; outside are half-a-dozen camels heavily laden with luggage; both in and out of the station are some singularly-attired sepoys in the pay of the Princess of Tanjore. These sepoys have huge chimney-pot hats, clumsily-painted, black, old match-locks, green coats, no trousers, and a few have boots. The band which accompanies them has the funniest collection of old brass instruments, tom-toms, and pipes. They are all on the tiptoe of expectation, and drawn up in as good order as their notions of drill will permit. Suddenly a train runs into the station with a centre saloon carriage, through the open windows of which may be seen a chieftain richly dressed and ornamented with jewels, and two little boys. At the sight of the train a number of native officials emerge from a room on the platform, and come forward with heads bent low, as though about to seek audience of some very distinguished personage. The door of the saloon carriage thereupon opens, and the Prince—for it is the Prime Minister and husband of the Princess herself—comes forward. A few moments' conversation, carried on with great show of condescension on the one side and of humility on the other, ensues, and then some attendants bring to the door of the saloon a curious canopy of yellow brocaded silk. Immediately the sepoys draw up to the canopy, and, while the four posts are being given to four bearers and the sides of the canopy let fall, they take precautions that the crowd shall not touch the screen. What can be the reason? A moment's enquiry shows that the Princess in passing her capital desires to descend from the train for refreshment, and that the guard of honour and the assemblage of her chiefs is in recognition of her rank. Yet no one on the platform may see the face of the ruler he so greatly respects. He may gaze upon the rustling, yellow, silk canopy, may even note the form of its fair occupant as her Highness unconsciously presses against the hanging sides; but, however much he may esteem and reverence her, however great his loyalty to her dynasty, he may only be granted the privilege of a glimpse of the outward sign of Royalty. So, too, when she returns to the carriage, a quarter of an hour later, what struggling of soldiery and canopy-bearers to prevent the eye of the curious from gazing upon the Royal lady's face! It so chances that they are not so clever as zealous, and that just as her Highness is being smuggled up the carriage steps the poles shift their position, and the eyes and forehead of a handsome dame of some thirty years are for a moment visible. But such a glimpse was by no means intended. The only Royal personage who might be looked upon at will at this moment in Trichinopoly is the son of another Royal lady—the Empress of India.

Trichinopoly has undergone many changes and witnessed many spectacles. Yet it is doubtful whether it has often been the scene of a more momentous event during its singular history than that which took place on Saturday. As a general rule it has figured in most of the wars of the district. It fell a victim to the ever-wandering Mahrattas in 1741; a little later the Nizam took possession of it; the French had it next; then Clive, after which the Tangerines held it for a time. Eventually the English came again, turned the Tangerines out, and settled down with the determination to remain masters of the district for ever. The result is that a collectorate is established there, that European troops and native soldiers under European officers parade its streets, that the British flag flies on the summit of the Rock, and English laws are obeyed with promptitude.

Never, however, so far as I can learn, has any representative of English Royalty appeared here. Trichinopoly was accordingly *en fête* to receive the Prince on his arrival, and European as well as Native residents did the best they could to express their loyalty. I may at once note that the chief characteristic of the Hindoo, next to his love for chandeliers—in which peculiarity he surpasses all rivals—is his love of painting. He has not the slightest idea of perspective, his notions of the human form are vastly inferior to the ideas which painters in the time of Sennacherib possessed; the faces he draws are the ugliest conceivable, and the colours he uses are the worst that can be found; but for all that he will paint whenever the opportunity occurs. He paints the outside of his house and the inside of his temples; he bedaubs the walls of his garden if he has a garden wall to daub, and he paints his neighbour's wall if he has none of his own. And when a procession—such as that which the Prince made—takes place, he paints the arches which are erected with all his energy. He did so in honour of the Royal visit, and the result was a little startling. Scarcely a house in the place has a roof; many dwellings boast only their walls; old temples with blackened walls, dilapidated palaces, and broken-down bridges are on every side. Here is a pagoda surmounted by a cross, there a mosque without a dome—it is a scene of hopeless desolation.

Yet even these ruins are very picturesque. They are found on the banks of an exquisitely pretty river, in the centre of a wide-spreading and well-wooded plain, superior to that on which Poona stands; and in the centre of all is a rock, which even a Scotchman would allow to be superior to Arthur's Seat. A great red mass of stone rises sharply from the ground to a harshly-defined point. On the sides are galleries constructed of white marble; on the top is a pillared structure, of great massiveness, but still of singular elegance, surmounted by a flag-staff. Nothing else of any height is near it; it rises about five hundred feet in an almost perpendicular fashion, sharply and abruptly. At a distance it looks like a huge building, so wonderfully does it shoot up from the centre of the town, like the great Athenian hill, though by many feet its superior. At its foot is a bright, clear lake, well filled with water, and encompassed by a marble terrace. And then, in a wider circle, lies the dilapidated, ruined town, and outside this are the walls that enclose the fort. The decorations consisted of such arches as have not hitherto been seen anywhere else. I have said they were painted; their colour was black. Span and supports alike were then divided into spaces some two feet square, and on these panels native artists exercised their ingenuity. At Baroda the energetic engineer, while encouraging the natives to erect triumphal trophies, decidedly curbed their passion for daubing; but at Trichinopoly the peculiarity was encouraged. As a result, the streets exhibited a series of the most extraordinary pictures ever seen. One arch was covered with delineations of animals—blue cats, green dogs, red tigers, purple lions, yellow elephants, and snakes with heads like crabs and continuations like quadrupeds. Another arch depicted the trades of Trichinopoly. Blue-faced men with pink hair were hammering, with green hammers, purple-coloured gold bracelets. The other pictures of artisans were in excellent keeping with this specimen. A third arch portrayed all the deities of the district—Shiva, Vishnu, and the rest of their pleasant company. I do not know the exact number of arms and legs which each particular god and goddess claims as a right; but I am sure that uglier faces were never portrayed, and that an English painter would have had some trouble in producing anything like them. At first I thought the climax of caricature was reached in what was intended as a likeness of the Queen; but later on I saw an arch which bore a "likeness" of the Prince, with the inscription underneath, "His Royal Highness did come after all," and was then obliged to admit that the painter of that picture had surpassed all his countrymen.

The Hall of the Thousand Pillars, at Srirangam, is known far and wide. It is dedicated to that very respectable deity Vishnu, is the centre of one of the finest temples in India, is surrounded by massive towers, and contains many precious treasures. A visit from the Prince therefore was a certainty, and the priests prepared accordingly. The road along which his Royal Highness had to pass was exceedingly beautiful. Date and cocoanut palms, with almost every other kind of tropical tree, overhung and shaded it; the varied costumes of the people added to the brightness of the scene, and, consequently, the drive was very enjoyable. Arrived at the pagoda, the Prince was received by the dignitaries of the temple with all possible pomp and show. Old men in long, white robes, accompanied by a number of nautch-girls, gaudily dressed, ornamented with spangles, rings, jewels in their hair, and wreaths of flowers on their heads, met the Prince at the end of a long corridor, and conducted him to the temple, the girls singing a low chant, and scattering flowers on the pathway. In this way the Royal party moved into a kind of reception saloon, where the treasures of the place were displayed on a table. As usual, they were of the most varied and curious kinds, valuable, apparently, only for their weight as pieces of embossed gold, and for the jewels which enriched them. No possible use, for instance, could be made of a golden hand eighteen inches long, and proportionately broad; or of a foot of even greater size. Nor were the ornaments available for personal decoration, unless a man felt inclined to hang himself in golden chains, when the assortment at Srirangam might be useful.

However, it was interesting to look at these curiosities; interesting also to watch the countenances of the priests, as with evident pride they directed the attention of the Prince to one article after another; and his Royal Highness courteously waited till the exhibition was concluded without the slightest sign of impatience. His patience may be better understood when it is known, that in addition to the delay already incurred, it was proposed to read an address. Smilingly his Royal Highness assented to this also, whereupon an old gentleman, with a wonderful name, read some mild platitudes and assurances of loyalty with great self-satisfaction. True that the words were engraved upon a sheet of gold. A Miss Kilmansegg might have valued the oration on that account. But the history of Trichinopoly scarcely needed to be told again, and we were all very glad when the priest had done reading it.

The inspection of the Hall of the Thousand Pillars followed, and was better appreciated. As an architectural work the singular apartment could scarcely be called a triumph. Half the number of pillars, better carved and more regularly arranged, would have produced a better effect; half that number again would have been a further improvement; the roof was irregular, the supports were crooked, and the vista very defective. So much for the interior. The view from the roof, to which the Prince was presently taken, was good. Here the towers of the temple, with their rich carving, were fully in view, and they repaid the trouble which the Prince had taken in mounting. A few minutes were accordingly spent enjoying the prospect, and then the Royal visitor departed.

All was not over, however, even as far as the temple was concerned; for a portly priest, whose eyes twinkled with delight at having been introduced to the Prince, proposed that the girls should dance in honour of the occasion. Whereupon they began the low chant and curious shuffle, which I have already described. There was a conspicuously ugly man who sang, or, to be more just, howled vigorously. There was a piper, and, you may be sure, a large gathering of spectators. The audience, in fact, seemed to spring out of the ground, so suddenly did it appear, and so numerously. In less than a minute there must have been an assemblage of some hundreds—men, women, and children—all crowding round to see the dance. Then, as though by some preconcerted signal, the great doors of the pagoda opened, and in bundled, all together, helter skelter, a number of elephants, a sacred buffalo or two, a donkey, and a great crowd of people of all ages. The animals made quickly for their resting-places. The people increased the dense mass of onlookers, and we, to avoid suffocation, struggled through the perspiring mass into the open air, much to the disappointment of the chief of the temple, who presently retired and wrote a long letter of eight quarto pages, which he forwarded to those who represented the English press.

A far more picturesque spectacle was that afforded by the rock when illuminated at night time. I don't know that any great talent was needed to produce a remarkable effect in the rugged outlines of the rock itself. The curious pagoda which crowns its summit, and the buildings on its sides only required to be lighted up in the most careless manner to ensure a spectacle worth looking at. The priests of the temple on the rock had, however, done their utmost to render the occasion memorable, and as a result the rock blazed with light. Coloured fires were lighted on each projecting point. Every line of the grand natural structure and of the temple was marked by hundreds of lamps; the whole standing out against the dark sky in bold relief. Daylight had scarcely gone when the Prince, attended by his suite, took up his position in a temporary building erected opposite the rock, for the special purpose of enabling his Royal Highness to witness the illumination and promised fireworks. A huge silver throne had been placed on a daïs under a marvellously worked canopy of gold and silver foil, crimson and blue paper, and such like decorative material. Here the Prince took his seat; his suit ranged themselves on both sides of him in velvet chairs, ladies and gentlemen of the district came in and stood behind the Royal party; a band which was situated in the road struck up, and then the entertainment began.

The rock itself was simply magnificent. The great square tank of water which intervened between the Prince and the temple was radiant with lamps; the masses of red and white turbaned people, the long lines of troops, and the occupants of the gardens were all parts of a very striking picture. But the fireworks were a dismal failure. It mattered little whether we enjoyed it or not; the people were delighted beyond description, and any unpleasant effects from the clouds of smoke which filled the air were more than compensated for when, as was the case every now and then, the noise ceased for a minute, the vapour cleared away, and we saw the rock once more blazing as brightly as ever. Once we saw a cataract of fire falling down one of the crevices of the rock, and now and then the colours of the lights changed, and the mountain, which was bright red a minute before, was suddenly brilliant in bright green. It was altogether a novel and pleasing sight, and one which attracted the Prince for two or three hours.

I do not know how the notion arose, but by some means

or other I had come to associate Madras in my mind with almost all that is objectionable. In praise of Bombay whole books had been written, for Calcutta there were always plenty to speak; but no one to say a good word for Madras. That you could not land on its surf-beaten shore without the certainty of a tossing, and the probability of a drenching; that the Black Town was as uninviting a spot as any on earth; that its climate was sultry and its atmosphere redolent of ague and cholera, everybody asserted. Consequently, when I entered the capital of the Southern Presidency my expectations were not great. Little did I expect to find a broad beach of bright sand some miles in length and many yards in depth, with a bright, blue sea in front, and the prettiest of watering-places behind. Nowhere did the Black Town, that great bugbear of the city, obtrude itself. There was scarcely anything to show that we were not enjoying a summer day's retreat on the English coast. Between us and even the English houses and Government buildings for the most part a wide promenade and spacious gardens extended. There were English children playing on the beach; English ships of war riding in the offing; the English flag was flying from the flagstaff of that famous old fort whence Clive was wont to sally; unmistakably English sailors were wandering along the shore; and the heat for the moment was scarcely more than that of an English July day.

Yet there were tokens that we were not in England. A glance at the boats coming ashore revealed those most singular crafts, the catamarans, with their intrepid boatmen and strange cargoes. Two pieces of wood fastened together somewhat after the fashion of an open raft, and a pole with a flat end, completed the boat equipment, forming altogether such a water-conveyance as one would scarcely care to travel in. The black fisherman, standing erect on their extraordinary craft, now riding over the surf, and next letting a heavy wave go over him, could scarcely be found off Hastings or Eastbourne; nor should we meet with such a group of coloured women engaged in drying fish at either Aldborough or Rhyl. For all that, the scene is not un-English, and the illusion is not altogether destroyed when we look inland. There are beautiful buildings such as could only have been designed by English architects. There is the spire of an English church, rising high in the air; you come upon English shops immediately upon leaving the strand, and the drums of your ears are being rent by salutes from English guns. Of course you can be under no mistake when once you have crossed the park-like space which runs down to the shore, and enter the Black Town. You are then in the very blackest of black places that can be imagined. The marvel is how the inhabitants who are crowded together within its walls contrive to live in such an atmosphere as they breathe. Let me describe the sort of house they dwell in.

In Bombay two-storied tenements, with great windows, fronted by a brick terrace or seat, on which the friends of the shopkeeper can squat and talk, form the native bazaar. In Madras, however, the houses have only one story, boast no windows whatever, and are fronted by two terraces, raised about eighten inches above each other, the door, which is the only mode of ingress, light, or ventilation, being always a very subsidiary consideration. Along each side of the road runs a broad gutter, somewhat after the fashion which obtains in Baroda. Into this the sewage of the town runs freely, with such effect as need not be detailed. On the terraces the population eat, drink, and sleep. I saw a school of jabbering, naked children on one terace; the school-master sat apparently fast asleep in their midst, while they kept up a monotonous hubbub such as no other children in the world could have surpassed; on another ledge there lay a corpse, over which a number of women—professional mourners—were making loud lamentations; while on a third a lady of exceptionally dirty appearance was frying some cakes of dough and fat, coloured apparently with turmeric. I did not attempt to enter their dwellings; a glance through the open door showed that they were rather more objectionable than an ordinary English pig-stye, and almost as small. Nor was it necessary to inquire as to the actual prevalence of cholera in the town. If it did not exist just then, it did very lately, and with the return of very hot weather would probably appear again.

Madras Races were a great success. If a drawback attended them it was the necessity for turning out at five o'clock in the morning—for, if Madras gets up early, it has no idea of going to bed at a reasonable hour. No matter whether you are fortunate enough to dine at the house of the Honourable Mr. Ellis, the well-known member of Council—than whom I know no more genial host—or at the hospitable Madras Club, famed for its curries and its balls, you cannot find your couch till long after midnight is past. The dinner at Madras is a sacred institution, held in the highest consideration. Course follows course with the regularity of clockwork, yet not with unseemly speed; and by the time that coffee and the *petit verre* arrive your night is gone and morning has come. Yet races cannot be run in a mid-day sun, and rest must therefore be deferred. Grumble, however, though one may very justly at all this, the scene on the course more than repaid for the trouble experienced in reaching it. Like their more northern brethren, the Arabs, the Hindoos are passionately attached to horses. So they sallied out by thousands before even the day broke; and when we reached the ground, had taken up their positions all along the course, adding their coloured costumes to the bright green of the landscape.

The course is a long oval in shape, well within view of the Grand Stand all the way. On this Stand, by a little after six o'clock, the English residents of Madras had assembled, and I am bound to say that their number comprised the prettiest bevy of ladies we have yet met in the East. But if the ladies and their costumes were striking, how much more so the native chieftains who occupied the very centre of the Stand. There were the brother of the Rajah of Cochin, grand in a golden robe and turban; the Rajah of Johdpore, irreverently named the savage Rajah, leaning on his sword; we missed for a time the Maharajah of Vizianagram, but in place of him the Rajah of Arcot was to be seen, umbrella in hand, looking about him with great curiosity. Then there was a number of minor potentates—all fine handsome men, and not boys like those we saw at Bombay—sitting amicably in the little railed-off space appointed for native royalty, their countenances beaming with delight.

Presently the Prince, accompanied by Lord Alfred Paget, Lord Charles Beresford, Lord Carington, Lord Aylesford, Major Bradford, and some of the less important members of his staff, drove up, attended by an escort of cavalry. The races at once began. Gambling was not a characteristic of the meeting. Not a betting man was in sight; the sounds of "Two to one" or "Four against the field" were missed. I do not think a bet was made on the course. Members of the Madras Club were allowed to risk ten shillings in a sweepstakes on each race, depositing cards in a box which will be opened on Christmas Day; but beyond this you could not stake a sixpence. Many of the horses, too, were ridden by their owners, so that the meeting partook very much of the nature of a series of private races. The Prince could and did leave the seat provided for him, and walk into the saddling enclosure without fear of being mobbed; he could chat with the English residents and others who chanced to be near, while the course was being cleared and the judges were taking their places. Everything was admirably ordered, even to a refreshment buffet, from which hot coffee and tea with toast and fruit came to all who thought fit to breakfast on the ground. Nothing, in fact, could be more enjoyable or satisfactory; the racing was good, the steeplechasing was better, and the conduct of all present, if possible, better still. Now and then a funny incident occurred. Wandering about in the enclosure, in a disconsolate manner, was a man attired in a very extraordinary costume. His bearing was that of one disconsolate, and enquiry resulted: what did he want—why his misery? At length it turned out that he wanted to ride in a race from which the committee had excluded him on account of his singular dress. They held that a man in a red turban, green coat, blue continuations, and white petticoat, was not attired suitably as a jockey; he on his part asserted that the two horses he had entered for two consecutive races would beat everything else on the ground. At last it was ruled that he should try, and try he did accordingly. The results to that doleful man were conclusive. The limping animal he bestrode vainly endeavoured to take part in the race; his red turban was seen nearly a quarter of a mile behind the black and red caps of his jockey competitors, and when at leangth he did reach the goal, he received such a derisive greeting from both natives and Englishmen that he slunk away quickly, and was seen no more.

The event of the meeting was the Sandringham Steeplechase, for a cup given by the Maharajah of Jeypore. Nine horses were entered, Arabs and Mysore breds; the natives gathered at the jumps, and every fieldglass on the stand was brought into requisition. I believe that every soul on Madras Racecourse would have willingly foregone all the other races rather than have surrendered that steeplechase. Nine such horses, too, are not often to be found. There was a veteran named Phantom, on whom an enthusiastic sportsman from the Neilgherries announced his readiness to stake his coat; there was a steed called Red Deer, ridden by a Captain Bullen, on which any number of tickets were put into the Pari Mutuel box. There were some who would have liked to risk five hundred instead of five rupees on the pretty chestnut owned and ridden by Captain Bullen. There was a mare called Gazelle, who presently behaved very unlike the type of swiftness and good temper, refusing absolutely to go to the starting post, despite all the efforts of her Hindoo admirers to coax her. I do not think the Gazelle was heavily backed; her reputation was well known, and tickets bearing her name were not numerous in the box. There is always a dark horse at such a time about which, though nobody knows much, there is a good deal of whispering and winking. We had that horse at our steeplechase; his name was Artaxerxes. The Prince was clearly anxious to see the end, for he left the place of State and bounded up to the top of the stand with a readiness which spoke more for his physical powers than the longest possible certificate from Dr. Fayrer.

At last eight horses were got into position, the Gazelle having by this time been given up as a bad job. Somebody said that Captain Bullen's horse in going to the starting post had suffered a tumble; but to the relief of at least a third of those on the Grand Stand, Red Deer could be seen mounted by her gallant owner in rose-coloured jacket and black cap, ready to be off in a moment. And off he was, with all his rivals, directly afterwards, without a false start, steering straight for the first jump of a good high hedge. On went Red Deer, cutting out the pace in terrible fashion, flying over earthen walls, ditches, hedges, one after another as though Captain Bullen was a feather-weight. The rest were "nowhere;" Phantom was last of all, and the dark horse only just in front of him. The horses were now approaching the water jump, about half a mile from home; it was the crucial test, and their riders knew it. A horse called Warwick suddenly shot to the front, cleared the water, and then stopped as though that leap was the end of the race. Phantom was not far behind—say about fourth. Red Deer was second. Then ensued a struggle. The old favourite carried a heavy weight, and his rider strove in vain to catch Captain Bullen and his fleet horse; yet the race seemed to be between them, and some were calling for Phantom, while the majority shouted Red Deer, when that terrible dark horse with colours of black and crimson forged ahead away from the rear, passed the striving pair in front, and cantered in first as easily and carelessly as though it had simply been out for a morning's exercise, and was just finishing an agreeable gallop. "Artaxerxes!" screamed the crowd. It was quite true; Mr. Taafe, the owner, had won by about a dozen lengths, leaving Red Deer and Phantom to finish in a neck-and-neck struggle. This was the last of the sport; it was nearly nine o'clock, and the Rothesay Plate, the Denmark Plate, and the Prince of Wales' Plate, the Alexandra Plate, and the Sandringham Cup, all given by native Rajahs, in honour of the Prince and his home, were handed to their winners; the people cheered, as the Prince entered his carriage and drove away.

"Reception" is at best a vague term. There are, in ordinary life, cold receptions and warm receptions; there are formal receptions and informal ones; and in Indian State phraseology a "reception" may mean anything. Hence the cards which were sent round by the courteous Major Hobart, military secretary to the Duke of Buckingham, and which invited those who were favoured to a "reception," were subjects of some discussion.

A great feature in apartments of all kinds built by Europeans in India is that they are lofty and well ventilated; the reception-room at Madras is no exception to the rule. A fine saloon, admirably lit, decorated with paintings of some merit, fitted up with a daïs at one end, and a prettily-arranged orchestral stand at the other, was the place in which the Duke of Buckingham met his guests. From one wing the fire-works, for which Madras had paid £1,000, could be seen to advantage; in the other a refreshment buffet offered attractions which residents in India well appreciate. Inside the hall the Prince was already on the daïs, attended by his suite, when ten o'clock struck; the orchestra was singing a chorale of no ordinary merit, composed in honour of his Royal Highness, and in commemoration of his visit. The space between was occupied by ladies and gentlemen in evening dress, officers in uniform, a number of the Rajahs at present in Madras, and their principal chieftains. Sometimes some one more noteable than the rest was taken to the daïs, and presented to the Prince. Occasionally his Royal Highness, recognising some one whom he had seen before, descended to the floor, and honoured the individual with a word of greeting. All the advantages of a private gathering—for everybody knew everybody else—with all the grandeur of a State ceremonial were there; and if anything is remembered with satisfaction during the visit of the Prince—and I think the arrangements have been very satisfactory—it must surely be this "Reception." Midnight was long past before the carriages were called for and the guests separated, and we then went to our respective destinations, through long lines of illuminated streets, lit by oil lamps arranged in all kinds of devices, with mottoes of the usually loyal description.

In a city so famous for jugglers, snake-charmers, acrobats, and *chevaliers d'industrie* generally, ladies and gentlemen who live by their wits, in the most proper sense of the word, and who apparently make a very good living, it was scarcely likely that the Prince of Wales would be permitted to stay long without witnessing the feats of skill for which these wandering Madrassees are celebrated. The Thursday of the week of his stay being a comparatively open day, therefore, the morning was selected for an *al fresco* exhibition of this kind. The town lost the nomads, Government House gardens received them.

Amongst them was a savage who appeared to make the dried skin of a cobra live. It is a favourite trick—you may see it done twenty times a day in the streets of Madras. You may examine the apparatus closely every time and watch the operation as carefully as you please, yet you cannot detect the *modus operandi.* The performer hands you a little, flat, wicker basket, some eight inches in diameter, and asks you to inspect it, while he folds the cobra skin, which you have previously well examined, into a square, leaving only the tail unfolded. So soon as you have given the basket back, the juggler places it on the ground in full view, and under the lid puts the folded part of the serpent's skin, the tail being in your sight all the while. You may, at this stage, lift the lid once more to see that nothing but the serpent's skin is in the basket, after which you must rest content. A white cloth is taken by the man and placed over the basket, after having been well shaken so that you may be assured nothing is in it. A pipe is produced, and with it a horrible noise, similar to that always made by snake-charmers, and not unlike the sound a cracked and badly made bagpipe would emit, is made. No one goes near the cloth or basket, except the almost naked man, who cannot possibly hide any live snake in his sleeves, for the simple and sufficient reason that he has neither sleeves nor jacket, nor, indeed, any other kind of clothing than a small waistcloth, which would certainly be a most inconvenient hiding-place for a lively young cobra. The sheet is lifted, you look at the basket and see the tail of a living snake being gradually drawn into it, and on the lid being opened a most distinctly energetic serpent is discovered. No sooner is it stirred than it rises on its tail, spreads out its hood, and strikes with its fangs and tongue at the charmer. No one would care to examine that basket now with a cobra four feet long, making vicious snaps at the juggler. The charmer takes good care that the snake comes near you, for with a dexterous movement he seizes the reptile by the head, and holding it in one hand comes to you with his basket in the other, while you put a rupee into the receptacle, if only to induce him to go away.

The snake gone, a stout, strong girl comes forward, makes a

deep obeisance, and then stepping back throws a man weighing fully 11 st. over her shoulders. Nor does she stop here, for she seizes her victim once more, places him crossways on her back, and then tosses him into the air as though he were made of feathers, and not a broad-shouldered human being. Turning backwards on her feet, she picks up straws with her eye-lids, throws somersaults and lifts weights which would astonish the ordinary London acrobat. While she is thus performing, jugglers are changing pebbles into birds, birds into eggs, and eggs into plants; men thread beads with their tongues, join innumerable pieces of cotton into one long cord, keep half-a-score of sharp knives in the air at once, throw cannon balls with their toes, and spin tops on the end of twigs. Pandemonium reigns, the clatter is unbearable, and one is compelled, as was the Prince, to dismiss the tribe of vagrants without further delay.

Supposing the visit of the Prince to result anywhere in the commencement of works of utility, as it has already in most of the places his Royal Highness has touched at, the working population of India will have cause to be permanently grateful. Foundation stones of asylums and hospitals, inaugurations of railways, and memorial stones of breakwaters and harbours, all tend to the employment of thousands, and, as such, should undoubtedly be valued. But at Madras the work begun was peculiarly useful. It will not only be the means of transferring rupees and annas from the pockets of the trading community to the waistcloths of the estimable artisans of the Black Town, but it will be a "joy for ever" to the thousands of travellers who in years to come have to land at Madras. It would require the most devoted attachment to ancient customs for anyone to reason that, because for ages it has been the fashion to get a drenching in the surf before the esplanade at Madras is reached, it would be well to continue the custom; and as the inhabitants of this city are by no means wedded to antiquity, it was suggested that a harbour should be constructed, and that the Prince should lay the first stone.

How admirably the ceremony was managed may be told in a very few words. Everything was arranged on the principle that "silence is golden," a maxim which other places the Prince has yet to visit would do well to bear in mind. The stone was hung in its place under a frame prettily decorated, a cloth covered with the plans of the harbour was laid upon a table, while the mortar-board and trowel were arranged so that as soon as his Royal Highness should arrive the formality of fixing the stone might be got through expeditiously. The ladies were ranged in tiers of seats on either side of the stone; in front were two other stands for less distinguished persons, troops lined the road, and the preparations were complete. The people and the sea filled in the picture, and a strikingly pretty one it was. In sight of everybody the foam on the shore and the huge waves breaking over tossed and tossing catamarans supplied an ever-recurring reason for the enterprise. All along the line of route tens of thousands of people testified to the interest with which the work was regarded.

It was a different crowd from what we had seen anywhere else. The Mahratta turban in which the native of Bombay delights could nowhere be seen; the hideous Parsee headdress was, greatly to our relief, absent, too; nor could the Cingalese comb be discovered anywhere; the full Madras turban, sometimes red and sometimes white, frequently trimmed with gold, and always cleverly made, was almost the only kind of head-dress. But if the turbans were not of a very varied hue—if the pink, green, blue, and yellow of the Mahratta were wanting, there was plenty of colour after all. A pleasant practice of staining the face bright yellow is much in favour with the native dames and damsels of Madras. Most of the men wear a device in white and red on their foreheads as a token of piety. There are as many shades of difference in the skins of the dwellers on the Coromandel coast as could be found between Nubia and Italy, and the dresses which are worn on high days and holidays boast every hue of the rainbow. As they packed themselves together to await the coming of the Prince, the women grouped by hundreds, the men in similar numbers, the front rank seated on the ground, those behind kneeling, while the rearmost of all stood up and peered over the heads of the others, they formed a vast and far-extending mass, to see which a journey of even eleven thousand miles was not too much. Every now and then carriages containing Rajahs and Maharajahs is picturesque costumes, escorted by the Governor's body-guard in bright scarlet and gold uniforms, and followed by parties of their own wild-looking horsemen, drove past; and at last the Prince himself came, cheered vociferously by the crowd. The spreading of the mortar and the lowering of the stone occupied the slightest possible time, and before most ceremonies would have begun this was over, and the Prince well on his way back to Government House.

Old Indians will, however, ask one question, which must perforce be answered—what of the Madras Club ball? For of all the clubs in India that of Madras, at once the oldest and widest known, is held to be the best. In competition with it are the famous Byculla Club at Bombay, and the Bengal Club at Calcutta; but these are held by the men of Southern India to be inferior to the famous home of curries. Such high claims bring with them high obligations. It is not enough to boast of being the best; it is necessary to prove it. If the Madras Club understands anything, however, it is the art of good living. Let others boast larger billiard-rooms or finer libraries; the Madras Club places side by side with these advantages, for the judgment of the thoughtful and the hungry, the best dinner in India, in the handsomest dining-room. For several days past the Club had been turned upside down for the purpose of decoration and preparation. The dining-saloon was converted into a ball-room, the library became a drawing-room, and the whole magnificent building was lit up with lamps, and wreathed with foliage and flowers. From the time that the arrival of a funny little captain was mistaken for that of the Prince of Wales, and honoured by the formation of a long lane down the room, soon to be closed amid a peal of laughter, to half-past two o'clock, when the Prince left, everything was the very perfection of enjoyment. Wherever a corner could be found, dancers availed themselves of it, covering not only the floor of the ball-room itself, but the passage which ran between it and the library, and extending into this last-named room itself. Nor was this difficult, for wide archways united the three into one, and from any given point the whole could be seen. At the supper the Madras Club held its own bravely, vindicating its claim to be the best of providers; and so the ball was a grand success, and one of which the Club and the city are alike proud. The capital of the Presidency did well; and the encomium which the Prince passed on the ball extends to all that has been achieved during the week that was spent at Madras.

CHAPTER XIV.

INDIAN AMUSEMENTS.

It is the old air of "Bonnie Dundee." At first you could scarcely recognize it. The six semi-frantic Hindoo musicians who are performing on a discordant violin, a pipe, a tom-tom, and some conch shells, make a fearsome noise; but now and then the old tune crops up for a bar or two, though it "crops" down for a good many bars directly afterwards. Were sturdy old Claverhouse here, he would make short work of such minstrel boys with that claymore of his. It is enough to make the blood of a Scotchman tingle again. Yet listening patiently, and even smilingly, to this terrible burlesque of the good stirrup song, is the Prince of Wales, Duke of Rothesay, and Lord of the Isles, surrounded and supported by a hundred Scotch ladies and gentlemen, to say nothing of two or three hundred English residents of Madras, and, at least, four thousand native gentlemen. Perhaps the peculiarity of the occasion may account for this extraordinary placidity under such very irritating circumstances. Let us see where we are, and judge for ourselves.

In a great hall, some five hundred feet long, and a hundred and fifty feet broad, are gathered together the rank and fashion, native and European, of the Presidency of Madras. English officers in scarlet rub shoulders with aged Mohammedans dressed in white and gold. European ladies sit next to young Tamil beaux; Hindoo princes and chieftains, who probably never heard of each other before, fill every line of chairs on a raised daïs. French and English naval officers hob-nob at a refreshment buffet, the bright glasses of which can be seen through their muslin curtains, partially looped up, collectors of districts, and the people who have to pay the taxes, all are here decked out in full dress. In the centre of the daïs, which, by the way, is on the right centre of the room, sits the Prince of Wales, on a golden throne. His suite are clustered behind him. On his left is the Duke of Buckingham, in the full uniform of a Governor of Madras; on his right Mrs. Shaw Stewart and the Maharajah of Travancore, who, by the bye, is just such another quick-eyed little gentleman as Sir Madava Rao, of Baroda; also the Maharajah of Vizianagram, and the Prince of Arcot, all glittering with diamonds, rubies, emeralds, and gold. On either side of the Prince, below the daïs, is a great sea of upturned faces; in front of his Royal Highness is, first of all, a little table, bearing an immense gold casket, the lid of which is surmounted by a silver tiger, then an open raised platform, in the centre of which hang a dozen coloured ropes, fastened together at the top; while farther back still is a stage, on which are squatted some fifty natives, male and female, all attired in the most fantastic fashion; a screen fastened to the wall in rear of them depicting a jungle scene and a springing tiger. As your eye wanders round the building you notice that the roof is one of extraordinary beauty, ornamented with flowers, stars, circles, and all kinds of devices by the artists, evidently of Tanjore. The gold, silver, and crimson foil in this remarkable ceiling, as well as on the sides of the pillars which support it, glitter and glisten in the light which scores of chandeliers throw upon them; but more than ever when flashes of limelight thrown from four points in the building hurl a dazzling gleam across the hall. You might perchance wish that the gentlemen who have charge of the latter knew how to manage it, and that they would not blind you at one moment and leave you in comparative darkness the next, but you must not complain.

This is a native entertainment given to the Prince, managed by natives from the doors to the limelights, in a place with a very native name—to wit, Royapooram—having for its chief entrance a door leading into a way called in native parlance Thumboo Chetty, decorated by natives, arranged, controlled, and now almost filled by natives. The programme promises an entirely native performance, the presentation of a native casket, Kôlâttam or Plait dances, concerted pieces on the Saranthé Sittár, Vina and Dol, and a native drama in four acts. You might wish that the native plan of smiling and making a present quickly had been pursued in regard to that casket, instead of a tedious imitation of that most trying of all customs, the presentation of an address; but this is an innovation insisted upon by the long-robed, red-turbaned gentlemen who flock up to the daïs just before the band strikes up, and read and stand in front of the Prince; while one of their number, happy man, reads a long rigmarole, of which we cannot hear even the purport were we so disposed. Of course the Prince replies pleasantly, as is his wont, using almost the same words, however, as have been put into his lips twenty times already; and then the entertainment begins.

Looking at the matter from a purely metaphysical point of view, it may, perhaps, be conceded that not only lights, but even shades, are advantageous in our pleasures. The easy chair which suddenly discovers a broken spring, the comfortable cot which presently lets you down on the hard deck below, the buck-jumping horse, and even a voyage like that in the "Nagotna," all have their useful lessons, all aid to make unalloyed pleasures the more appreciated. Viewed thus, the native entertainment was a complete success. It was in itself the most dismal and trying performance ever witnessed, yet the memory of the misery endured during its continuance may tend to make those who sat in that tinselled hall, from nine in the evening till two the next morning, a little less captious in future.

But while I digress the music, if music it can be called, is going on, and "Bonnie Dundee" on pipes and tom-toms, conch shell and fiddle, is being murdered. At last a dozen girls, strangely attired, come away from the throng squatted down in front of the screen, and walk up to the coloured ropes. Unlike the celebrated lady of Banbury Cross, they have not only "rings on their fingers and bells on their toes," but they have rings, great pearl-adorned rings in their noses, rings in their ears, rings of bells on their ankles, and wreaths of flowers on their heads. Strictly speaking, not one of them can be styled pretty; their features are regular and their forms fairly good, but these beauties of Madras, selected on account of their personal attractions to dance before the Prince, are neither graceful in appearance nor lithe in movement. Their dress, which could not be more resplendent, so entirely covered is it with gold, silver, and jewels, has a cumbersome look about it which by no means adds to the facility of motion, and the long red trousers which each damsel wears hang in a slovenly manner over the naked feet, and occasionally impede the *danseuse* in the very midst of her steps. Still it must not be denied that these nautch girls are picturesque in appearance. Their long black hair, worn in plaited tresses, their olive-coloured skins and great white eyes, their curious costume, and their wonderful ornaments, lend them in the flashing lime-light a fictitious weirdness which the three witches whom Macbeth saw might have sighed for in vain. And when they seize each a coloured rope, and to the tune of that extraordinarily rendered "Bonnie Dundee" fly round in a frantic dance, twirling in and out and backwards and forwards, till the ropes are all twisted and they are brought close together, and then, with more dancing, unravelling what appeared to be a very Gordian knot, and so gradually bringing the ropes into their first order, you have good cause for wondering, and, were they to stop now, reason to be pleased.

But neither the dancers nor the conch-shell players have any idea of ceasing yet, and the girls occasionally joining in the chant, hop and skip and twirl till you are giddy with looking on, and long for an end of the Kôlâttam. You are, however, in the hands of a stolid old gentleman in a long green gown and a great purple turban, who occasionally looks at the dancers and then at the Prince, a look of honest delight and pride beaming through his great round spectacles as he says most unmistakably by his self-satisfied grin, "See what a tremendous discord they can make, and how admirably they can keep it up." They do "keep it up" for nearly an hour, during which many Europeans enjoy a nap—the most wakeful, and certainly the most graciously patient, being the Prince himself. At last the purple-robed stage-manager finds his troupe exhausted, whereupon he orders forward a fresh supply of players, and a celebrated nautch-girl named Gnyáná who is to dance a Carnatic *pas seul.*

I need not describe the appearance of this damsel. Had her charms only equalled her excessive vanity and astonishing powers of endurance, we might not have objected possibly to her prolonged gyrations. Nor would the everlasting drumming on conch shells, tom-tomming, pipe-playing, and fiddle-scraping which accompanied her movements have been so unbearable as they presently became had they not been accompanied by the hideous noise which the six players were good enough to call singing. I have said something about Hindoo music, how it is all that we hold to be most objectionable in England, exaggerated to the utmost extent of human power. The principal vocalist of the six, this time, was the most terrible of his class. All of them dispensed with the nose in singing; he did without nose or mouth either, and sang apparently from the pit of his stomach, sending a volume of sound up his open throat that completely astonished even experienced Anglo-Indians. And as for power of lungs, he must have borrowed a pair of bellows from Vulcan to have maintained such a howl for so long a timo as he did. In a feeble way his companions attempted to accompany him, and occasionally the girl ceased her dancing, and yelled at the top of her voico too; but he needed no assistance, the pair of conch shells he clapped together and his incomparable windpipe did all that was necessary, and it needed the most frantic efforts of the tom-tom beater to create the slightest impression. We could see the fiddler playing as though he had orders to go at a rate of a hundred strokes a minute and was working against time, but the result of his efforts troubled us not, we could see the pipe-player's dark face getting darker still as he fought despairingly against the man with the voice; but whether he was going on with "Bonnie Dundee" or giving a selection from Weber, we never knew. All was swallowed up by that man in the white turban and long white gown. His face worked convulsively, his body bowed and bent; he would lean forward and then backward; throw his arms frantically into the air, and then turn round upon his comrades as though he could remonstrate with them if only he dared stop shouting for a moment—without wearying or pausing, much less stopping. And the strangest thing was that the natives smiled and gibbered as though they were being pleasingly enchanted by the soft song of a syren. As for the manager of the stage, he was simply beside himself with joy, and nodded his head with satisfaction till his spectacles tumbled on to the floor.

I do not know how the Prince went through that trying ordeal. He said, I was afterwards told by an enthusiastic native, that he was very much astonished, and no doubt he was; but nothing except his most imperturbable good humour could have carried him through it. Yet he continued to look pleased as the girl squatted down, and jumped up, turned round with one arm raised, and then strutted up to the edge of the Royal daïs; or, moving backwards on her heels, joined her screeching companions and helped them to "sing;" although for more than an hour she continued the same monotonous movement, and the musicians the same wonderful noise, the Prince neither remonstrated, nor for a moment looked weary. At length, as it was now getting far into the morning and there were five other pieces on the programme, the old gentleman in purple essayed to stop the Carnatic dame, and this, after much rebellious conduct on the part of the white-turbaned singer, he was enabled to do.

So soon as Gnyáná and her companions could he moved off, a fresh set of musicians accompanied another and a darker girl to the foot of the daïs, and then squatted down, while she, sitting in their midst, began a "Vinah" solo. Apparently this was too much for the Prince, and she had not squealed and beaten a tom-tom which was placed in front of her more than ten minutes when the Prince bowed, rose, and led Mrs. Stewart to supper. This was a signal for the Vinah solo to stop, and for another batch of Kôlâttam or Plait dancers to gather round the coloured ropes; but when the Prince presently came back, he stayed for a few moments only and then took his departure. I never heard whether the programme was continued afterwards —whether the song by Krishna, the concerted piece, or the drama in four acts, were even attempted. If so, and each occupied the time of that Carnatic dance, they must be going on now. I had already determined that at what time I heard the Saranthé, Sittár, Vinah, and Dol, I would call for my carriage and set out on the five miles' journey which lay before me; but the departure of the Prince stifled any scruples which a strict adherence to the demands of etiquette previously required, and in company with the rest of the European portion of the audience, I quitted the Royapooram Hall.

While in this city the Prince of Wales paid a visit to the Madras Club, and there tasted some thirteen curries and eight chutnies; his cook also had lessons in the Club kitchen, with a view to introducing the best-made curry into the Marlborough House cuisine. The record of Madras loyalty and hospitality, therefore, fitly closes here.

CHAPTER XV.

THE PRINCE IN BENGAL.

Three times the Prince of Wales landed on Indian soil—first of all at Bombay; next at Tuticorin, the most southerly part of the Peninsula; and lastly at Calcutta, the capital of the Empire and the seat of the Viceroy of India.

Let us transport ourselves at once to the landing-place, at Prinseps Ghaut, where on Christmas Eve the entry of the Prince was effected. It is three o'clock in the afternoon; we are in the centre of an open space which lies between two open pavilions. In front is the Hooghly, looking marvellously like the Thames on a bright summer's day. The sun plays upon the waters, upon the thousands of boats that crowd together close to the pier, and the roofs of the warehouses which stand in a long line on the opposite shore, just as they do on the Surrey side of the grand old London river. The warehouses are shut, however, and yonder crowd of boats are full of holiday-makers; the ships are gay in colours; and the throng, which reaches to the water's edge in one direction, and right away through the city of Calcutta in the other, is no ordinary gathering, but comprises all that is alive in this great Bengal capital. It is commonly said that Calcutta crowds lack the colour which makes an assemblage of Bombay natives so picturesque. If so, the ordinary aspect differs from that of to-day, for the dark faces of the sightseers, and their red hats, flowing robes, and strange decorations, combine to form a notable display hardly inferior to anything I have seen elsewhere. No combs are visible in the heads of the men, nor many Mahratta turbans with the curious distinguishing point in the centre thereof. One looks almost in vain for the Parsee hat and the Madras puggaree; yet there are fine, handsome, manly faces, and the graceful Bengal hat is worn in every conceivable colour; rich shawls, too, and costly dresses are not uncommon, so that the natives of Calcutta may well be proud of their appearance to-day. My point of view, however, is outside the crowd, next a pillar hidden away in palm leaves, which helps to support both the pavilions on either side. A crimson carpet leads down to the end of the pier; behind is a huge triumphal arch, whereon a welcome to the Prince is inscribed in roses—artificial, perhaps, but still roses; floating on the river, immediately opposite, is the "Serapis," clad in bunting, and on either side, at some distance removed, are the belles and beaux of Calcutta. I have said at some distance, because between my standpoint and them are all the Rajah and Maharajah-dom of the Bengal Presidency, together with princes and princelets from the South and North, who are come hither to see the Prince, and, if possible, to greet him. The Viceroy is moving about, shaking hands with his feudatories; it is a time of great rejoicing, and everybody is glad.

An air of ease and comfort characterises the reception pavilions. By placing the English residents, both ladies and gentlemen, on seats which, while rising one above another, abut upon the walls of the pavilions on either side, a broad square space is formed, in which the native dignitaries can move about at pleasure. Here movable couches, sofas, easy chairs, and lounges are scattered about, and any one may sit or stand. The Bengal wolf may lie down with the Madras lamb. Maharajahs and sirdars can meet on an equal footing. Thus the Maharajah of Puttiala, a short stout gentleman in a white turban and a bright blue satin coat, stands next to the good Bishop of Calcutta in shovel hat and shorts; and not far off are the three members of the Burmese Embassy, who look, for all the world, as though they were victims of the Spanish Inquisition. High conical hats, long, crimson, purple, velvet gowns, ornamented in extraordinary fashion, with bright gold braid, and the funniest faces that could be drawn, are the characteristics of these well-born, highly honoured, and very excellent representatives of the Lord of the Golden Foot. The peculiarity of their costume is perhaps heightened by the yellow-plumed, helmeted, and blue-trousered French officer from Pondicherry who now and then turns a pirouette on his high-heeled boots. A curious group that, and one to be regarded attentively.

Then there are the Maharajah of Cashmere, the Maharajah of Benares, and the three sons of Jung Bahadoor, all in friendly conversation. He of Cashmere is quietly dressed in white and gold, is a portly person of some sixty years, and is happy in the possession of two very handsome daggers which he wears in his cummerband or girdle. His compeer of Benares is older—a very patriarch in fact, grey, bent, palsied—yet withal a grand old fellow, gorgeously arrayed in the far-famed Khin-khob cloth, which is a handsome mixture of silk and cloth of gold, and would make the eyes of any English dame of fashion glisten with delight. The three young gentlemen from Nepaul are stout, nor do they present any striking contrast to the other notables here, except that these youngsters are more brilliant in diamonds than most of their seniors. On the Maharajah of Cashmere's neck is certainly a row of pearls, costly in their way, yet only small pearls; but in the turban of yonder round-faced Bahadoor, just above the two little black eyes which can scarcely be seen to twinkle for the fat which surrounds them, is a diamond aigrette such as the Maharajah of Mysore would view with interest and delight. He is not so *distingué* with jewels as the chief whom we just now saw close to the prelate of Calcutta. That potentate bought, it will be remembered, the jewels of the Empress Eugénie, and as he stands there he is worth three hundred thousand pounds. Still the representatives of Jung Bahadoor are eminently respectable, and, I should say, could sell their diamonds for as much as would buy a considerable street in the West-end of London.

There is, however, another *posse* of young men who have claims to distinction. They are three melancholy youths, not stout, but thin, standing close together, but otherwise alone. Nobody goes near them; they are not pressed to the left and right breasts of Rajah or Maharajah, as are all the rest we see. Save that some political agent now and then accosts them, they say nothing to anybody, but stand still and look on at all that passes with quiet interest. In attire they resemble the old pictures of Martin Luther—black, velvet caps, somewhat like the old biretta with earlaps standing out straight, long black velvet gowns, sandalled feet, no ornaments, not even a pearl or a diamond. Who can they be? I turn to the courteous Colonel Martin Dillon, the secretary of Lord Napier, who, like his chieftain, is in full dress covered with medals and decorations, and from him learn that these are the grandsons of Tippoo Sahib. Shades of the great, what a different scene do their eyes look upon to-day from that which they would probably have witnessed but for the valour of British and native soldiers, and the skill of Arthur Wellesley! They might have been gazing at a successor of that most unfortunate captive, Sir David Baird, who not so many years ago was placed in a water-wheel and made to work it for the amusement of Tippoo and his ladies. *Quien sabe?* To-day, these unhappy ones, ejected from Mysore, no longer rulers of Seringapatam, stand meekly in the background to see the Prince of the race which annihilated their family's greatness pass by in state. They are not even honoured by a nod or a shake of the hand. When Tippoo fell, the grandeur of the dynasty fell with him; that thrust of the private soldier's bayonet in the fatal gateway not only killed Tippoo, but upset his successors to all time. Those young men would not be here to-day had the Treaty of 1793 been observed. In such case they would have been received with a twenty-one gun salute at Madras, met on the edge of the carpet, conducted to a grand seat at the right hand of the Prince, and been favoured with the pleasant conversation which is now reserved for those who are greater than they.

But moralising is out of place here, for we must look round before the Prince lands. There is the Maharajah of Rewah, a fine tall man, with an astonishing aigrette of diamonds in his cap, and splendidly clad in bright colours. A certain lankness about the hair and whiskers of this notability perhaps awakens suspicions; but few are prepared to see anything half so forbidding as his countenance when he turns round. His face is painted red; he must surely be a descendant of the Sandwich or savage islanders, so curiously tattooed are his cheeks and his forehead. No such thing. He is a victim to leprosy; his terrible face is the sign, and his feeble walk the result. Yet he is not avoided. How could a man who carries thirty thousand pounds' worth of brilliants on his turban be shunned? See, the Maharajah of Cashmere clasps the leprous Rewah to his bosom; and a little stout Rajah, in a red turban, bright purple satin coat, and light green trousers, trots up full of joy at being next saluted. That amusing person who carries his sword before him so carefully wrapped up in silk that it looks as bulbous as a teapot, squeezes the red-faced Maharajah to his breast, and then runs off as pleased as though he had embraced Shiva, and Parvati into the bargain. It is clearly a great thing to be a Maharajah.

Not far distant is a tall, fine, clear-complexioned gentleman in a long green robe spotted with golden stars. On his head is a small golden crown, just like those depicted upon the school-history likenesses of William Rufus. He has a high forehead, a noble expression, a skin quite unsullied by leprosy; yet there he stands all unnoticed. Why? He is not a Prince, "only one of those fellows from Oude," says an officer; and splendid fellow though he is, even the tainted ruler of Rewah would not vouchsafe to give him one salute. He might wear fifty crowns, he will not be squeezed to the breast of anybody here. Just now Lord Napier of Magdala spoke to him, and here comes the veteran Commander-in-Chief leading somebody else up to Scindiah, who, with a yellow hat, and a white robe, with diamond armlets and the riband of the Star of India over his shoulder, is sitting on a sofa. Who can help regretting that India is about to lose the services of so far-seeing a general and so careful a diplomatist—more so than ever, indeed, when he grasps you by the hand, bids you welcome to Bengal, and tells you that on your arrival at Delhi there shall be a tent for yourself, a peg and a rope for your horse, and a restaurant to save you the six miles' ride into the city when the daily fighting is over and you need rest? A rare old soldier is Lord Napier, and you honour him for what he has done. Close behind him is Sir Richard Temple, who but lately jumped from his horse, then falling over a precipice, and so saved his life, and near him are Colonel Earle, Captain Evelyn Baring, and Captain F. Baring. A group of favoured ladies and gentlemen admire the case in which the address to the Prince will be placed, a fine gold box, much ornamented, the treasure casket of Calcutta eloquence and loyalty.

Meanwhile the guns of the men-of-war blazed away, the old sixty-four converted making but a feeble boom when compared with the ear-splitting crash of their seven-inch rivals; and his Royal Highness made for the shore, followed and preceded by his followers and retainers. At length they landed, and a number of Baboos, officers, gentlemen in cocked hats, who belonged to the Legislative Council, and others, crowded round his Royal Highness, while the chief policeman, Mr. Stuart Hogg, read very deliberately. This is however, mere guesswork. From my coign of vantage I could see the deputation nod their heads at what appeared to be paragraphs in a much-admired address; the Prince also bowed in return, and it was

NATIVE PRINCES AT THE CHAPTER OF THE STAR OF INDIA, CALCUTTA.

evident that he was saying something. When the inaudible business was over, all joined in the cheer which saluted his Royal Highness, as he moved towards the pavilions. There was very little enthusiasm at Bombay, less at Colombo, still less at Madras; here there was a genuine English shout of joyous greeting, and it was prolonged long after the Royal party reached the pavilion.

In the midst of all this there are presentations—the Viceroy presenting the Rajah of Cashmere and Holkar, next Rewah, and after that Prince Scindiah, who all stand in the order they themselves choose, and shake hands with the Prince with great cordiality. How for each the Prince has a pleasant word, how it takes nearly twenty minutes to shake hands with them all, and how, when his Royal Highness left the arch, a louder cheer than ever was given, can be imagined. Nor need the order of the procession be given, since the Viceroy and the Prince must necessarily occupy the same carriage; and it boots not for the English people to know whether the members of Council rode before or behind his Royal Highness. Suffice it to say that, escorted by volunteers and native troops, always cheered by the people, and at one place saluted by the school children of Calcutta, who sang a new version of the National Anthem, he at length passed the gates of Government House, and took up residence in that magnificent building.. I should not omit to mention that next day a local newspaper appeared in deep mourning, in consequence of the address having been read by the police superintendent.

That night the streets and squares of Calcutta were in a blaze of light. The place which has been justly called the city of palaces, was lit up in so artistic a style as to bring to mind the grandest tales of the "Thousand and One Nights." In the luminous atmosphere, dusky forms, clad in Oriental garments, flitted about noiselessly by thousands; palankeen bearers, coaches, buggies, and bullock vehicles were carrying unwonted loads; and Christmas Eve was a night of joviality in honour of the Prince. I wish I could portray to you, as vividly as I saw it, the beauty of the scene. No Aladdin was needed to cry new lamps in exchange for old; every building seemed to be one vast lamp full of oil and light. The resources of the East and West were brought into play together, Hindoos and Mohammedans, under a celebrated local firm, and English makers and designers, joining to decorate this already handsome city. There were stars and crosses, all kinds of devices, such as Birmingham, Sheffield, and London delight in on great days of festivity, in gas, and in addition to these, thousands of oil lamps hung in festoons and loops, or stretched over the roads in arches, covering fronts of houses and walls, and the railings of the squares. It was, without doubt, the grandest Christmas Eve Calcutta had ever seen, a night of great and unalloyed rejoicing. And Christmas Day itself was to be kept this year in real English fashion by a Prince and his followers, and by hundreds of Englishmen and Englishwomen, in the Empire city of Calcutta; while that night we began the festivity by lighting up the streets, as they never had been before, in honour of the Royal visitor and the Royal visit.

CHAPTER XVI.

A SUNDAY IN CALCUTTA.

Sundays in Calcutta are not spent at the Zoo for the very sufficient reason that Calcutta has till lately had no Zoological Gardens in which to spend its after-church Sunday. But it has long had its own fashionable resort, for all that; and while people in England were buttoning their overcoats and putting thick gloves on, preparatory to taking their favourite race through the frost-bitten gardens in Regent's Park, Calcutta—that is to say, of course, European Calcutta—having achieved its devotions at cathedral, church, and chapel, in accordance with the fashionable method out here, was getting ready to move off to the Botanical Gardens, which lie on the opposite side of the grand river Hooghly. It was Christmas-tide, and the good old Bishop, since dead, had droned out the last sentence of what at one time promised to be an endless sermon; the choir had sung the fifth and last hymn; the offertory had been made, and sixpences had been furtively slipped into red velvet bags which certainly should have opened to nothing less than rupees; and the organist was thundering "For unto us a Child is born," when one of the gentlemen who had just made the collection stepped across the aisle of the church and invited me to luncheon. All innocent of Botanical Gardens, and far away from the guidance of any member of the Sunday Observance Society, my thoughts naturally turned in the direction of a sober meal within four white walls, under a waving breeze-making punkah, somewhere in the suburbs of Calcutta. But, to my surprise, the carriage of this estimable and hospitable person stopped neither at staid-looking bungalow nor white-faced house; but, passing under the triumphal arch which had welcomed the Prince on the day of his landing, pulled up at the water's edge, close to a dingy, in which sat four or five semi-nude boatmen.

Would you know what a dingy is? Then take the shabbiest gondola that Venice can furnish, knock off all that is ornamental in the shape of carved prow or stern, move the covered seats in the centre to one end of the craft, give it a flush deck, and thereupon place four not handsome native rowers, and you have a first-class dingy—just such a one as we entered on that bright Sunday afternoon.

We were not alone in our expedition, for already seated in the dingy were four or five gentlemen who, unlike ourselves, had not been to cathedral, and from whom I learnt that our ultimate destination was the Botanical Gardens, where we should have to lunch on the grass "the same," my informant continued, "as everybody in Calcutta does." Onward the boat sped towards the other side of the river, where the sail was to be hoisted. On the Hooghly was many another craft of the same description; some with parties of intending lunch-takers, and others with parties of intended lunch-makers; namely, servants who were carrying boatloads of provisions and wine to the place for which we were bound. Still, there was no unseemly noise; nothing like the hideous cackle of the catamaran rowers at Colombo. There, if you would be quiet on the water, you would have to beg your boatmen as a particular favour not to sing the songs they love, else you would be treated to a series of yells compared with which a London street singer's melodies would be agreeable music. And even then you would be startled every minute or so by the eternal "La illa, la, la, la," wafted from some other boat on those troublous waters. Here, however, there was no "singing," only the steady plash of the oars in the water as we passed along the bank of the river.

Respecting the Hooghly at the point where it pierces Calcutta, there is not much to be said. It is rather more uninteresting than the Thames below Gravesend; about as wide, but less turbulent, though more turbid. On one hand stands the city proper—on the other a long line of cotton-spining factories, which promise some day or another, according to local prophets, to be an exceeding trouble to Manchester and a great source of supply for the London market. But as you pass down the river you find the scenery more diversified. On one side is the present residence of the ex-King of Oude, with its gardens and pleasaunces, on the other the Botanical Gardens. It was at a little landing-stage attached to these last that we stepped ashore, walking now up a slight incline to a shady spot, where, under aromatic trees of great beauty, we found seats and a tablecloth spread on the grass, with a luncheon fit for the Prince himself. Guards, too, there were—coloured gentlemen armed with sticks, who were waving them about as fiercely as though a band of Dacoits were somewhere in the bushes. Yet there could not be Dacoits in the gardens, and the bunch of squalid Hindoos who were squatted on the pathway some little distance off scarcely required such a display of force to keep them from the cold game-pie or the sherry. They looked hungry enough—were hungry, too, Heaven knows; and their reason for squatting in the pathway was, without doubt, the hope of getting just one mouthful of something to eat presently—just as a pariah dog close by them came there in search of a bone; but they no more dared to seize upon the boiled leg of mutton, steaming hot and savoury, with the turnips and carrots artistically and temptingly arrayed on a great dish, than they would dream of plundering Government House.

Where was the enemy, then? We had scarcely sat down when we discovered that recondite foe. One of the party had helped himself to a choice slice of beef. On the joint itself was a Government mark of undoubted genuineness, indicating that the beef was of the very best quality, in accordance with rules laid down for the guidance of meat inspectors in the Calcutta markets from time immemorial. But neither inspector's mark —the corner of the cross was on that identical slice—nor the sticks of the guardians of the feast could save that unlucky morsel. Down from the sky above us, at a moment when least expected, swooped a voracious kite. Like a flash of lightning that unconscionable bird, utterly regardless of the rights of property, and not caring a single snap of the bill for inspector or proprietor, came through the picnic party, and, seizing that choice cut of beef, flew aloft and away before we could utter the Hindostanee equivalent of the proverbial "Jack Robinson." That was the thief, then, against whom the men with the sticks were warring; that was the marauder against whom they had to fight; and, worse than all, his friends and acquaintances were hovering by the score, about forty feet above us, ready to seize the rest of the provisions if only we would let them. Had we only got one of the descendants of the Lord Cardinal of Rheims there, he might have "solemnly cursed that rascally thief," and, perchance, brought him to repentance, just as the great Lord Cardinal himself dealt with the jackdaw that stole the ring; but we had no one amongst us who could lay the slightest claim to belonging to the Rheims Cardinal's family. So we had to sit a little closer, advise the guards to wave their sticks more fiercely, and to watch the kites more closely. It was necessary, I firmly believe, to eat things as quickly as possible; even the beer seemed in danger, though, so far as I could learn, the most voracious and reckless kite had never been seen to fly away with a bottle of Allsopp. Yet, with the Darwinian theory of natural selection before us, and the possibility that in course of time some elderly kite might possibly have advanced from the seizing of eatables to the purloining of drinkables, we disposed of what potions we had brought with us, and presently adjourned to the great banyan tree, of which Calcutta and the chief of the Botanical Gardens are proud.

There is always some satisfaction in seeing the largest specimen of any particular class—the biggest baloon, the highest mountain, the hugest ship. We went to the largest banyan tree in the world. I know that in Guzerat there is a tree of this class which claims the premier place; also, that at Barrackpore there is a banyan of undoubted respectability. But the Calcutta specimen is, after all, the king. You could bivouac a whole regiment of soldiers comfortably under its branches; if you had it in your garden there would be room for nothing else, but you might live under its shade and call it your "roof tree" with some propriety. Indeed, in one respect, it is not altogether unlike the Hall of a Thousand Pillars—for the banyan tree has one great peculiarity which is not generally known in England. From its branches drop feelers or hangers, somewhat in the way that the strawberry plant's feelers spread out, and, there taking root, become eventually strong trunks themselves, several feet in girth, and the parents of other roots again. In this way the space under the tree is filled with pillars of wood, behind which you could hide, and between which lovers were seated, and—what is still more sad—some were playing what Cromwell designated "that most ungodly game of kiss-in-the-ring." Others, too, were picnicing under the umbrageous shade of this grand tree, which is never aught but green summer or winter, while more were perched on the branches which extend in almost every direction for very many yards. I say "almost," because the tree, curiously enough, has not shot out a single tendril towards the north, but confines its leafy shade to other parts of the compass. But that scarcely detracts from its beauty; it covers a huge circular space from the heat of the sun, and constitutes a marvel of which Calcutta may well be proud.

Of the gardens themselves, I scarcely think so much could be said. They are not to be compared with those of Kandy, either in beauty of landscape or rarity of plants. Palms are plentiful;

but where are the vanilla, with its wonderful pods, the picturesque plantain, the lovely pommelo, or the leafy nutmeg tree? Where are the groves which make Peradinya so lovely—where the rich clusters of flowers that load the air with perfume? There is nothing like that here. The groves are thin, even the fernery is small; a vast expanse of plain, barely covered with trees and plants, constitutes these gardens. Yet bordering on the Hooghly, they are a great source of comfort to European Calcutta on Sunday, and we, in going thither, only did what all the world and his wife in these warm regions do. Before night had set in, or the church bells for evening service had sounded, we had once more landed on the opposite shore, all the fresher and more gladsome for our pleasant picnic on the grass.

CHAPTER XVII.

POLC PLAYING AND SNAKE-CHARMING.

Cricket at Lord's, lawn tennis at Prince's, football at Rugby, racing at Epsom—are seen at their best. But to learn how polo should be played you should have spent an hour on the Maidan at Calcutta, a large, open, grass-covered space, when there were galloping there at a terrific pace fourteen semi-savage Munipuris. I do not for a moment desire to disparage the feats of Mr. Murietta, or any of the other gentlemen whose powers with the polo stick are undoubted. But of this I am sure, that there is not an admirer of polo at home or in India who would grudge to award the palm of superiority to these masters of the game. It was with no small feeling of pleasure that I received an invitation to attend a polo match, at which it was expected the Prince and Viceroy would be present. To see the Munipuris play would be to see the style of the tribes who first taught India, and, through India, England, this pleasant athletic diversion. How well their skill had been maintained had been already shown, when the savages beat the skilled horsemen of Calcutta with a rapidity and ease that greatly surprised the Europeans.

It was four o'clock in the afternoon when, by the aid of a policeman, who gently whipped my recalcitrant coachman, I reached the Maidan. The driver having an eye to that honest penny which it is the ambition of every Hindoo to turn as frequently as possible, had made arrangements to use the vehicle which I had hired for the day as a hack carriage for people attending the Prince's levée, and at such moments as he found himself unwatched carried out his project with considerable energy. An unexpected demand, therefore, that he should bend the carriage wheels in the direction of the Maidan met with something very like rebellion—a reprehensible state of affairs which it was necessary to deal with. Reason at length prevailed; the troublesome worshipper of Siva was persuaded to do his duty, and an hour's drive brought us to the place where we would be.

There was no overlooking the workmanlike appearance of the Munipuris; both they and their ponies were ready for anything. These latter were scarcely over 11 hands high, but as strong as lions and as fleet as deer, somewhat shaggy, but under extraordinary control. The saddles were broad, and had the fronts turned over in such a way as to give the rider the strongest possible grip; the stirrup leathers so short that the knees of the player were actually higher than the top of the saddle. To guard the flanks of the pony, on either side a thick piece of hide, about eighteen inches deep and two feet long, was hung, strongly secured by thongs of leather, and, to give additional protection to the knees of the rider, this hide was also turned round at the ends. For the rest, the trappings of the ponies were very ornate. Woollen rosettes and balls of varied colours hung all round them, giving a pretty effect when the animals were in rapid motion. The men were habited in a turban tightly fastened on to the head, close-fitting jackets, seven dark and seven light, ornamented with golden spangles. On their legs were thick leather guards, extending a little above their knees. Fastened to their left wrists were the thongs of a whip. A short white gown completed their dress. The sticks they carried were about 4ft. 6in. in length, made of the lightest bamboo, with the cross-piece at the end rather more slanted than those used at Hurlingham, or, indeed, in Calcutta. There were three ridiculously-dressed men for keeping the ground, each clad in a long white gown, and a cap with three points of the exact pattern worn by English clowns, and wanting only the bells to be the perfection of ugliness. The ball used was about the size of a cricket ball, and was made from the root of the bamboo, being subjected to a drying process lasting over nearly a year before fit for use. There were no goal posts; the area, which was in the form of a parallelogram, was marked out by a deeply-cut line in the grass, over which the players did not hesitate to rush occasionally, to the discomfiture and terror of on-lookers.

While all this was being noted, those invited were gathering. The Viceroy and his staff—whether the Prince eventually came I do not know—a few Maharajahs, some American generals who chanced to be in Calcutta, a few officers from the camp, and a carriage or two full of ladies, together with a score or so of gentlemen from Calcutta, composed the spectators. The contest had been kept secret, in order that the Prince, in case he might find time to attend, might do so without being mobbed. At length the players range themselves up on two sides, very close to each other, the dark jackets facing the north. The ball is thrown in, and the game begins. We notice that it is caught up and sent whirling over the heads of the dark jackets. Helter-skelter they go into a terrible rush, the leather flank guards clattering against the sides of the saddle with a noise like that of small drums, the white ball constantly in the air, but still getting nearer and nearer the goal of the dark jackets. They fight with tremendous bravery, and at one moment rally so strongly as to force their opponents back some yards. But it is only for an instant; the next sees a white jacket, standing in the stirrups, with his head bent lower than that of his horse, fly past, and then, turning round, swing his arm over the hind-quarters of his pony, and, achieving that most difficult stroke known to polo-players, land the ball in the enemy's goal.

Back they go at once to the centre of the ground, and again the ball is thrown. This time the struggle is even more exciting, for the ponies have entered thoroughly into the spirit of the game, and require no lashes from the whip-thongs which are on the left wrists of the riders. Indeed, it would go ill with the players if they did; for, curiously enough the game is almost wholly a left-handed fight, and is won by a left-hand stroke, given by a white jacket again. The friends of the dark jackets are somewhat disheartened this time, and a Calcutta polo-player who is seated on a splendid little pony of about 12 hands gives it as his opinion that he could beat "any of those fellows easily." Not so easily, though; for the next goal and the next are won by them, and now comes the conquering game.

I do not think there is a single spectator who is not carried away by the enthusiasm of the moment. The sound of martial music in the camp close at hand; the red orb of the sun as just before it goes to rest it lights up the open work of a neighbouring church steeple; the palatial houses of Calcutta in the distance; the long lines of green trees which surround the Maidan; and more than all, the appearance of that little corps of horsemen and their steeds panting alike for excitement and want of breath, all combine to give interest to the scene. I could conceive of Mr. Pickwick himself hazarding a rupee on the chances of the struggle. At last the ball is thrown once more, and before we can get out of the way the ponies are nearly upon us, for the white bamboo-root comes skimming along over the boundary, and is out. Back it goes again only to meet with a like fate; and a third time expectation is at its highest. This time the issue is decided. For nearly five minutes the struggle continues. A great dog rushes away from its master into the very thick of the fray, and speedily comes back sadder and wiser. Then the group breaks, and there is a rush to the white goal which bids fair to succeed; but unhappily at the supreme moment two green jackets cannon against each other, and roll over on the grass. Though they rise at once, and join in the battle, the ball speeds its way towards the other goal. One desperate effort is made. A white jacket is tearing along in chase of the little sphere, and about to strike it a final blow, when an opponent catches him and entangles his stick in his own. It is useless. Another white jacket is close behind, and with a tremendous cut he sends the ball over the heads of the rivals, and gains the fifth victory. Of course, we applaud this feat, and, as it is rapidly becoming dark, hasten across the grass to congratulate the riders and pat the ponies, which, strange to say, after the stupendous efforts they have made, are still fresh and just as ready as ever to rush into the fight once more. It is too late; in the distance the triumphal arches are being lit up; lights are rapidly extending along the streets. We must return to the city.

To leave Calcutta without seeing the snakes at the General Hospital would have been an omission of which, at any rate, we could not be guilty. Accordingly it was with great pleasure that I accepted an invitation to visit the collection. Bear in mind that no snake-charmer was present, that neither pipe nor whistle was used, that every snake had its poison fangs or teeth in capital order, and that no means save the marvellous skill of the native operators was employed in the exhibition which followed, and you will have a good idea of the peril through which those Hindoos passed.

It was early in the morning—not, however, before the snakes, which were in a series of wire-covered boxes, were awake and lively—that we were shown into a stone-floored room some twenty feet long and twelve broad. In the boxes were the strongest and deadliest snakes in India: pythons, ophiophagi, cobras, korites, Russel snakes, and many others. The Hindoos who had charge of them were two slim, wiry, little men, nude to the waist, as most of their countrymen are. They wore neither gloves nor any other protection, and had no instrument of any kind in the place. After showing the varied collection under their care, they proceeded to open the python cage, and one of them, putting his hand in, seized a monster serpent and threw him upon the floor close to our feet. The python objected to such treatment, and began to hiss, making at the same time a vigorous effort to rise. But the snake-keeper was waiting for this, and no sooner did that huge shining back begin to curve than the keeper put out his hand, and seizing the creature's tail, pulled it back with a jerk. Instantly the python was powerless—hissing, but unable to move; the more he struggled the more tenaciously did the keeper hold his tail, explaining meanwhile that so long as the reptile was controlled in that fashion there was no danger of its doing mischief; then, just as its rage was becoming ungovernable, the man lifted it quickly, and with a jerk deposited it in the box. Its companion was now taken out in similar manner, and slapped and buffeted till throughout its entire length, some twelve feet, it quivered with passion, but all to no purpose; it, too, was presently replaced in the cage, and shut up to hiss at its leisure.

The fact that an ophiophagus is in the Regent's Park Zoological Gardens, rendered the next exhibition more interesting, although it may be doubted whether the sudden throwing into so small a room of a snake seven feet long was agreeable to the visitors. However, there was really no danger, for the venomous creature was so completely in its keeper's power that we had no occasion for fear. One bite from the reptile, and any one of us would have been dead in five minutes, for it was exceptionally strong and lively; but it was no more able to bite us than the little mongoose caged outside the door. Up rose its head, out came its slithering tongue, its eyes dilated, its huge throat swelled, and all seemed ready for a desperate attack, when the keeper struck the reptile's mouth with the back of his hand, and, before it could strike him, had seized it just under the head. Then it struggled, but only to get away —it had met that native before, and did not at all approve of his treatment. The other native now seized its centre and tail, and, without more ado, the terrible creature was hoisted into the air as harmless as a butterfly, and its fangs exposed by the aid of a small piece of wire. Those teeth were literally full of poison—enough to have killed a dozen persons. At length, our curiosity satisfied, this monster was put into his cage, and his brother plucked out by the naked native, with the hand, and thrown on the floor. He, too, was truculent for a minute, endeavouring to follow the unpantalooned Hindoo round the room; but he had reckoned without his host, or rather his keeper, for he was seized presently by the tail and hoisted up just as the other had been. In vain he hissed and spat. His tongue might move in and out as often as it pleased, but all to no purpose; whether on the floor or in the air its efforts to bite were perfectly unavailing, and when the cage was opened it slunk in, a disconcerted serpent.

A cobra was the next to be turned out, a strong, healthy snake, nearly five feet in length, with a hood the power of moving which somewhat startled us. But move as it might, the agile native was too quick for it. He would put his knee within a foot of it, as it stood up ready to strike, and it would make a dart as futile, however, as it was sudden. Then it would hiss, as though hoping to frighten its adversary; it might as well have hissed at the wall. And, just when it had got up again, and was so enraged that it could scarcely wait for a good opportunity to strike at the native's knee, which was moving before it in a most tantalizing manner, the keeper's hand was quietly placed under its head, and it was removed like its predecessors. "Will it bite?" I asked. "See," said the native. Taking up a piece of bamboo stretched across a shell, he held the wood to the serpent's mouth. Instantly the reptile seized the proffered bait, its eyes glistening, its neck distended, and crunched the wood as though it was tinder. Two or three moments elapsed as the teeth penetrated further into the fibre, and then we saw the poison falling in white drops into the shell, which acted as a kind of saucer. I was particular in noticing two points in regard to this incident: first, that the poison did not come from the fangs immediately the bite was inflicted—a fact which will account for the mongoose living sometimes after he is bitten by the cobra; and, next, that the quantity of venom emitted was much greater than is generally supposed. There were five or six large white drops in the shell, and probably one or two absorbed in the bamboo. When forced to surrender the wood the serpent seemed by no means exhausted; the fibre was much torn, for the teeth had penetrated nearly a quarter of an inch.

For all that, I should mention that when presently another cobra equally large was examined, it was shown that the teeth were set back some distance in the head, and that they were by no means so large as those of a viper which was shown afterwards, and which was so quick in its movements that it had to be lifted out of its box by means of a hooked stick. Cobras and ophiophagi might be seized by the hand, but not so this huge viper, which made such desperate attempts to strike one or two of us, that we were by no means sorry when the keeper seized him by the neck and tail and opened his mouth. His fangs were undoubtedly large—larger than the cobra's by one half, and very strong. They must have contained a great quantity of venom. However, he was not invited to try them, and by the time he got back into his box, was, I think, heartily tired of the exhibition. A Russell snake, with a golden spotted back, was the next on the floor, and it hissed violently, but was taken up just as easily as the others after it had been provoked to a great rage for several minutes. A korite, proverbially deadly, had been played so many tricks before that it was slow to take part in the fun. Once or twice it struck viciously at the keeper, but without any effect, and at last ceased to make any effort to bite the Hindoo. There was no need to play a pipe or tom-tom to awe that snake. It was only too glad to get away into his blanket and box again.

The exhibition was ended by the showing a biscobra, or small guava. What cared we for a wretched snake-charmer, who, with a few serpents whose fangs had been abstracted, a lot of pipes and charming sticks, and all kinds of protections, waited outside, and offered to give us an entertainment? After such an exhibition as we had witnessed the cleverest snake-charmer was the merest impostor. Passing across the grounds, a valuable piece of information was given us. Chained to a wall was a pariah dog, with a severe wound on one of its legs. This animal, we were informed, had been experimented upon by Dr. Wall with wonderful success; a large quantity of cobra poison had been injected under its skin, and yet it had been recovered by an antidote which Dr. Wall is said to have discovered. More may probably be heard of this. In the hospital visitors' book was a note in the writing of the Prince: "I am very much pleased with the hospital, which I find in good order, and well ventilated. ALBERT EDWARD, Jan. 1.,"—the signature of the Duke of Sutherland being also appended. A little lower down was a similar certificate from Dr. Fayrer. The hospital certainly deserves the highest encomium.

CHAPTER XVIII.

A CAPTIVE KING.

Wajid Alee, ex-King of Oude, is too well known in history to need much description; but of what sort is the Royal prison in which he is now confined very few out of the precincts of Calcutta appear to have any idea; and it was with this impression that I accepted the kind permission of Colonel Mowbray Thompson to visit the residence of the ex-King.

A drive of nearly an hour by the side of the Hooghly brought me to an imposing gateway, guarded by troops. Not English soldiers, mark, nor, indeed, sepoys in English pay, but men belonging to his ex-Majesty of Oude, of the same type and costume as those good fellows who committed the butcheries at Cawnpore and elsewhere. However, they were undoubtedly civil, and I was quickly admitted to what at first sight appeared to be an admirably designed garden. I think it is Miss Carpenter who advocates the plan of endeavouring to reform criminals by making delightful residences of gaols. If her theory is right, Wajid Alee should certainly be reformed by this time, for a more lovely succession of groves, parterres, miniature park-like plots of grass and pleasant terraces I have never seen. And what was more astonishing still to me was to discover in these grounds a zoological collection surpassing in many respects the grand menagerie in Regent's Park. At first the prospect, however, was forgotten for a moment in the contemplation of one of those extraordinary pictures for which India is famous. Hung in a large window in such a manner that all its beauty, or rather ugliness, should burst upon the spectator at once, this wonderful daub portrayed a battle-piece, of which the locale might perhaps be the Crimea. One thing was charming about the object, and only one—its absolute impartiality. A Russian officer, with a lobster-coloured face, was cutting down a French soldier; while an English infantryman was bayoneting in the most satisfactory manner a Russian who had injudiciously planted his back against the side of a gun. I think the fight might be described as ending in the defeat of the French by the Russians and the rout of the Russians by the English, which doubtless appeared the most satisfactory result of the struggle to the artist engaged.

A step more, and the celebrated pigeons of the ex-King were in full view. I do not wonder at their being famous; you in England have no idea of what Wajid Alee has achieved. It would be no exaggeration to say that many scores of varieties, most of them surpassingly beautiful, appear in every direction. I am not an ornithologist—I do not know the name of a single pigeon; yet my uninstructed eye was delighted with the success of the Royal breeder. If he did not succeed as a potentate, it was because he was accidentally placed in a position for which nature did not intend him. He should have been a gentleman of moderate means residing somewhere in the South of England; his skill and his patience would have astonished his rivals; he would have gained prizes everywhere, and everybody would have united to praise him. He was unfortunately a King, and all his excellencies are forgotten in the one fact that he was a Royal failure. He is as fond of the birds as ever, and here, in the centre of the garden set apart for them, has a pretty little bungalow, furnished in Oriental fashion, with a couch at each window, on which he can recline and look at the pets that brought him into trouble. There are not many men who, if they lost a kingdom for the sake of pigeon-breeding, would take great pleasure in that particular hobby afterwards. Thus thinking, we passed into another garden, walled in, and in its centre boasting of a marble tank of extraordinary dimensions. I should say, roughly speaking, that it is a hundred and fifty yards square; it is very deep, the water is clear, and on its surface and at its sides are ducks and fowl of all kinds. Scores of pelicans, divers, teal, swans, curious ducks with wonderful plumage, storks, cranes, and peacocks wander all over the garden or go to the tank as they please. They are in no confined cage, cramped up in a space of twenty feet square as in London, but roam all about the delightful square in the bright sunshine, chirping, cackling, hissing, and chattering, and withal as happy as though all the world was before them. Here and there an unruly one is confined in a large pagoda-like cage till he learns to do well; but these moral lessons do not appear to be often needed, for there are only some twenty ne'er-do-wells in custody. Perhaps the prisoner of Oude is tender to evil-doers.

Our next step was into another walled-off space which is even more noteworthy. Here there are several large tanks, trees of abundant foliage offer opportunities of shade, and luxuriant climbing plants cover the sides of the enclosure. Here are buffaloes, goats, deer, and almost every species of herbivorous animal in nature, and the larger birds as well. As you stand under a tree you may be gently brushed by the feathers of a passing ostrich, who winks at you confidentially as he makes his way to a choice box of food he sees at a little distance, and which a cousin for whom it was brought has not noticed yet; or you may be prodded in the back by the horn of a sacred bull as he hints to you the necessity of getting out of his way. Indeed, if you would avoid having to beg the pardon of a resident bird or beast, you must be careful not to walk about quickly, for they are all around you, and, as the weather is exceedingly pleasant, are apparently taking a "constitutional" preparatory to the afternoon dinner. It is a grand idea of the ex-King to give his mute subjects so much liberty; human beings would not have had the same amount had the mutiny succeeded and he remained at Lucknow. But that is a detail into which we need not enquire too deeply. Less fortunate are the feræ which are in an adjoining enclosure. It clearly would be a mistake to let half-a-dozen energetic panthers, or a leopard or two, loose in any garden, particularly if visitors were invited to enter promiscuously. I saw a couple of cheetahs in a cage who would soon clear the place of its attendants —three Rajahs, who, in purple and gold, were seated comfortably under an arbour, and a Hindoo gentlemen, who was apparently engaged in worshipping the sacred Beble tree. Of tigers, there are, singularly enough, none; the two that were here have just died; but there is a pair of wolves who would do nearly as much mischief if turned loose, and, fastened under a tree by a strong iron chain, is an enormous stag, with antlers nearly two yards long, who would be only too happy to be liberated for a moment; indeed, he made several attempts to reach the Hindoo gentleman, but fortunately failed. Of jackals, too, there are some good specimens, but that is a superfluity, for you can see as many as you wish any night in the less-frequented streets of Calcutta, and will certainly be awakened by them unless you live in the busiest part of the city. Hyenas and foxes, porcupines, and many other uncomfortable animals, from the lion to the mongoose, are here, and, if this collection is not so large as the other, its deficiencies are more than compensated for by what we next see.

In the centre of anotber garden, beautifully laid out, and superior in point of style to most of those in England or France, there is a structure of singular description. In form at a short distance it looks like a magnified ant-hill, in three conical portions, and the fact that its sides are full of round holes confirms for a moment the suspicion that it has been produced by some huge insects, and must now be their abode. But it is nothing of the sort. Constructed with enormous care, this extraordinary building is seen on closer inspection to be the work of human hands. Its base is fixed in a large square well, and is surrounded by water; you note, too, that the sides of the excavation arch inward, as though to prevent the escape of something or other, but of what it is not very clear. All over these cones, which rise to a height of about thirty feet, and are more than six times that distance in circumference, are little spikes of iron; the holes are about three inches in diameter, and are very numerous. While we are wondering what can be the use of this building, our eyes light on a couple of big cages in the centre, looking into which we descry two of the largest pythons ever captured. At a rough guess they must be thirty or forty feet long, and their bulk is tremendous. We at once divine that the structure is a snake-house, and, looking up again, remark that in almost every hole the head of a snake may be seen. While we watch, too, a long cobra slowly emerges into the sunlight, clasps one of the iron spikes by its tail, and so swings himself into an opening a little lower down. Every minute, too, serpents are to be seen moving in and out as though they are engaged in morning calls or shopping. It is by no means a pleasant idea that creeps over us just then. What if that arched wall and narrow stream of water failed to suffice for the imprisonment of these animals? There are five hundred of them in all, of which I learn that half are venomous, and they all look strong and healthy enough when two men come up with some baskets of frogs, and throw the chirping struggling creatures to the snakes. Out rushes every member of the colony, and, for a few moments, the frogs have a very uncomfortable time. Some of them are seized by two serpents at once, and are rent in halves forthwith; some are bolted before they have time to jump an inch, and all of them are disposed of in ten minutes. Then the snakes go back to their holes, some pieces of meat are given to the pythons, and you move away. Not out of the gardens yet, however, for we must first of all go through an immense series of huge cages, full of small birds of lovely and varied plumage, and past another of the six residences belonging to the Maharajah. There is little here, however, that we do not see in every rich Hindoo's house; scores of shilling German-manufactured coloured prints representing girls smoking cigarettes, the Madonna and Child, the Emperor William, and Teuton farmers and dairymaids; a collection of chandeliers, such as would fill a large shop, and a great number of couches. Gubbins, in his "Mutinies of Oude," says that Wajid Alee was a man of considerable taste. If that is so, he must have left the furnishing of his domicile to some such genius as he who decorated the palaces of the Guicowar of Baroda. The gardens, the zoological collection, the bungalows themselves, are well-nigh enchanting; and we are careful not to lose so pleasant an impression by a prolonged inspection of the interior of the habitations. In such a mood we pass once more through the gateway, leaving the ex-King of Oude alone in his glory.

CHAPTER XIX.

LIFE IN CALCUTTA.

It has been properly remarked that a ball is a ball all the world over. There is the eternal quadrille to begin with; you are sure to waltz, galop, and polka; and although now and then the air may be different, the measure is the same, and such a thing as a new kind of dance seems unknown to the polished floor of conventional society. For this reason it is absolutely unnecessary to describe at any length the ball which was given at Government House, Calcutta. That the Prince danced heartily and laughed merrily, that there was a tremendous crush in ball-room and supper-room alike, and that the tune of "We won't go home till morning" might have been appropriately hummed by everybody present, is all that need be said. But a garden party at Calcutta is a different thing from an English *fête champêtre*. At a garden party at home you have the same pathways to traverse, the same flower-beds to admire, the same people to converse with, the same tent for champagne and ice, time after time; the same band plays the same tunes; you go at the same hour and you leave at the same moment; there is nothing fresh except the breeze, which makes a garden party pleasant. In India all this is reversed. Let us repair to Belvedere, the residence of Sir Richard Temple, Lieutenant Governor of the Bengal Presidency.

Unless you have been in an Indian equestrian crowd before, your patience will be sorely tried. Oriental imperturbability may not be yours, any more than it belongs to an artillery officer who is close to us, and who is just now yelling at his driver. A thousand vehicles of all kinds are jammed together in a very narrow road, and can only move over the ground at a snail's pace. Even the Maharajah of Benares, all unused as he is to being stopped anywhere, sees that it is useless to storm, and, leaning back, lets a benign smile play upon his countenance. He knows Sir Salar Jung is a good forty feet ahead of him, and will get the best seat in the gardens without fail, yet he never fumes nor frowns. Very differently does a particularly fat Rajah in a very small gig behave. The gentleman who has the honour of driving his horses has a sore back, I trow, by this time; the Rajah's stick has been by no means idle for the last five minutes. I do not see the Maharajah of Cashmere, however, although he is yet a great distance from the gate, conferring any such distinction upon anybody. He is apparently only too delighted with the novelty of the scene to wish to be out of it for a moment; and the three stout sons of Jung Bahadoor are models of patient bearing. Not so a civilian official in the next carriage to us, who is in a frenzy of fear lest he shall miss the opportunity of displaying himself. If he could see himself as others see him, he might perchance sit down quietly; as it is, he gesticulates as violently as though he were endeavouring to address a noisy constituency from a very high hustings. However, he is kept in countenance by a hundred others who are behaving in pretty much the same manner, and one only wishes that a photograph could be taken of fashionable Calcutta going to Sir Richard Temple's garden party. At last the gateway is reached, a ticket is given your carriage—which, by the way, you see no more—and you pass over a carpeted walk on to a grass plateau. Possibly after three hours spent in gaining the gardens, the refreshment tent, which is pretty much like what one would see in England, offers most attraction, were it not that the sound of the tom-tom is heard. It is certain to be the accompaniment of some entertainment; the sound of a gong in a well-ordered house no more surely betokens dinner than does the noise of the black man's thumb and fingers on the tightly-drawn parchment, performances more or less amusing. Besides, yonder wide circle of people, all craning their necks forward, betokens what the vulgar would call "high jinks." Jinks, indeed, they are too—pretty much such as one would expect to see were the inmates of Dante's Inferno giving a holiday, and urged to lose no time but be merry.

At a moment when we enter the crowd, about a dozen of the most hideously-arrayed natives are engaged in a dance. To dance before the Prince—who, by the way is seated on one side of the enclosure, with the Viceroy, the Governor of Ceylon, Miss Baring, and a host of Maharajahs on one hand or the other—Sir Richard Temple has forty or fifty men and women, not all attired exactly alike, but varying their costume according to their individual taste. Some wear their hair very long, reaching down to their waists, and adequately supplied with the stickiest of mud; others are cropped as closely as though the whole period of their dubious lives had been past in a convict prison. Some bind their foreheads with rings of metal, others wear an arrangement of coloured feathers that would move an Ojibbeway to a paroxysm of envy. In the matter of painting, too, they are not guided by any hard and fast social line, but are allowed to be as artistic and prodigal of paint as they please, which also produces an effect all its own. The weapons differ as widely as the attire; some have bows and arrows, some swords of a cumbersome and ugly pattern; others again hide a club behind their backs, or clasp the handles of small daggers. In facial expression, however, they are very much alike; they come from the hills of Assam, and are therefore Mongolians, though not of pure blood. We hear various bystanders bestowing upon them all kinds of technical names; but as these authorities differ amongst themselves, and are moreover not at all likely to be right, we leave that detail and watch the dance. We are told that the twelve fellows who are now jumping about in front of the Prince are illustrating their mode of attempting to avoid the arrows of their enemies. They could not make more ugly contortions of face or body if their enemies' arrows hit them. When they move off, they are replaced by some of their musical kinsfolk, who pipe and tom-tom for five minutes, and then are induced to pack up and begone, only to be followed, however, by four other musicians who come up with a kind of three-stringed fiddle and scrape away with great energy. They, too, have leave to retire, whereupon another posse of savages hop into the ring, and are beginning to dance, when the Prince, always patient, but now very tired, rises, and, leading the way to the refreshment tent, stops the performance. Night is coming on, the sun is down; and all around us, lighting up the Lieutenant-Governor's mansion, his trees, his ponds, and his gravel-walks, are almost innumerable oil-lamps. It is a happy finish to the spectacle in the ring; and though we may have to wait hours for our carriage, or possibly walk home five or six miles in consequence of not finding it, there can be no doubt that Sir Richard Temple's garden party has been a novelty and a success.

Whatever else is missed, native entertainments given to the Prince must be attended. With a feeling of this sort I quitted a dinner table at which sat the most genial of company, to penetrate the native town and to discover the place known as Belgatchia Villa. Its history alone—printed on a large sheet of paper—could not have warranted any extraordinary effort, although to a native the record was doubtles flattering. The place had at one time belonged to a gentleman with the name the spelling and pronunciation of which might take rank as a puzzle, who once had the honour of entertaining Lord Auckland. To please this excellent native, the kindly Governor-General went, it appears, in a grand style, "making," to quote an extant letter of his sister, "all the noise we could;" and, as such another trip to the Belgatchia Villa would please the natives exceedingly, the Prince determined to go to the fête.

There is a great deal in an attractive programme. That issued by the managers of the fête was uncommonly attractive. A present was to be made to the Prince; his Royal Highness was to be "blessed" in a Jajur Vedic Mantra—whatever that might be—by three Vedic students; a gentleman who called himself Pandit Satyavrata Samaswami, had promised to chant a hymn; four native amateurs had volunteered to sing a welcome song in Bengali; a native musical concert was down on the list, after which the Baboo Kally Prosmo Bannerjee was to play on two flutes at once by blowing, not with his mouth, but with his neck, and another gentleman, named Gopal Chuckerbutty, was to sing a song. I hope I shall never hear Chuckerbutty sing any more. A trio on the sitar was promised by three other native instrumentalists; a Nautch dance, a supper, and fireworks were moreover announced.

To hear the music, and see the Prince, nearly two thousand natives had assembled, in a hall built expressly for the purpose, near the villa, nearly two hours before the arrival of the Prince. The apartment itself would bear some inspection, with its blue star-spangled roof, and its green star-spangled pillars. The arrangement of the place was a little peculiar too. For the Prince a throne, with two chairs on either side, was placed, with tiers of seats behind, rising one above another, intended for the use of the Prince's suite. Facing the carpeted gangway which led to the throne, and was not very wide, were the seats, in equal numbers on each side, whereon visitors sat. There was no platform, no raised daïs for the performers—simply the pathway; the result being that of the performance itself scarcely anybody but the Prince and his attendants saw anything. Long before the entertainment began there was a great excitement amongst the managers. Baboos were flitting about hither and thither, as though they had to march up and down the hall a certain number of times before the Prince arrived, and were afraid their task would scarcely be completed. More objectionable, perhaps, than their continual movement, was a constant, droning sound, which penetrated the building, and told of Baboos and instrumentalists rehearsing their music. Was it the sultan Mahmoud who delighted in the noise of fiddle-tuning? He would have been enchanted with the preparations of our Hindoo musicians. We, whose tastes were not thus educated, were less pleased.

At length the Prince's arrival was heralded by a fanfare of trumpets outside; we could hear an order given to the Sikh regiment, drawn up at the door, to present arms, and then in came the Prince, leading Miss Baring, and followed by the Viceroy, Sir William Gregory, and most of the minor members of his suite. The Duke of Sutherland came later. You may now spend a moment in looking at the audience. Yonder is Sir Richard Temple in a cocked hat and feathers of wonderful dimensions, just such a hat, in fact, as an alderman might view with envy; hard by is the descendant of Tippoo Sahib, with a sort of Lutheran hat on his head, but a dress as unlike that of the sober-minded German reformer as may well be. Still that solemn face and that velvet cap cannot be disassociated from the idea. It is Luther still; but Luther going to races or a ball. He would have been the last man in the world to wear cloth of gold in a church, whatever his Protestant followers may do nowadays. And then, seated quite with a crowd—it is a very fashionable, albeit native crowd—is the Maharajah of Jheend; an ancient gentleman, with a long beard, who delights in a golden turban and a white dress. He is not alone in his princely glory; for there are at least twenty of his compeers here; the Maharajah of Travancore is not twenty feet away, and his Highness of Cashmere is close by, smiling as pleasantly as ever. I fancy the aged chieftain of Benares is, after all, the happiest. How he rubs his hands, and peers through his spectacles at all that is going on around him. I verily believe that even the Baboos, who are hopping past us every moment, and whose claim to be elected to the Wanderers' Club should be incontestable, please him. Why should he not enjoy it all? Time, which has dealt kindly with him, cannot long continue its favours. In looking at his happy face one almost forgets the banging and cracking that are going on outdoors. When the Prince visited Kandy, gallant Captain Byrde, who had no cannon, and could not bear the idea of receiving a Prince without a Royal salute, manufactured twenty-one bamboo guns, and, filling them with powder, burst them one after another in honour of the Royal traveller. So, too, at Baroda Station, the traffic superintendent, also a man of resource, laid fog signals on the line over which the Royal train ran, and thus caused sufficient noise to satisfy the most exigeant. Outside the hall to-night they are doing something of the sort, and the delighted countenances of the managers show that the noise is quite equalling their most sanguine anticipations. Inside, just in front of the Prince, the three Vedic students are going through their "blessing," an edifying process, of which we cannot catch a word. Directly after these are gone the hymn is chanted from the Sama Veda.

I think I might be chary of criticism thus far; the professionals are bearable, but alas for those who have to listen to the four amateurs. There is no doubt about the song, the words are in print on huge cards, already given us, and the refrain in Bengali runs:

> "Though humble our reception be,
> And though our strains may halting run,
> The loyal heart we bring to thee
> Is warmer than our Eastern sun."

Perhaps it is; so we pardon the noise the amateurs make for the sake of the words they sing. They should have very loyal hearts. Their lungs are undoubtedly powerful, though nature forgot to give them any vocal ability. But another crowd is forcing its way up the aisle—a crowd of determined-looking old men who carry under their arms and on their shoulders all kinds of instruments. Their smile is portentous. They are going to play before a Prince; not a man in the dozen or so now passing up the hall would leave off playing till the end of the tune, if death itself threatened. And they do play too; no mere short-lived galop or waltz, but a good set piece with plenty of all kinds of bars in it, except bars of rest, an omission for which we heap malediction on the head of the composer when a quarter of an hour of thumping and scraping had passed. However, they cease at last, and then the gentleman with the two flutes stands before the Prince, and certainly does produce a singular effect therewith. The two tin tubes are placed on either side of his neck, he shuts his mouth and turns red in the face, whereupon the flutes emit sounds, and a tune is played. Then comes the redoubtable Chuckerbutty, who, sitting down, begins the vocal music promised. To attempt to describe his "music" is impossible. He appears to have shut his mouth off from all communication with the nose, and to be shouting from the pit of his stomach. Enough, Chuckerbutty, the Prince longs to be delivered from thee. Nautch girls come now, some half dozen in number, and begin such a shuffle as I have previously described. They are not pretty, but their movements are graceful, and they have the good sense to divine when it is time to go. Thankfully we now repair to the refreshment room, on the tables of which is spread a liberal supper, and from the windows of which the fireworks may be seen. Tell it not how we were nearly all asphyxiated with the fumes of gunpowder, and how at three o'clock in the morning we waited for our carriages, Rajahs, Maharajahs, Baboos, Parsees, all. To learn what native entertainments are, it is necessary to go to them. But they should not take place too often.

CHAPTER XX.

KNIGHT-MAKING.

Would you know how Knights of the Star of India are made? Then imagine that you are in Calcutta on the 1st of January in the year of Grace 1876. The scene is an enclosure the form of which is an oblong square, encompassing a space nearly a quarter of a mile in length and about half as broad. It stands in the centre of an extensive mead, is itself carpeted with the greenest turf. And not only the northern and southern extremities, but those also which point to the east and west, are gates wide enough to admit several horsemen abreast. At each of these portals are stationed guards—strong bodies of men-at-arms—for the purpose of maintaining order, and ascertaining also the quality of those who present themselves at the entrances. Along the inner sides of the enclosure looking north and south are sixteen pavilions, adorned with pennons, the chosen colours of the knights to whom they belong. Beside these pavilions also stand the squires of the knights, many of them quaintly attired in fantastic dress, in each case according to the taste of his master. At the eastern end of the enclosure is a pavilion raised higher and more richly decorated than the others, graced by two thrones and canopy, on which the Royal arms are emblazoned. Squires, pages, and yeomen in rich liveries wait around the place of honour, which is clearly designed for personages of high degree. Galleries on either side are filled with knights and nobles in their robes of peace, whose rich tints contrast with the splendid habits of the ladies, who, in greater numbers than the men, have come hither to witness the sport. In a yet lower space are such of the lesser gentry as from modesty, poverty, or dubious title, to say nothing of inability to persuade somebody in office to give them a more desirable post, dare not assume any higher place.

This tented field is within a mile of the city of Calcutta. Yonder thrones of silver and blue—the one surmounted by the crown, and the other by three feathers; both of them placed on a daïs raised three steps from the ground, and under a canopy of the same material as the thrones themselves—are intended for the Viceroy of India and the Queen's son. The tents, at the doors of which stand clusters of singularly attired retainers, hide Knights of the Star of India, Grand Commanders from Scinde, Cashmere, Travancore, and Indore; the guards at the gates are battalions of Sikhs, bronzed warriors from the Punjab, athletic soldiers of Bengal. Inside, the helmets of white and glittering weapons are those of British troops and British sailors, drawn up in strong lines in front of the tents, and forming a guard of honour on either side of the pathway which leads to the Royal pavilion. The splendid spectacle is not only romantic in itself, but to persons acquainted with the style and title of all that are notable here, it is an extraordinary but very intelligible scene. Inside the Royal pavilion, and on either side of the daïs, no less than at the back of it, were tiers of seats filled with native grandees, English generals and naval captains, political officers, and ladies, the beauty of whose uniforms and dresses was marvellous to behold. Scarlet, blue, cloth of gold, silks of the brightest hues, all combined to give warmth and colour to this delightful picture. The pale blue of the Order, which was apparent everywhere, on throne and canopy, in banners pendant from the roof, and in the cloaks of those who were about to be invested as Knights Grand Commanders—the recipients, as yet invisible—actually relieved the eye, so overwhelming was the assemblage of gaudy colours. Nor were "Queen's of Beauty" wanting; there were many here whose beauty entitled them to be every whit a queen; it was an assemblage of all the fair and all the brave in Bengal. Allowing your eye to run along the red carpet, on which was emblazoned the Royal arms, and so looking right and left, you found at the entrance to the Royal tent other galleries erected for and filled by those whose rank or deeds were not sufficient to entitle them to the premier places. Yet even these were much to be envied, and, indeed, were envied accordingly by those whose fortune it had not been to receive an invitation. They were content to sit under insufficient canopies, braving the hot sun for hours, rather than lose an opportunity of being present at the greatest fête which India witnessed in modern times. It is a long and striking vista—the vastness of the enclosure and the brightness of the sunlight render objects somewhat less distinct, mellow down the tones of colour outside the pavilion, and give to the whole spectacle more than may be easily imagined the attributes of an admirably painted picture or a fairy scene, rather than the idea of life and reality, "Nothing shall be omitted which will redound to the dignity of the said Order," says the Royal Warrant which commands the Prince to hold the chapter.

Standing, as we do, in the Royal pavilion, then, this splendid morning, before the Prince arrives and the chapter is opened, there is much to notice. Of the tents outside this throne-room, but, of course, inside the enclosure, that on the right-hand side looking towards the entrance is reserved for the Viceroy, who, as Grand Master of the Order, has the chief place; the opposite one belongs to the Prince of Wales. Next to that of Lord Northbrook is the tent of the Maharajah Scindia; next to the Prince of Wales' the pavilion of the ruler of Cashmere. In order of precedence as follows are the tents of the Maharajah Holkar, the Maharajah of Jeypore, the Maharajah of Rewah, Sir Bartle Frere, the Maharajah of Travancore, Lord Napier, the Maharajah of Puttiala, Sir Salar Jung, and the Begum of Bhopal. Round the doors of these tents, for their occupants have already arrived in order appointed, stand their retainers, in all the costumes of the Indies. There are two more large tents, one for Knights Commanders and another for Companions of the Order. Pathways to all of these have been marked by red carpet; their doorways are all guarded by English troops. Inside the pavilion fresh arrivals are swelling the already crowded audience every moment. Several of the Prince's suite, headed by the Duke of Sutherland—who wears the scarlet coat and plaid of a Highland regiment, the plaid being fastened to his Grace's epaulettes by the aid of white ribbon—and Lord Alfred Paget, in a general's uniform and sash, stroll in at one door at the precise moment that Sir William Gregory, brave in his Governor's gold-embroidered uniform and newly acquired collar of St. Michael and St. George, enters by another, leading Miss Baring and followed by his aide-de-camp. Miss Baring stands and chats with the Duke, Lord Alfred Paget and Sir William Gregory are apparently wishing each other a happy new year, when a stir at the door betokens the arrival of somebody of great importance. One marvels who it can be, and has reason to marvel still more when the apparition makes its way into open view.

Surely nothing more grotesque was ever seen before. Four olive-coloured gentlemen with Mongolian faces, attired in fashions so fantastic as to provoke a general murmur of surprise, even from people somewhat used to singular dresses, are waiting for seats. Golden hats, red collars, green robes, dragon-headed swords, all belong to the representatives of his Majesty of Burmah. What reason for wonder that the subjects of that potentate occasionally commit little excesses if the magnates of his empire wear dresses like these. The sons of Jung Badoor are just entering, and are led to a post of honour. Their aigrettes of diamonds and horsehair plumes are no mean addition to the head-dresses of the audience; besides which one of them is to be decorated presently. There is a native officer, too, of the Viceroy's staff—a fine, soldierly man, dressed like a

European, save that he wears a turban and a short plaid petticoat, and he is placed in a good seat; and another native—this time a civilian, one of those who is to receive the medal of the Order—by name Baboo Degumber Mitter, follows, and is placed close to Colonel Ramsay, who, like his native friend, will shortly be called up and be publicly honoured. At length, however, a far more notable incident occurs. Amid heavy salvoes of artillery, the presenting of arms by the troops, playing of bands, and hurrying of umbrella bearers and aides-de-camp, the entrance of the Prince and the Viceroy to the enclosure is announced, and they are conducted to their tents preparatory to the forming of a procession to the Royal pavilion. For a moment there is a pause; the chiefs of the Order are seen moving from their tents across the enclosed plain, while a lively march is played and distant guns are firing.

The first Knight Grand Commander of the Star of India is just upon the point of entering the tent, heralded as becomes the possessor of titles and dignity so undoubted, by a goodly array of men-at-arms. Turbaned warriors in pairs, eight in number, two of them Nawabs in their own right, precede the knight, while an officer of rank bears the Bhopal escutcheon. Fancy pictures a stalwart soldier in rear of that silken sheet of blue and gold—a broad-shouldered, fierce-looking winner of honours, when following the banner, which by this time has entered the tent, totters forward a native lady, so closely muffled-up and veiled in blue silk that not a hair of her head or a feature of her face can be descried by the most inquisitive; a little Mahommedan dame, dressed in the blue robe of the Order, with a shield in the place where her right arm should be, an embroidered star on her left side, the medal of the Order hung round the mufflers which cover her neck, and the star of brilliants pinned to her breast. It is certain that she can in some way or other, to us unknowm, peer through that thick, blue veil, or that tottering shuffle would degenerate into a helpless halt. As it is, she moves slowly forward, her train being held up by two little pages in yellow turbans, till she finds her chair of state, and subsides. But another group is coming forward, and we have not time to look longer at the little Begum of Bhopal. Make way for Sir Salar Jung, who is preceded by eight attendants. Clad in a black velvet coat richly embroidered with gold, and with the blue robe of the Order thrown over his shoulders, the great Minister of the Nizam steps slowly forward, a single page upholding his train, and takes his place exactly opposite to the Begum of Bhopal who, by the way, is standing up once more. Then his Magnificence of Puttiala, with banner and attendants, appears in the way. A broad-shouldered potentate, truly; the front of his turban and of his coat alike nearly covered with those famous brilliants which once glittered at the Tuileries, and at St. Cloud, at the assemblies of the Knights of the Legion of Honour, when the Empress Eugénie looked on the grandest pageant which France could afford. Their owner stands by the side of the tiny lady Knight, a very tower of strength—a giant magnified the more by the contrast he makes with the Begum of Bhopal. Behind him, not very far behind, is a more notable Knight than he, Lord Napier of Magdala, eight English officers heralding him, and one bearing his banner aloft—a broad silk flag of brown and gold. For pages this hero of many fights has a midshipman from the "Immortalité," in navy blue, and a sub-lieutenant in bright scarlet uniform; fit followers of one who has achieved so much by sea and by land. The little Maharajah of Travancore, with only four heralds and two little boys attired in Bengalee fashion, is close behind, moving in as graceful a manner as though he had all his life long made Chesterfield and Brummell his models and study. Sir Bartle Frere follows, and then the Maharajah of Rewah, preceded by his banner of black and gold, and having pages prettily attired in cloth of gold. Jeypore the Rajpoot is next, with a banner of curious kind. Divided lengthwise into strips of various colours, it portrays at once yellow, blue, white, green, red, and black. His train is supported by boys in hats like sugar loaves—yellow hats, and extremely ugly. Holkar's red puggaree is in view a minute later—Holkar, the plainly-dressed Maharajah, clad wholly in white, excepting the blue robe which he wears in common with all Knights Grand Commanders—and then the Maharajah of Cashmere, whose banner is of gold and white, and whose little pages wear tiny pink turbans. Scindia the senior now approaches, wearing a white Tyrolese hat trimmed with a yellow feather, and as he follows his blue and yellow banner, stops here to shake hands with Lord Napier, there to bow to his Highness of Travancore, then to exchange a word with his *vis à vis* of Cashmere, and lastly to speak to Holkar, whose seat is next his own. All the Knights Grand Commanders are then in their places; the band plays the march still; all are now in suspense, for the Prince and Viceroy are coming; their processions are moving towards the tent.

About the dignity connected with an umbrella, many great authorities, from King Coffee in the West to the Jam of Nowanuggur in the East, are agreed. But when there are not only one, but three umbrellas, when one of these is of gold, and the two others of blue and red, with massive gold broideries, there can be no manner of doubt in the minds of the most ignorant in such matters as to the amount of dignity and honour they confer. In front of these insignia of pomp march with steady tread twelve chosen esquires, attendants on the Knight Grand Commander whose banner it is which is seen in the distance. That banner, too, is worthily borne, for it is carried by no less a warrior than General Probyn, to whose name attaches all that is dear to a soldier. And close behind, under the gold umbrella, comes the Prince of Wales, clad in a general's scarlet uniform, with the blue cloak of the Star of India over his shoulders, the gold chain of the Order about his neck, and that of the Garter beside it. Following this procession is that of the Viceroy, very similar and quite as grand, boasting two other little pages almost the counterparts of those who follow the Prince. His Excellency takes his seat on the daïs, the audience sits down, there is a short consultation between Lord Northbrook and his Foreign Secretary, and then Mr. Aitchison stands forward, a long roll in his hand, and proceeds to call out the names of the members of the chapters. He begins with Albert Edward, Prince of Wales, and the Prince, in a loud tone of voice, says "Here!" Lord Northbrook comes next on the roll. "Here!" Then the Duke of Edinburgh, to whose name there is no response. So the roll goes, on, each Knight present answering to his name, until at length it is finished, and then the chapter is declared open, and we wait with curiosity for further proceedings.

In a loud, clear voice Mr. Aitchison reads the warrant authorising "our well-beloved son" to hold a ceremony of investiture of the Order on behalf of her Majesty, and details by all those repetitions of which lawyers are so fond, but of which all other people are so tired, the separate rights and powers to which certain and sundry chosen already for the honour will hereafter be entitled, "all statute, rule, or usage to the contrary notwithstanding." After which satisfactory statement, there is silence while the Prince and all present stand up, and his Royal Highness is saluted. Hereupon Mr. Aitchison moves forward again—he is the principal personage here after all, and will appear very often, but he is a good and untiring official, and deserves all prominence—and hands to the Prince the warrant, which by his Royal Highness is transferred to the hands of one of the pages at the back of the throne, and the ceremony proceeds.

Mr. Aitchison now goes in quest of the Maharajah of Jodpore, who is hidden away in a tent in the dim distance, taking with him four macebearers, the Under-Secretary of the Foreign

Department, and two junior Knights-Commanders, while the bands outside strike up a quick march. It is a long distance that has to be traversed, and it is some time ere the little procession has turned to the left and gone towards the pavilion of the waiting Maharajah. But as time passes it is seen returning, this time swelled by the attendants and person of his Highness of Jodpore, who with pages and bannermen is now coming up. It may be that you are tempted to laugh outright as that extraordinary party from the tent approaches, till you remember that you are in the very presence of Royalty and in the chapter of a lodge of Knights. Six very fat men, with long pink gowns drawn tight to the knees, so that they can scarcely walk, but bulging out thence, and frilled so stiffly as to resemble a large Chinese umbrella, are not, perhaps, stately objects, albeit that one of them is a Maharajah. However, the soldiers and sailors present arms as the cortége passes, the bands play a slow march, and it enters the Royal pavilion with all state and show. Conducted to the foot of the daïs, where he makes profound bows, kissing his hand in approved style, the Maharajah hears the warrant for his decoration read over, is then taken to a table on one side, where he receives his cloak and badge, then back to the Prince, who, ejaculating the words, "In the name of the Queen, and by her Majesty's command, I here invest you with the honourable insignia of the Star of India, of which most exalted order her Majesty has been graciously pleased to appoint you to be a Knight Grand Commander," places the chain round the bent neck of the recipient without himself rising from the throne. Immediately a salute of seventeen guns is begun; the newly-made Knight bows to the Prince and Viceroy, who both remain seated with their helmets on; a blast of trumpets heralds the proclamation of his style and title, and Jodpore of the red petticoat is led to his seat.

Then another pause ensues; Mr. Aitchison sallies forth again, this time in search of the Rajah of Theend. He presently appears, followed by the Foreign Secretary, clad in cloth of gold, and wearing a golden turban. He is a grand man, in appearance firstly, for his long, grey beard and manly carriage betoken a patriarchal warrior; in repute secondly, for he it was who first led Sikh troops to conquer the fiends at Delhi. The ceremony of his investiture is the same as in the case of his predecessor of Jodpore, save that eleven guns only are fired in his honour. And then the Knights Commanders are brought up. The first is Mr. Robinson, of Madras, who immediately receives a collar of blue silk and medal from the hands of the Prince, and then is made a Knight Bachelor of Great Britain by the placing of a sword, which General Probyn has ready, on his left and right shoulders. The rest, with the exception of Colonel Ramsay, who receives the same honours as Mr. Robinson, are unknown to the English public. Companions of the Order are next nominated, the Prince handing the medal to Mr. Aitchison, who pins it upon the breast of the selected one, who bows reverently, and so the ceremony draws to an end. The newly-made Companions take their appointed places; their names are called out and responded to with much humility: the Secretary informs the Prince that there is no further business before the chapter, whereupon he is commanded to declare the lodge dissolved; a Royal procession is once more marshalled; the guards of honour present arms; bands play a grand march; one more Royal salute is fired, and the Prince and Viceroy leave the pavilion, stopping in their way out to speak to the great chieftains as they pass. A few minutes later, and the enclosure itself has been quitted by the Royal party, and the rest of us are moving to the gates on our way home. The chapter of the most exalted Order of the Star of India is dissolved

CHAPTER XXI.

THE SACRED CITY OF BENARES.

Benares is undoubtedly a fine city. The view from the river is perfect; but a person beholding it for the first time on a chilly moonlight night, in a rickety vehicle that threatened to turn over every moment on a bridge of boats, with only a very vague idea of where he would find a bed for the night—that bed being, at all events, quite six miles off—might fail at that particular moment to recognise the attraction of Benares. On the other hand, a believer in Shiva, a red-turbaned, shuffling, white-petticoated, olive-coloured native of Hindostan, with his heart set upon visiting the sacred city of India, would leap for joy; would forget the mist and the dimness, the chilly wind and clammy air, the chance of having no bed, and possibly no board either, and rejoice with exceeding joy at the prospect of plunging in the Ganges next morning, and washing away what peccadilloes and worse might cling to his soul. The slow-moving, shrunken stream—for the rains are long since past—would assume a new appearance. Yonder innumerable steps down to the river would be but as Jacob's ladder reversed; not, indeed, leading upwards to glory, but downwards to happiness here and hereafter.

A grand position is that of a Hindoo pilgrim to Benares—a lot to be envied by the myriads who live in the far North, and the millions who inhabit the distant South, the natives of the Malabar Coast and those whose vista is a view of the Coromandel Sea. These may yearly send their roll of fortunate men—men who have done wrong and had misgivings, but who come hither to bathe and be morally clean henceforth and for ever; but the vast majority can hope for no shriving, no indulgence, no pardon; the waters of the Bombay Abana or the Madras Pharpar may be blue and beautiful; but the Benares Ganges, the sacred river, can alone do good to the crowds of natives whose dread is Shiva the destroyer. Of course, the wealthy of the land can come hither and be blest. "See Naples and die," say the Italians, "See Benares and die," echo the Hindoos; and, in hope of dying here and being consumed by fire on the river shore, many a rich native hurries up, despite agony of body indescribable. What becomes of him when he reaches the sacred city? Visit the river banks, and entering a dingy, or covered boat, move slowly down the stream, and see.

On the right bank is a wide plain, somewhat similar to the Essex marshes which skirt the Thames below Tilbury; there is the palace of the Maharajah of Benares at a distant point, but with this exception the right side of the Ganges is deserted. On the left, however, a very different picture presents itself, and such a one as cannot be forgotten so long as memory lasts. A great city suddenly fronts us—a city not only sacred, but grand in its edifices of palaces and temples, the chief of which are on the water's edge. Here are hundreds of flights of stone steps forty or fifty feet broad, rising high up the river bank. The steps, or "ghauts," lead to magnificent Oriental buildings. Here is the Ghaut Scindia, with the palace of the Ruler of Gwalior above; there the Ghaut Nagpore, with the Rajah's house at the summit; a little further on the Ghauts of Vizianagram, Benares, Nagpore, and Peshwa, with the mansions attached. The subsisting Maharajahs and Rajahs, having always an eye to the possibilities of fate, and anxious to make "the best of both worlds," have a house in the sacred city, where they can comfortably retire when the warning comes and preparation for departure is judicious. Poorer people must manage without all this, and indeed do so manage. In view at this moment are thousands of them bathing in the water, lapping it, washing their clothes—if a waistcloth can be called "clothes" —and taking up a vesselful of the sacred water for the benefit of their friends. The water is not bright or clean. It might, were it not so sacred, be called very dirty. And there are, just now at any rate, some thousands of people bathing in it continually. But that matters not; it is the holy river, and the worshippers of the Ganges fill their mouths with the water, lave in it, drink of it, quite happily. Every dip they take, every drop they swallow, washes off moral uncleanliness. To us strangers the sight is amazing. Under the shadow of temple and mansion alike, troops of men, women, and children are coming down the steps. A short prayer, a momentary uplifting of the hands, a certain, or rather uncertain, rolling of the eye-balls, and then a plunge into the river. All along the bank, huddled together against the landing stages, in the stream up to their necks, clinging to the bamboo posts to which boats are fastened, every devotee is happy, each ready to pay for a garland of yellow flowers, each determined to make the most of a liberation from the ill-deeds of the past.

While thinking about this unwonted scene, the boatman attracts attention by a touch on the arm, to say we are opposite the burning ghaut. To be burnt at Calcutta or Bombay may be a satisfactory contemplation for the dying native; but to be placed on the funeral pyre at Benares, to be first of all washed in the Ganges, and then to have his ashes thrown into the sacred river, is indeed a happiness. As we look on the shore, the boat being drawn close to the edge, a curious sight meets our eyes. In a little space, fashioned somewhat after the shape of an amphitheatre, are three burning heaps of wood. Looking down upon these, quite thirty feet high above the pyres, and enveloped in the smoke, are some forty or fifty men and women, perched on the steps like so many rooks, looking complacently down while the remains of their relatives are being consumed. Down at the water's edge, partly in the water indeed, are two human bodies. One is that of a woman, the other of a man; each is wrapped in white linen. Very little ceremony is needed, but that little is observed. The fire pile has been prepared for the reception of the corpse to be burnt. The body is therefore placed by the side of the river, and then dipped into the water, so that all the sheet is covered. Lest there should be any doubt about this, however, a vessel of water is twice emptied over the head of the corpse before it is removed, and then the two men in attendance, lifting the body, place it upon the pyre; logs of wood thrown to them by assistants are laid on it; light, dry chips placed beneath; a torch is fetched, and the light applied; there is a blaze, and—of the rest nothing need be said.

Our boat is now propelled a little further down the stream, till the Great Mohammedan mosque is reached. Two minarets, one of which may be ascended without danger, stand on either side of it; but we decline the proffered opportunity.

I have said that Benares is a holy city; it is notable in many other respects. Were nothing more to be seen, its Observatory, its Golden Temple, its sacred well, and its strange bazaar, would give it the title to be ranked amongst the most notable places in the world. But it has, in addition to all these, and the most holy point of the Ganges, long groves of trees—orange, citron, plantain, and palm; and the most singular monkey temple in the world. On arriving at the temple the Prince was supplied with a plate of parched peas and a number of white sweetmeats, of which it was said that the monkeys had many times signified their approbation, and thus furnished, his Royal Highness entered the temple. We had been told that on stepping inside a great assemblage of monkeys might be expected, and sundry signs had not been wanting that monkeys were somewhere about in great numbers. Up in the neighbouring trees, on the walls and roofs of houses, in the roads, chasing luckless children, and on the fronts of the shops, these creatures seemed to be everywhere. That they were mischievous was also undoubted, for now and then they would hurl stones or pieces of wood at passers-by with an aim by no means to be despised, or would lean over the wall and quietly snap off the turban of some thoughtless pedestian, who might shout, and call not only the monkey but the monkey's sister and mother—the approved style of abuse here—all kinds of unpleasant names; but his turban might be considered as gone, all efforts of its owner notwithstanding, and the best thing he could do would be to buy another puggaree as quickly as possible. Our entry to the temple was the signal for a general assemblage of these pleasant animals. They tumbled down from the minarets of the temple, they came over the walks by scores, they wriggled through holes and crevices, rushed in at the doorways, and, in short, so readily obeyed the summons as to form a body that could, without the slightest trouble, have had a great piece of fun with the Prince and his suite. Fortunately, they were peaceably inclined, and as the stock of sweetmeats and peas was large, and their hunger not great—for they are fed on an average fifty times a day by pilgrims and worshippers—they were content to take what was thrown them, and filling their cheeks as full as possible, make off. I am not sure that at times the gold lace on the Prince's coat was not a temptation, for the monkeys' eyes glistened as they looked at the Royal uniform. But the visitors were, fortunately, on three steps, kept clear by energetic priests, and the Royal party came away without any accident.

Not far from here is the celebrated Golden Temple, to visit which is the ambition of every Hindoo. To see it thoroughly, the Prince was, on arrival, conducted to an adjacent window, whence the golden dome, with its surrounding minarets, one of them golden also, could be inspected. The stone carving of this edifice is very rich, and so minute as to cause a feeling of considerable surprise in the minds of all strangers. It is as neatly

THE MONKEY TEMPLE AT BENARES.

carved as the finest ivory boxes, and the sharpness of the figures, although they were fashioned hundreds of years ago, remains to this day. Inside, some hundreds of Hindoos were going through their worship as they did in the days when the carvings were new, without variation or alteration.

There is a well here which, as the residence of a deity—no less a personage than Shiva himself—is greatly worshipped.

The proper thing for a pilgrim on arrival at Benares is to do "Poojah" in the first instance to this well. This he accomplishes in two ways—by throwing holy Ganges water and flowers into the well, and as much money as he can scrape together into a bright silver box, which a thoughtful priest is careful to point out. One may look at the well without throwing anything into it, and be just as much rewarded as if he had brought the Ganges into the temple, provided that he place something in the box. But if you throw all the flowers in Benares into the tank, and only look at the box, be good enough to remember that you are still an unregenerate Hindoo, and not at all a favourite of the very respectable deity who, strange to say, prefers for a dwelling-place one of the most horrible stench-holes in the universe. We, as pilgrims, held our noses and gave up our purses. It was an act of homage which the priests understood and approved—the most effective way of doing Poojah at the Gyan Bapee.

Other wells in Benares are almost equally holy—one named Mankarnika, which is said to have been built by divine hands, and sanctified by the dropping of one of Parvati's earrings into the water. The dropping of flowers and refuse into the water since that memorable moment has made it so unbearable a cesspool that one glance is sufficient, and a hasty retreat necessary. We did no Poojah here—perhaps we were good enough already. A Brahmin told me—he was a highly educated man —that originally the well was filled with the perspiration from Vishnu's body; but it was his belief, and here he became quite confidential, that Vishnu had not visited the well for some time —a statement which credits Vishnu with great good sense. But the Brahmin was an attendant on a rival well, so he must not be implicitly trusted.

From the well a move was made to the Observatory, where a considerable number of interesting objects were to be viewed. There was a stone wall eleven feet high, nine feet one inch broad, in the plain of the meridian, which is used as a quadrant, and I was told that the sun's altitude and zenith distance at noon, as well as its greatest declination, and the latitude of the place, could all be ascertained by the help of this instrument—if so a stone wall can be named—by a very aged and excessively dingy astronomer, who was chattering in Tamil to one of the party. There were two large circles of stone, and a square, and another arrangement of stone in the shape of a staircase, by all of which various astronomical problems may, it is said, be worked. The staircase was called Yantrasamrat, or Prince of Instruments; and a very knowing old gentleman was pointed out who could tell the declination or right ascension of a star by the aid of it. As a staircase, I may impartially admit that it was respectably constructed, and not difficult of ascent; moreover, that it afforded an admirable view of the city and the river, when once we were perched on the topmost step. As to its use as an astronomical "guide, philosopher, and friend," I can say nothing. The old gentleman tried to explain something to me, but as his language was not similar to mine, the conversation was of a very one-sided character. However, the sum of two annas, politely offered and gratefully received, was at least understood and accepted in lieu of learned discourse.

CHAPTER XXII.

A LEVEE OF THE BRAVE.

Lucknow saw the levée of the Brave. Not a dress exhibition of such braves as may be found anywhere ready to march past a Prince—the brave in gold and tinsel, in moustaches and uniforms; but the brave who, at the peril of their lives, and despite the entreaties of friends, remained true to the flag at a moment when fidelity promised nothing but suffering.

It was about four o'clock in the afternoon when a sharp drive landed me in the midst of an extraordinary scene. In the background stood a pile of charred ruins, bullet-seamed, shell-beaten, fire-broken heaps of stones. A circle of trees enclosed the whole scene—trees heavy with foliage, deep groves of bright green leaves. In the centre was a mound of earth, on the top of which was a triangle of wood, surmounted by two Union Jacks. In front and on the two other sides, the third of which was the ruin I have referred to, were long lines of troops; those in front Sikh and Punjabee regiments, attired somewhat after the fashion of Highland soldiers, except that they wear "breeks," while those at the sides were European battalions. In rear of the Sikhs, and under the shade of the trees, two batteries of artillery were drawn up ready to salute. Inside the space thus held by the soldiers, and close to the mound, were ladies and gentlemen in brilliant costumes. Natives, too, in the bright-hued dresses of holiday attire, helped to fill in the already striking picture by clustering round the lines of the troops and endeavouring to peer over their shoulders and between their fixed bayonets. But neither ladies nor gentlemen, English nor Punjabee soldiers, were the most notable of those present. The dark hues of the artillery and Sikhs contrasted with the bright scarlet of the Line; the deep, full turbans of the Punjabees and the helmets of the English, with the snowy white puggarees of the Bengalese—all this and much more might have been noted, but they were not all. Only as a setting to a rich gem such as might be gazed at again and again, could all this be considered. You wonder what this may be. On the top of the mound, close by the foundation stone, stand some two hundred veterans, grizzled and grey, their breasts covered with medals and stars of valour. Their uniforms are as varied as are their castes and races. Sikhs tall and stalwart, Bengalese small and wiry, Portuguese and half-caste, Punjabees and natives of the Malabar coast, all are there. These are the brave of Lucknow, the natives who kept yonder charred ruined in those dark days when death stared them in the face and escape seemed only possible by treachery.

Suddenly the guns under the trees thunder out a salute. How the buildings rattle, how the noise echoes through the corridors of the ruin! From the very spot where that artillery is placed—not one gun at a time, but fifty, loaded to the muzzle with grape and canister, or crammed with heavy shot, hurled missiles against those trembling walls. Ladies and men, too, are actually shaking their heads at the clatter and the din which these little nine-pounder Armstrongs make as they are discharged singly. The veterans on the mound swerve not; they could tell you of an hour when the earth trembled with the vibration of artillery, when thousands of blood-thirsty ruffians, hidden away under the trees round the mound, were discharging their muskets every moment at anything that appeared like a human being on the walls of the Residency. One gun, forsooth!—that pandemonium of 1857 cannot be forgotten in the clatter and the din of to-day. The firing is not intended, however, to remind us of the terrible noise of the Lucknow siege; it is a salute—a sound of joy. The Prince is coming, attended by his suite, to lay the foundation-stone of a memorial to the native brave who fell in the fight, in the presence of the brave who survive.

All on a sudden the word of command is given for a Royal salute; arms are presented along the lines; the bands united play the National Anthem, and the Prince and his suite, the Duke of Sutherland, Lord Alfred Paget, Lord Suffield, Lord Aylesford, Colonel Owen Williams, Major Sartorius, Mr. Knollys, and some other persons, come past the corner of the ruins, and so upon the mound. The veterans raise their hands to their foreheads; the spectators bare their heads; the Prince bows; and then Mr. Cooper, himself one of the members of the brave band who held the Residency, steps forward and delivers an oration on the merits of the grey soldiers who stand before the Prince. It is a subject upon which he may well be eloquent. Who could not wax warm when dwelling on that fight of heroes? His address, too, is extempore, and, what is more to the purpose, at times impassioned. He remembers the dark days when, had yonder brave men faltered, the dark sea of rebellion had swallowed them up alive; and, mindful of the fact that he is one of those who owe their lives to the fidelity of the *vieux soldats*, he stints not language in telling of their deeds of valour. You and I have heard addresses of which we grew tired; many a time we have wished the laboured speech could be "taken as read." But in presence of the dark ruins, in presence of the piece of stone which, hanging from the triangle of wood, is to commemorate forever, telling to generations unborn the grand deeds which faithful natives achieved, he may well be careless of time. How one turns round and looks with new interest at the tiny fortress, the mere house in fact, which for five months sustained that terrible siege! How shut out from all the world it seems by that dense circle of trees! Why, it is in a hollow, that hollow in the centre of a wide-stretching plain which it has taken you hours in a swift morning train to pass over. You remember that when these veterans were in those battered walls, help was far away, and vengeance very near. You need not fancy to paint the myriads of bloodthirsty villains in the groves, or working under cover of huts and broken houses, close by the Residency. Gaze around you ; place a musket in the hands of the thousands who are now quietly looking on this peaceful scence; send 500 men, women, and children into the "fort" once more, give to the Sikhs and Punjabee regiments, with many more of their comrades, plenty or artillery, an unlimited supply of ammunition, and leave to kill and destroy—thought need travel no further—yet you have not then half pictured the scene which Lucknow beheld before Havelock had reached it, while yet Lawrence lived.

The Prince as he stands there is evidently no careless listener. Without any sign of weariness he hears Mr. Cooper to the end, and then, without notes of any kind, touches his hat and replies. Brief but to the point are the words he chooses. He acknowledges the bravery of the men he meets to-day; he praises them for their fidelity, and then points out that such monuments as that about to be constructed must tend to the good of all, must act as incentives to bravery and fidelity to Europeans and natives alike. Then, moving back to the stone, His Royal Highness takes the trowel in hand with all the air of an accomplished mason, and spreading the mortar carefully, while the veterans look curiously and inquisitively on, himself superintends the placing of the stone, gives it three taps with the mallet, and declares it well and truly laid.

Then comes the levée of the brave. There is no raised daïs, no servants with maces, no punkah-bearers, no carriers of umbrellas, no clerkly person to call over a roll of names. There are those on the Prince's suite who would like something a little more stately—some fitting ceremony in a proper place—somewhere from which the common herd could be excluded and from which special correspondents might be shut out. This is scarcely dignified enough for such exquisites; and one or two of them do not fail to say so. But the Prince is of more sensible stuff, is more of a man than many around him, and he holds his levée of the brave in sight of the place where their glorious deeds were done. Standing, then, on the green mound—a little in advance of his suite—his Royal Highness awaits the introduction of his courtiers. Major Cubitt at once steps forward to act as Master of the Ceremonies; Canon Duckworth, minister of peace, but none the less admirer of the brave, assumes the *rôle* of Assistant-Master of Ceremonies; Lord Alfred Paget and General Probyn are close at hand to direct the movements of the veterans as they pass by, and thus the Court is formed.

The first who have the honour of being introduced to the Prince are a number of scarlet-coated Jemindars and Soubadhars who have since the memorable days of 1857 risen from the ranks to the dignity of officers. As they go by they salute the Prince, and then, at the bidding of General Probyn, hold out the handles of their swords, whereupon the Prince touches them, and the veterans, saluting again, move on slowly. These officers know their duty, are well disciplined, and have not forgotten the rules of the service. Not so those who follow them. These have, since the days when they were on parade—years ago in the case of many of them—lost sight of the golden maxim of strict obedience, and are altogether unmindful of the injunction to "move on." They linger, indeed, as long as they possibly can, gazing wistfully into the face of the "Burra Sahib," the Prince, for whose Royal mother they once fought so well. They are not content with one salute, or two even, but raise their withered hands over and over again to their grey heads, and smilingly bow to the great stranger without so much as a notion of leaving the mound and making room for some one else. The Prince, too, shows no haste to be rid of them, but good-naturedly bows to each of them several times, smiling at their honest, loyal enthusiasm, and forgetting for the moment that the sun is setting. Very differently, however, does the stern, though kindly General Probyn view the matter. All must pass the Prince, or endless jealousies would be aroused and grievous wrong done—therefore all must obey the rule of motion, and go forward. So when one lingers long he is taken gently by the arm, and passed quietly along to the rear of the mound, generally receiving in such a case a kindly word from Lord Alfred Paget or a pressure of the hand from the worthy Canon Duckworth. The old soldiers seem to understand it all—at any rate, they are the last men in the world to mutiny now that they know what the Sahibs wish.

Then come by a number of turbaned veterans, in light brown uniforms. Many of them have four medals on their breasts; they are now officers in the police, and admirable fellows they are. They, too, hold out their sword-handles, which are touched. After them come a number of old men, whose appearance fills the eyes of many present with tears. There is one who can only walk with the aid of his two sons, for he is blind; a splinter of shell within the walls of the ruins deprived him of sight; another, who cannot walk at all, even with help, but who comes by on the palms of his hands, swinging a crippled body as he moves along. How that poor face lights up with joy as he is addressed by the Prince, and actually asked to extend his hand that his Royal Highness may touch it! This is, indeed, an honour which he had never expected—to have his hand taken by one who is greater than the greatest Princes of his own land. To be spoken to at all seems too great an honour to one poor old fellow, who forthwith bursts out crying, and has to be led away sobbing by Canon Duckworth. It is, indeed, too much for many of the poor souls, who quite forget the necessity for going on, and, lost in amazement, stand chattering and gibbering like bewildered monkeys. Sometimes, however, a smile is raised by the furtive attempt of some disappointed one who has carefully prepared a petition which he intends to present to the Prince. Furtively he conceals it in the palm of his hand, and just when he thinks General Probyn's quick eye is a little less wakeful than usual, he pushes the paper into the Prince's hand. But it is all to no purpose. The Prince would look at it, perhaps; but he must not. The crumpled, soiled document is promptly handed back to its owner, who shuffles away full of disappointment. What is his grievance? Can it be that some of those brave ones who saved India for us are in actual want? I hear a whisper that such is the case. Would that that whisper could be proved untrue! I fear it cannot.

In this way the procession moves past. There is a man with only one leg and another with a curiously wounded foot, which he shows the Prince; another has no legs at all; several have only one arm. In uniforms they vary, as I have said, very greatly. One old gentleman has got on a coat which looks as though it belonged to a field-marshals uniform; another looks like a Frenchman of Pondicherry. They totter up one after another; some are touched on the hands; others are specially introduced to the Prince by Major Cubitt. Men who carried messages through the enemy's camp; men who risked their lives over and over again in open conflict; men who were patiently faithful in the presence of all kinds of temptation and danger—such were honourably mentioned as they went by. Two hundred men of an Old Guard, superior in point of bravery to the windy corps that made its boast that it died but never surrendered; two hundred faithful followers of Horatius, who in days of old kept the bridge; two hundred valiant ones thus passed by the Prince in presence of many thousands of their countrymen just outside the city of Lucknow. Then, the levée over, the troops once more presented arms, and again the band played. The guns rattled out a Royal salute, and the Prince passed to his carriage. While many a one, mindful of the days in which the veterans gained their honours, wandered into the Residency, through the vaults, between the bullet-scarred pillars, and past the loopholed walls, wondering how so frail a structure, riddled as it was with shot and shell, could be held for an hour against the hordes of the rebellious soldiers—what thoughts came into our minds at such a moment time forbids to tell. How the tablet which marks where Lawrence fell, the board which points out where the Baillie guard was stationed, the charred walls and the sashless windows, affected such of us as had never looked on so thrilling a scene before, need not be dwelt upon. The levée of the brave was over; darkness was coming on; it was high time to leave the scene of England's pride and her enemies' humiliation.

The next day was partly spent in an inspection of the ruins of Lucknow, and partly in a pig-sticking expedition, which was about as unsuccessful as the previous attempts of the Royal party, and resulted in an accident to Lord Carington, who broke his collar-bone while attempting to spear a boar.

On the previous evening, however, a short ceremony took place in the Kaiser Bagh, or King's Residence, which deserves some notice.

The Talukdars of Oude are, without doubt, a noble set of men; their dresses may be eccentric and their habits objectionable, but in their veins runs the blood of the barons who had titles when our respected ancestors lived upon acorns and made their toilets with the aid of blue pigment. When, therefore, a gilt card was received announcing that the Talukdars of Oude "requested the honour" of my company, I looked upon the missive with about the same feelings that would animate a *caballero* of Spain were he invited by all their worships of Castile to favour them with his company. There was nothing on the document to denote the nature of the ceremony contemplated. It might be a Nautch dance and a song or two from the rival of Mr. Chuckerbutty, of Calcutta. It could not well be a banquet, for the hour was too late; and if only an address were to be presented to the Prince, the occasion could scarcely be styled a *fête*. There was something very mysterious about it, and I accordingly set off early in search of the famous hall, was ushered in with equal expedition by a mute giant who carried a sword, and so entered the apartment in which the entertainment was to take place.

I remember, when very young, receiving as a present from a thoughtful friend a box of wooden slabs on which were imprinted representations of the Kings and Queens of England. But for the knowledge that I was actually with the Talukdars of Oude, I should have imagined that those slabs had been vivified in some unknown way, and that the Kings of England were all walking about in the room. There were no Queens. Elizabeth with her abnormally long bodice and huge frill, and the much meeker Queen Anne, were neither of them to be seen; but King John most distinctly sat in a corner with the very crown he always used to wear, according to those painted bricks, on his head and his sceptre in his left hand, also like the ancient picture. King Richard, a little dark perhaps, but undoubtedly the original Cœur de Lion, marched up and down with a great hatchet in his belt and a very serviceable-looking steel coronet on his head; and although I could not detect Rufus of the red hair, I came across Edward II. two minutes afterwards. Indeed, had I still had those bricks with me, I could have fixed upon the names of every one present in a few minutes, for the twenty or thirty gentlemen present all wore crowns, and though some were seated on chairs and others squatted on the floor, they looked all of them kings "every inch." One, however, attracted my particular attention, and, without minute reference to history, I named him Edmund the Uneasy. Incessantly this worthy monarch wandered about as though he were the troubled ghost of somebody who, having centuries ago hidden his crown, had come back to tell treasure-seekers where to find it. His mission, however, turned out to be the very reverse of this, and what that was will presently transpire. Up to this the Kings were all alone—no one else had had the curiosity to come early —but now the company began to arrive and to be placed. The natives who came found no difficulty in this. The floor was wide; it was only necessary to preserve the line of march to a throne which stood at one end of the room, so they pleasantly sat down on the boards, crossed their feet and their hands, and were happy. As for the Europeans, they stood in the rear, or walked out on to a large balcony where chairs were placed, and whence they could see the illuminations of Lucknow.

All this time Edmund the Uneasy flitted about anxiously. At length he appeared to gain confidence, and after some consideration invited several of us into an inner room where lay the treasure he so carefully guarded. There were golden vessels for betel nut and pan leaves, intended specially, we were told, for the use of the Princess of Wales, though in what way her Royal Highness is to use them we were not told. But these were only subsidiary gifts. The real present was a great crown of crimson velvet and gold, covered with gems of considerable value, and decorated with all the skill that natives could devise. We were not allowed to touch the precious head-dress—only to look, being kept at a very respectful distance, while the crown was lifted an inch or so out of its case, and then popped back as quickly as though it had been a sensitive plate which could not bear the light. Just at this moment a band announced the approach of the Prince, whereupon five or six Talukdars entered the apartment and proceeded at once to take charge of the treasure. Then a procession was formed, which, between the rows of people seated on the floor, passed up to where the Prince was with the crown, and the betel nut and pan-leaf cases, and a huge address on an enormous roll. I do not know what the Prince thought of the apparition; but he had plenty of time to recover his composure before the address was finished; for the declaration of loyalty from the Barons of Oude was not a light or insignificant document, but a work of considerable labour, and as such required to be read slowly and with emphasis. At length it ended, the crown and other presents were produced and accepted, the Prince returned thanks, and then a general move was made first of all to the balcony for a peep at the fire-works, and then to the supper table, where Talukdars and people who till that night were not even aware that such notabilities existed sat down together and feasted. A notable fact in connection with the visit to Lucknow might here be mentioned. Both on coming to and departing from the *fête* the Prince received a royal salute of artillery; his every movement, indeed, was the signal for heavy firing—an arrangement which seemed to impress the native mind most satisfactorily.

"I was standing by this well, sir," said an old Sikh to me as we passed through the Residency, "saying prayers to my God, when two bullets came and killed an English officer who was on one side of me, and a comrade who stood on the other. I come to this well every year now to say a prayer, and that is why I am here to-day." It was a grand old veteran who thus spoke, one who had been presented to the Prince the previous day, on whose breast four medals and the star, which bears the words "For Valour," hung; so we thankfully accepted his offer to guide our portion of the party over the ground so bravely held by Sir Henry Lawrence.

Lucknow Residency has been too often described for a detailed account of what the Prince saw to be written. Yet there are several facts to be mentioned. We found the ruins themselves in excellent preservation; the tops of the broken walls had been covered with a composition which retained the loose stones in their places; and the Residency bids fair to stand, black, shot-riddled, ruin as it is, as a monument of English endurance. Here and there plants have climbed the walls, found their way through holes, and covered desolate corners with a warm covering of leaves; but this does not affect the appearance of the place. These bare walls tell their own tale, though the ground round them is now converted into one of the loveliest gardens, and roses and honeysuckles are being trained up the tower. Happily the spot where each particularly brave action and heroic deed occurred has been fixed, so that the Prince as he went along could learn, from tables fixed on little pillars specially erected, which was Sikh-square, where were Inglis' quarters, where the celebrated house in which Mr. Gubbins lived, and in what room the brave Sir Henry Lawrence died. Even the rent by which that fatal shell entered was pointed out, and the places struck by pieces of the fragments noted. Some one complained that the monument which was erected some years ago inside the garden, had been placed upon a mound, and by that means a full view of the position was obstructed. But when the celebrated tower was ascended the whole was seen at once, and the fearful odds against which the handful of British soldiers fought appreciated.

A field of moderate size, partly enclosed by a wall, partly by a hedge, containing two or three buildings of no very solid description—such was the place which these brave people held. They were shut out from all the world, could see nothing but the trees and the enemy, except when they ascended the tower, where the distant river and the stone bride by which the mutineers eventually escaped could be descried. I do not think the Prince went down into the cellars in which the women and children were placed, but some of us did, and found the place in the same condition as they left it in, except for the fact that all the Smiths, Browns, Joneses, and Robinsons in the world appear to have written their names on the wall with a number of remarks, amongst which passages of Scripture are frequent. It is a pity that for such an outrage they were not shut up in the vaults for a few days in the hot weather—their loquacity would have diminished with considerable rapidity.

The Secunder Bagh, where two thousand rebels were caught and put to death, a great square enclosed by a high wall, remains as it was, save that a road has been run through at one end. Still the walls are otherwise untouched; the loopholes which the Sepoys made are there yet; the gate is a ruin, and the tomb inside, a wreck. All over the ground a number of young trees are shooting up, so that in process of time the scene of the massacre will be exceedingly pretty. Where Havelock rests in the Alumbagh roses cover the ground; the walls here, too, are untouched, the breaches made in them have been left as they were, and the palace itself has not been repaired. Most of the party received from the hands of a native who takes charge of the grave a bunch of roses and other blossoms as a souvenir of the place.

At Cawnpore the Prince's visit was a very short one. His Royal Highness arrived late in the afternoon, dined at the house of one of the local civilians, visited the scenes of the massacre, the Memorial Gardens, the river, and the church, and then took his departure for Delhi. A full moon had risen in a cloudless sky when we started for these historic places. Of course there was a certain order to be observed, quite different from what the chronologial course of events would warrant, but in the end everything was shown us.

The first place to which we drove was the well, situated in the centre of magnificent gardens, at the gates of which all natives were requested to remain. Slowly moving up the pathway between richly-flowering beds of roses, the cuttings for which had come from England, we came at last to the Memorial, "sacred to the perpetual memory" of the slain. As is already well known, the well is covered with a marble seraph, which, with outstretched wings, watches over the place where the dead were hidden. I cannot describe the effect of the bright moon's rays on the white marble work—how the whole memorial stood out in its lonely grandeur on that delightful night. They did well to exclude natives from the place; the feeling aroused by the sight of that memorial and the adjacent graveyard is not congenial to them. The slaughter-house where women and children were hacked to pieces is gone, but scores of graves, some with monuments erected by "passers-by," by "brother-soldiers," by "men of the regiment," and some without either name or date, tell their own story. Over each hang roses from England; the grass is carefully tended, the pathway admirably kept. If they must be buried in alien soil, no more beautiful spot could be discovered in the world.

From thence to the Memorial Church, which is an extremely pretty red brick building, and built on the site of Wheeler's entrenchment, was no very great distance. It has only just been consecrated, and has therefore an appearance of newness, which does not quite accord with the objects around it. It also boasts an echo, which, I am told, bewilders the clergyman and astonishes his hearers, so that, en the whole it is scarcely a success. But we had little time for a prolonged inspection, having to hurry away to the river side where the Nana began his miserable butcheries.

Coming to the top of a slope which led down to the water's edge, we were requested to dismount, there being no road for carriages; and quitting the vehicles, therefore, at the corner where the victims first gave themselves into the hands of their destroyers, and where later on the brother of the Nana was hanged on a gallows, we passed down the gully which was before us. It was no great length, some two hundred yards perhaps, and then the Hindoo temple in which the Nana planted his cannon was reached. The scene of so much villainy is happily a ruin, yet not so greatly destroyed as to prevent a full appreciation of what took place on that memorable day. On the left of the pile was the place at which the fugitives embarked; their desire was to pass the temple, and so go down the river. The Nana had stationed his men all along the shore on the opposite side of the river, and in the temple too, and how he used them need not be related again. An aged Hindoo said that the Nana, after giving the order for the massacre, ran away. I connot trust myself to give expression to the feelings which we experienced as we looked at the astonishing scene in the bright moonlight.

CHAPTER XXIII.

A REVIEW OF DELHI.

Although it is unnecessary to describe at length the Prince's entry into Delhi, there can be no doubt that of all places in India this city of the Moguls boasts historic recollections most dear to Englishmen. It was the scene of fighting such as must ever stamp our soldiers as the bravest of the brave, the centre and the stronghold of the mutiny, the key to the possession of India; and when it was proposed, therefore to hold a grand review on the plains where less than twenty years ago the great struggle took place, English from all parts of the land, from the plains of Madras to the hills of Simla, from the mouth of the Hooghly and the frontier of the Punjab, from Bombay, and even from Ceylon, came to see and be seen. Nor were these all the strangers. A goodly number had come out from the mother country itself to be present at the spectacle; there were American Generals and a German Count; a nervous little man whispered, too, that there were Russian spies, which was very likely true, but also very possibly only the creation of the imagination. Foremost among the spectators of course was the Prince, in whose honour, indeed, the *fête* was to take place—one which will long be remembered in military annals.

Six o'clock had scarcely struck, when, driving into the road which leads to the Cashmere State, I found myself in a motley throng such as could not be met with outside of India. People in every description of clothing, from the simple waistcloth to the thick quilt, people with turbans and people with hats, people on horseback and people afoot, riding on elephants, on camels, on mules, on cows, some in open carriages, and others in the pleasant vehicles of the country—contrivances somewhat of the shape of parrot cages, very little larger, and much less inviting —some again in bullock gharries, and others in nondescript carts, which, for the want of a better generic title, must be called gigs, hundreds in close oblong boxes, light cabs, and many more in palanquins, all crowded together in the road, hustling, shouting, shrieking at each other, beating their animals, occasionally thrashing each other, and always regardless of the comfort or convenience of everybody else save themselves and friends, so anxious were they to be at the review. For many reasons it is well that the streets of Delhi are not narrow. They might be the hiding-place of rebels; they would certainly be the receptacle of much that is equally objectionable, and, what is more to my purpose just now, would have been simply impassable to such a mass of struggling life as filled them that morning. The elephants would have trodden down the mules, the camels would have cannoned against the horses, bullocks would have run wild, gharries been upset, and soldiers and civilians alike, horsemen and footmen too, would have been mingled in disaster. Happily this was not the case. We grumbled, we shouted; some, sad to relate, used expressions which would have shocked good Lord Chesterfield; we now and then grazed wheels, trod on each other's corns—it was just as well not to tread on the elephant's toes—but, though we all made everybody else and ourselves supremely uncomfortable, open collision was avoided, and, like a very troubled stream, we slowly rolled along. Still the place was conveniently fitted for a struggle—the very air seemed to smell of powder.

We were in the exact place where in 1857 the most desperate fights on record took place. For were we not under the shelter of the Cashmere Gate, that terrible entrance which witnessed the slaughter and the final entry of the British troops—the place where deeds of valour were done at which both listener and recounter even to-day turn pale? Why, yonder was the breach made by the English guns, now filled up by mud, but never to be rebuilt, fit monument of English pluck and Mohammedan defeat. We can fancy how the crowd of treacherous Sepoys fled as red-coated soldiers poured in at this gate and over the wall, catching them at the base of a stone triangle and bayonetting them as they ran. Some such struggling as then was seen we are suffering now. Ours, however, is, after all, a peaceful fight, a bloodless war, a strife for place, not for life—we are not revengeful or despairing; we only wish to get away from each other to be the best of friends for ever. Fortunately for us, no battery is placed on the ridge opposite to meet us as we pass through the gate, and throw us into more confusion than ever; we cross the breach in the wall and the mosque from whence it was made, and so into the open country, though not into an open road. There is no space anywhere—it is going to the Derby in the good old days, in company with a more disorderly throng than ever filled the way to Epsom. A very Babel, too, is this place, so great is the confusion of tongues, and so intent is everybody upon making as much noise as possible. Our onward progress is more due to the fright of the draught animals than to any skill on the part of their drivers, as many a broken panel and splintered pole abundantly testify. As we go along we see long lines of elephants drawn up on either side. One is for the Prince; its head is covered with a mantle of gold made wholly of gold mohurs, worth at least thirty shillings a piece, and not so large on the face as an English sovereign—you may guess the value. Its howdah is of scarlet cloth, richly embroidered with gold; the Imperial crown is on one side of its trappings, the three feathers are on the opposite one. Other elephants have less splendid equipment, yet all are equally decorated, and seem to know it. A mile further on we find the Prince's horses waiting to take him on to the review ground; about a mile further still is the flag-staff itself.

Once in position we have time to survey the field. A wide-stretching plain surrounded by trees is that upon which you stand. In front of you are the troops drawn up, the infantry in columns of battalions, in their rear the cavalry, artillery, and siege train. At the distance which separates you from them, you might imagine yourself standing beside a huge table on which a kind of Kriegspiel is presently to be played, so level is the ground, so compact and toylike look the columns. Every kind of uniform is there—English, Affghan, Bengalee, and Sikh. There is unfortunately no control or transport service present; a hundred camels or so are close behind you, but they are not in review order, and will not be officially inspected.

In the immediate neighbourhood of the flagstaff an open space has been reserved for the Prince; on each side of this rows of carriages are drawn up, and then, extending in a long line, leaning over ropes as though they were expecting races rather than a review, are tens of thousands of natives. Had you time, this crowd is worthy of minute inspection. You would see men passing huge pipes one to the other, taking a prolonged draw and then handing them on; and scores who have brought out with them not dogs, but little birds, partridges, hawks, or, more proudly still, the jay, perched upon their arms. For the last, be it known, is the bird in whom Vishnu especially delights; it is his steed, carries the god, and is venerated accordingly. A curious fancy is this of the Hindoos for feathered pets; they stroke them, tend them, kiss them, talk to them, just as the Arab does to his horse, or you at home do to your pet dogs.

While you are looking at them, however, the noise of horses' feet behind you draws attention to the fact that Lord Napier and his staff are coming by, and the good old General, attended by Colonel Martin Dillon, his private secretary, dashes to the front at once. He has hardly taken his place before the Prince rides on to the ground, advances to the General, shakes hands with him, exchanges a word with Colonel Dillon, and then proceeds to inspect the troops. To us, who have to wait behind, this would in any other place be a tedious business. But on such ground as this what half-hour could be badly spent? The Prince is actually on the very soil where the first battle of the mutiny, excepting a slight skirmish at Meerut, was fought. You can just see the walls of Padlee Ke Serai, where the fearful struggle took place. An officer who stands by tells you how on that day two thousand English troops routed hosts of the enemy, captured twenty-six well-served guns, and drove the discomfited wretches headlong into the city—how, at one period of that action, he became so confused by the uniforms which the rebels wore—spick and span direct from the arsenal—that he gave orders to his men to cease firing, so nearly did the enemy resemble English troops. And another recounts hair-breadth escapes, relates to you how the deep seam across his face was made by one of a great party of Sepoys who cut him off from his men, and almost from the face of the land altogether; while a third, a Victoria Cross man, modestly describes the fighting which took place where he stood. They occupied the ridge which faces you before noon on that fearful day, and began the investment of Delhi which resulted in the suppression of the mutiny.

At length the bands have ceased to play the National Anthem in different keys, the Prince is returning to the flagstaff, and the musicians themselves are massing for the purpose of playing as the troops go by. Then you hear "Bonnie Dundee," and know that, if not the Campbells, at least the artillery are coming. With superb dressing the famous chestnut Troop A of the A Brigade sweeps past, the guns in exactest line, the men and equipment perfection itself, and the 2nd Battery, with Armstrong guns, is quite its equal. The 3rd Battery has some white horses in the centre of its line, and these somewhat spoil the effect; but the 4th Battery, under Major Fitzgerald, is simply superb. This completes the Horse Artillery, of whom it may be said that a finer brigade was never seen. The field batteries follow, headed by Colonel Corder, six of them all admirably turned out, and presenting a magnificent appearance—in all sixty guns, well horsed, well manned, perfectly disciplined, and fit for anything. It would be invidious to pick any out from amongst the others—they are all so good.

And now came a sight which could not be witnessed in England. A company of Bengal Infantry, in blue uniforms and red turbans, marched two deep, with their curved swords on their shoulders, followed by a number of mules bearing all kinds of curious and useful implements. There were six little mountain guns, with the use of which King Theodore became so well acquainted; there were engineering implements of all kinds, and generally all that is useful to the soldier in mountain warfare—in all thirty-six mules well equipped, after which came another company of men armed like the first. Then the huge forms of some particularly large elephants were seen approaching with people on their backs, carrying little steel picks in their hands. Wondering what use these particular animals were put to, we eagerly leant forward, and, in doing so, saw that three 40-pounder Armstrong guns, each drawn by two elephants, were being brought along as easily as though they were "unconsidered trifles light as air" in reality. On they came at a slow, measured pace, apparently quite oblivious of the fact that they were drawing a siege train which it would have taken twenty-four or thirty horses to have moved, and quite double that number to take for any distance over Indian roads and rough ground. Traction engines indeed! What need of engines at all in a country which boasts such natural means of locomotion, save when rapidity of transit is required? The elephants go by, a bullock train along with them, dragging three large howitzers and tumbrils for ammunition, and then we prepare for the cavalry, who are now coming on.

But what tune is that? It was "Bonnie Dundee" just now, reminding us sadly of that terrible hour we spent in the native entertainment at Madras, where four uncomfortable scarecrows sang it with a conch-shell and tom-tom accompaniment. There is some confusion, for the Scotch melody is not yet finished by some of the bands, and some of the players are not yet certain that "it's up wi' the bonnets o' bonnie Dundee." At length, however, the struggle ceases, and the tune, "Among our ancient mountains," rises above everything. The 10th Hussars are coming by, and the Prince's air salutes them. I need not say how the old rivals of the 12th Lancers looked; three such squadrons as theirs are scarcely to be seen anywhere, certainly nowhere but in the English Army. Yet they are worthily followed, for, to the "March of the Men of Harlech," the 4th Bengal Cavalry come by, their serviceable blue uniforms and turbans suiting them well. Lord Mark Kerr says he could lead such men against any troops in the world, and he is no mean judge. They are a Hussar regiment; those who come next are the 10th Bengal Lancers, coloured Uhlans, with red and black pennons, revolvers at their waist, and medals on the breast of nearly every one. They go past magnificently, quite equal to the 11th Hussars who follow, gay in their cherry-coloured breeches and high boots, and especially noticeable for the white squadron which comes second, which would be perfection were it not that they have a roan and two duns to make up the number. The 5th Bengal Hussars, whose officers have breast-plates of gold lace, march next. A buff regiment of exceptionally tall men follow; they are the Central India Horse. Somebody whispers that their commander has picked the best squadrons out of the two regiments he has, but perhaps they are only envious of their admirable appearance. We notice that the front rank of each squadron are lancers, while the rear rank are armed as hussars, with sword snd carbine.

We have heard of mounted infantry before, but what say

European soldiers to a cavalry regiment composed half of lancers and half of hussars? The helmets of the officers are of purple velvet and gold, the most superb head-dress I have ever seen. As to the 13th Hussars, who follow them, and whose officers, like their brethren of the 10th, have leopard skins on their saddles, but little can be said in praise; they are scarcely so good as the 6th Bengal Cavalry, who have made all their troop pivot men lancers, the rest being hussars. The 15th Mooltanees, in dark green dresses and red puggarees, a wild set of horsemen, go by in excellent order just afterwards, followed by the 15th Hussars, who are in good condition; and the rear is brought up by the 11th Bengal Lancers, in dark blue uniforms, the same regiment which Probyn once commanded, the name of which spread far and wide to the terror of the rebels. Without loss of time the infantry go by—English and native vieing with each other to do their best. Needless is it to specify each as they pass—all are good. Perhaps the 73rd of the line are the best, with the 15th Sikhs, tall, strong men in scarlet coats and yellow striped turbans, as formidable rivals. To the eyes of such of us as are used to military spectacles in England, the appearance of the Rifle Brigade, as it comes on in black helmets with black puggarees, looks strange, and, in good truth, they are almost outdone in their march past by two battalions of Ghoorkas, who are dressed in dark green with black forage caps, and step out as well as any troops in the service. They are not very big men; they are little fellows, of a Chinese type almost, very like the savages from Assam whom we saw a week or two ago at Sir Richard Temple's garden party. Yet that they are valiant in the fight we well know, for they were Ghoorkas with whom Sir Charles Reid held the ridge opposite Delhi for five long months in face of all the efforts of the rebels. Then, too, there is the 33rd Native Infantry, recruited almost entirely from herdsmen, and led by Colonel James Harris, of Chinese fame, who are as well drilled and set up as any regiment could well be, and an admirable proof of what can be effected by an intelligent commander who has skill and patience. Other regiments there are which deserve praise of the highest kind, but to recapitulate their names would be to write a long catalogue for which you would not care. Suffice it to say that the army corps thus placed in the field reflects the highest possible credit upon Lord Napier and his excellent secretary, Colonel Martin Dillon. The hero of Magdala and his *alter ego* may well be proud of the force which the Prince reviewed.

CHAPTER XXIV.

THE BATTLE ON THE RIDGE.

Were the fate of the Empire dependent—which happily it is not—upon the battle which took place just outside Delhi on the Friday and Saturday during the Prince's visit, it would doubtless be matter of greatest interest to know exactly how the contending forces were disposed, with a thousand other technical details dear to a soldier's heart. But as, after all, the fighting was unreal—very unreal indeed—and ended only in fiasco and smoke, I do not propose to trouble you with more of such particulars than are absolutely necessary, but to take you at once to the field in the capacity of a spectator who is quite indisposed to be critical, but anxious to see of what stuff are our troops in India, and of what capacity their commanders. To reach the scene of the struggle it is necessary that you should pass out by the Cashmere Gate, close by the famous breach, and so over the rocky ridge which, in 1857, was the vantage-ground from which English soldiers peppered their rebellious adversaries. This latter place would, in case of actual fighting, be a very difficult part to assail; in fact, it could be rendered impregnable by a force sufficient to hold it. Such being the case, it was not given to Sir Charles Reid, who commanded the army of defence, but was reckoned only as an ulterior line in case the troops whose object it was to prevent Delhi from assault should have to fall back in disorder. It is for this reason that we find the defenders a couple of miles in front of the ridge, occupying a straight line of ground, the left of which is on a canal, the centre on a village called Wazeerpore, situated in a wood just as was the German centre during the manœuvres of 1874 at Hildesdorf, and the right on another hamlet named Daheerpore. All round these points is a wide stretching plain, without cover for troops of any kind, and it is over this that General Hardinge has to advance to the attack. Reid's force is behind entrenchments in the line I have mentioned ; Hardinge's army in front of it, but some miles distant. It being now nearly eleven o'clock, we are able to take a view of our position. Away on the extreme right are the heavy Armstrong guns drawn by elephants, the mortar battery drawn by bullocks, a battery of horse artillery, and our cavalry, consisting of the 10th and 11th Hussars, the 4th and 5th Bengal Cavalry, the 2nd Punjab Cavalry, and the Central India Horse, all hidden away in a little wood. The 2nd Infantry Brigade, consisting of two battalions of Ghoorkas and the Rifles, are in the centre ; and on the extreme left, under Brigadier-General Brown, is the 1st Brigade, comprised of the 73rd Foot (English) and the 33rd and 11th Native Infantry. Two brigades of infantry are somewhere close to Daheerpore. They hold their ground well, do nothing very noteworthy, and in the end are held to have defeated the attempts of their opponents.

We who are just now on the extreme left have something very pretty and interesting to look at, for the commander there —Colonel Harris, of the 33rd Native Infantry—a soldier of great experience, one of those who fought on the ridges in 1857 and was desperately wounded. He has seen plenty of service in China and elsewhere, and earned many an honourable distinction, but while the army is in the hands of Society, he stands less chance of promotion than if he had done nothing more than rely on influential friends. Our left is, as I have said, the canal, and the two battalions of native infantry, half a battery of artillery, three companies of sappers, and a troop of native cavalry, are holding a long shelter-trench, which reaches from the water's edge to the wood of Wazeerpore. In that the 73rd Infantry, with half a battery of guns, are posted. The canal has a banked pathway on either side, and on this, the left side of the water, Colonel Harris has constructed an entrenchment capable of concealing the three guns he has with him; almost strong enough to resist the fire of artillery. Down in this temporary bastion are posted the trio of cannons, their muzzles peeping through tiny portholes just big enough to admit of their discharge and nothing more. In the low ground under the pathway the cavalry are hidden out of sight. The infantry men of the 33rd N.I. and the 11th crouch down in the shelter-trench, and two or three companies with some mortars that have been posted along the canal up to the point which has been fixed as the extremity of ground to be manœuvred over, are all in their places. Not a head is to be seen, not a sound is heard—all we want is an enemy. The brigade opposed to us, as our scouts tell us, is that commanded by Colonel Basden, a gentleman who has not apparently instilled much terror into the hearts of our men. They do not believe he can take the position, and they shake their black heads and show their white teeth as they look over the top of their shelter, and laugh at the English who are coming against them. For remember that to take this line of Sepoys Colonel Basden has a battery of artillery, three troops of horse, two battalions of English troops, the 1st of the 8th Foot and the 85th Foot, with the 32nd Native Infantry, to watch the 73rd, who are at Wazeerpore. Just while we are looking out the cavalry does make its appearance on the other side of the canal, but rushes away directly fifty shots are discharged, so that for another half-hour we are quiet, and can only hear a distant banging of guns. At length there is a movement in our front; it is certain the enemy is coming, for two miles distant we can descry by the aid of a glass the white faces, white helmets, scarlet coats, and bright bayonets of the English battalions, as they advance, in close skirmishing order, only one pace apart, upon the trench. Of course we expect to see their approach heralded by artillery fire; very naturally, we look round for the cavalry which but lately disappeared, but there are none of them present; so our men, without more ado, wait till the enemy is within range, and then open a rattling fire upon them such as no English or German troops could excel. Suddenly up rides an umpire out from the attacking force, one Colonel Chippendale, and in a confused manner gives us the order to retire. Of course our commander remonstrates, but this military Daniel come to judgment refuses to hear a word, and back we have to go, till Colonel Harris points out firmly that his force behind shelter is much superior to that of the enemy in the open, whereupon Colonel Chippendale is obliged to yield, and gallops away rather faster than he came, to tell our opponents that they must go back. In actual warfare they would never have done so; a few might perchance have escaped our rifles, artillery, and cavalry, but Colonel Basden and all his merry men who were not shot would have been taken prisoners to a certainty. It was altogether the most ridiculous exhibition I have ever seen. Two battalions of infantry marched two miles in the open to attack more than their own numbers snugly entrenched and supported by cavalry and artillery, with guns posted in Wazeerpore Wood raking the flank of the advancing force every moment.

But, grotesque as this spectacle is from a military point of view, something much more funny is about to follow. We are all in our trenches. A company and a half of the Englishmen, who came across the plain just now are ordered out of action, and we are wondering what will be the next move of the strategic Basden, when Captain Dyke, who, we know, commands the artillery of that gentleman's brigade, comes pleasantly along the path on our side of the canal, his charger caracoling as though it were heading a procession. There is no hesitation, no distrust; he gently ambles up to our trenches, and, pulling up, says, "Can you tell me where Basden's brigade is?" "Of course I can," is Colonel Harris' reply, as he lays hold of Captain Dyke's bridle-reins; "only, as you are my prisoner, the news won't be worth much to you," saying which he led the astonished Dyke gently into our enclosure, took his parole, and sent him to the rear. Now, where one sheep goes the rest are sure to follow, and we had not to wait long for Captain Dyke's battery. A quick-eyed Sepoy descried it, Colonel Harris prepared for it, and a gun was trained on to the pathway, as it came on. Why should it fear? Was not its commander in front, and had there been any alarm? So it trotted forward, with the canal on one side and a precipice of twelve feet on the other, until it got another four hundred yards, when our gun was discharged point blank at it. Had this been a real fight, yonder battery would have been overthrown at once, for seven hundred rifles are pointed at it, three guns cover it, and the Punjab Cavalry are all ready to rush upon its flank. Again the men, like their leader, are not distrustful. They imagine that a mistake has been made. They are determined to consider us as friends, and so they come on still further. We are determined to claim them as prisoners. Colonel Harris orders a company of the 33rd to spring from their trenches and run along the bank, and then calls to the gunners to surrender. There is no option—the native riflemen have every one of them at their mercy. They must submit—the choice is not pleasant, but what can they do in presence of five times their number? They accordingly give in; are conducted down the bank under the escort of half a company of sappers and half a company of infantry; hand up their linch-pins and washers, their ammunition and arms; and are then led to the rear, guns and all, guarded by native troops. What use are the boasted English artillery if they can walk into such a trap? And now we hide away once more in hopes of other wanderers. Nor are we disappointed. Five minutes elapse, a rumble of wheels is heard; we look up very cautiously, and see the spare ammunition wagons of the battery, their hospital doolies, and their provision carts, all coming along. No gun is fired this time, for the

Quartermaster-General of the enemy's camp can be seen in his cherry-coloured trousers riding at the head of the train—Captain Carnac, of the 11th Hussars. A troop of cavalry is got in readiness, a company of infantry fixes bayonets, and as soon as Captain Carnac shouts out, "Have you seen ——?" they are upon him. A bold man is this Quartermaster-General, used to fight and to danger, and without ado he makes a struggle for liberty. Down the bank, so steep that in descending it just now a gun was nearly upset, he dashes, cutting through the Sepoys, albeit that one discharges a rifle close to his ear, and for an instant it seems that he will get clear. But the cavalry close up round him, twenty Sepoys spring upon his bridle, and he is powerless at last, to be at once led in, sent to the rear, and offered some luncheon. So, too, are the drivers of the wagons with their charge all placed under guard of native soldiers. You need not look round to see how the Sepoys enjoy all this. The low chuckle which indicates satisfaction is heard on every side. What can be thought of white sahibs who run into such a snare? On the left, too are now perceived the enemy's cavalry, the three troops we saw before, just the other side of the canal, and almost within easy rifle range. A very few moments and they will be our own. The artillery is being trained on them, the infantry is being got ready, and the cavalry are in saddle, when an excited jemadar gives his men the order to fire; a musket or two is discharged, and the horsemen, taking the hint, wheel round, and rush away without ever finding the artillery of which they are in search. We should have liked to introduce them to each other in rear of our entrenchment, but that unfortunate jemadar has prevented a meeting.

While all this has been going on, the cavalry near Daheerpore have been preparing for a fight, and by this time are advancing in full force, excepting only the few squadrons which have been detailed for other duty, upon each other. Ten minutes' ride brings us to the village, from whence we are able to watch all that passes. On our right are the 11th Hussars, supported by the 10th. In front of the houses are three squadrons of the 5th Bengal Cavalry and three of the Central India Horse. All are in line, except one squadron of the latter, which is about a hundred yards in rear. The reserve is formed by the 2nd Punjab Cavalry and the 4th Bengal, and these are placed on the left of a village. Now, were these in the hands of an experienced cavalry general going into action, there can be no doubt as to how they should be used. Captain Chevenix Trench's admirable translation of the new German cavalry regulations and our own new orders, which, if I mistake not, were issued somewhere about last June, would dictate all that is required. You remember that we are in an open plain; that we are supported by the elephant train of 40-pounder Armstrongs; that we have a mortar battery to aid us, and a battery of horse artillery in rear. The enemy's cavalry are well in sight; already the huge guns drawn by the elephants have opened upon them, so effectually that the 15th Hussars are ordered on to fight, and any German cavalry officer would tell you in a moment how to overwhelm and destroy a whole force opposed to you. But, fortunately for the unmilitary spectator, the Prince has expressed a desire to see a charge, and although under actual circumstances this would not take place, and the enemy would be in full flight long before the horsemen had time to manœuvre upon their flank, the request must be listened to, and a piece of unsoldierly performance gone through. So we allow the squadron of the 15th Bengal Cavalry to approach our left flank, accompanied by two guns, the 13th Hussars to advance against our 11th, and the 6th Bengal Cavalry, with two squadrons of the 15th, to come towards our centre. Then the fun begins. You are perfectly well aware that nothing of the kind could possibly happen in war, and you are therefore not very much alarmed when you see the 13th and 11th Hussars rush full tilt at each other. On they go at a terrible charge, the 13th going through a little stream which runs by Daheepore at headlong speed. There is every prospect of a collision; when suddenly the charge is stopped, the men being at a distance of ten yards only from each other, and victory is declared in favour of the 13th. They cannot, however, advance, for the 10th is in front of them, so they scramble off the ground without more ado. By this time the Central India Horse and the 5th Bengal Infantry are forming up and preparing to charge the enemy, which consists, as I have already stated, of native horsemen. On they go, too, at a headlong speed, their turbaned heads lowered, their lances and swords ready, and a fight takes place which ends in the defeat of the enemy and the ordering out of action of a squadron or two of them. The extended line on our side is admitted to have won, and notwithstanding that the attacking force has dismounted some of its men for the purpose of using them as skirmishers, we are admitted to have outflanked and beaten them. Then, while everybody is wondering what will be the next ridiculous spectacle, the sound to cease firing is heard, and the battle all along the line is ended. Infantry regiments hear the word of command, and go home, officers jump into the saddles and ride away, while we join a pleasant tiffin party and lunch on the ground which but a few minutes before, was so hotly contested.

CHAPTER XXV.

FEATS OF SKILL AND STRENGTH.

Yet if the battle at Delhi was somewhat theatrically managed, there was a contest of a different nature on the following Monday which was very real indeed. It had been announced that after a cavalry parade in the morning the Prince would be present at some sports in the camp of the 15th Hussars, at which both English and native soldiers from the whole army would appear as competitors. As on the day of the review, therefore, all fashionable Delhi turned out; some on horses, elephants, and camels, others in vehicles, with multitudes on foot. For just then the native of Delhi was quite ready to don his most startling dress at a moment's notice, and would, I believe, have slept in it if that arrangement would have ensured his gazing at every sight engendered of the Royal visit. This being the case, he systematically appeared everywhere with his children and his birds, leaving only his wife at home. She never came out. Unlike the dame of Madras or Bombay, she might be curious, but she must not be visible; she might see, but must not be seen. No rows of handsomely-attired ladies with olive complexions and long oval eyes welcomed the entry of the Prince to the old capital of India; no bullock-gharries full of native damsels, rolled and jolted on the camp-ground to look at the sports. Had the revelry been held in front of the houses in the Chadni Chauk, inquisitive faces might have been pressed against the gratings which act as windows in the native houses. But, there being no houses near from which they could look, the Hindoo and Mahommedan ladies were shut out from witnessing the sports;

while their lords put on the best puggaree and quilted coat, and sallied forth for the day. However, it was not for them that the *fête* took place, but for the English ladies and gentlemen, who came up in hundreds, and began a grand pic-nic an hour before the time announced for the sports. It was a bright day. The space was pleasantly shut in by trees; all round, under the shade, well-appointed equipages might be seen. There were luncheon-baskets of all shapes and sizes; the sound of the champagne-cork was heard in the land, and brilliantly dressed ladies might be seen everywhere. Those huge elephants with gold and scarlet howdahs, those camels with trappings of bright colours, those black servants, that singular crowd of dusky faces, and those broad-shouldered Sikhs with gold-striped turbans, belonged to no English city. Where the Prince was to sit long lines of native infantry were drawn up to keep the ground, and there the native horsemen, preparing for the contest, were also in full view. I remember how varied were the feelings with which I waited by the arena at Baroda to see the fights between wild beasts. There was all the curiosity which belonged to ignorance. One wondered what a rhinoceros contest would be like—after what fashion elephants would struggle; but withal there was a strong sense of the brutal which would crop up every moment and spoil all interest in the sport. But here was a sight which could be regarded with unmixed satisfaction; the swordsmen of India were to be pitted against the Hussars of England, the Lances of the Punjab against the best horsemen from home. Then too, there were to be races afoot, high jumps and low jumps, tournaments with blunted spears, and many another diversion. Oddly enough, a band of European strollers, their faces bedaubed with lamp-black, their heads covered with woolly wigs, in their hands the familiar banjo, concertina, and bones, and on the backs of their necks the old, old hats, which we used to look at with amazement when very young indeed, appeared close to the Prince's daïs, and favoured his Royal Highness with a version of "I'm off to Charlestown," from a Christy's Minstrel melody book. The effect was almost too ridiculous for anybody to request them to go to Charlestown at once. They sang their song in a villainous fashion, held out their shabby hats for money, and forthwith departed to frighten elephants, camels, and horses with their discordant shouts.

The National Anthem sounded the arrival of the Prince, and immediately afterwards the bands—there was plenty of them—struck up a more lively tune, and the competitors entered the lists. The first champion, a broad-shouldered Sikh, wore a blue puggaree round his head, and a blue linen coat. On the head of the lance he carried was a huge piece of cork or indiarubber, and on his breast shone many a medal; the star, with the magic words, "For Valour," glittering on his dress; at the sight of him many a caitiff rebel had fled; his lance had in days not very long gone by been couched at stubborn foes, and had overthrown them. To meet him there came another no mean antagonist, a burly Punjabee, with his puggaree curled round his head in military fashion, with a red end turned over the front. He, too, led by the gallant Nicholson, had used his lance against Sepoy foemen. No child's play was the thrust of his arm when his blood was up. The spectator looked on with some awe. Both warriors were well matched, and it was a great question who should win. The chargers of the opponents were pawing the ground waiting for the signal. At last it was given, and each dashed against the other. Thud! Thud! but to no purpose; the shock has effected nothing, for the horsemen have wheeled round. Once more they rush, and again without success, though you and I, and less marvellous horsemen, would have been hurled out of the enclosure. No fear is there that their lances will shiver; as well might you expect to see a Muniporee's polo stick break. They clash and then charge again, they strike each other on the backs as they wheel round, they plunge their lances into each other's stomachs, but all to no purpose, till after some minutes the Sikh contrives to get upon the flank of his antagonist. Only for a minute, but what a minute is that! Out goes his arm, in goes the spear. His opponent receives the head in his ribs, his horse staggers, rocks, and the rider falls to the ground, as the lance is pressed home by that terrible Sikh. Cossack, or Uhlan, would that you could hear the crash of that falling man.

Nor was the scene less exciting in another part of the arena. Those who have not seen tent-pegging as practised in India may like to know what the work for the competitors was. Driven into the ground so as to remain about six inches above the surface was a genuine tent-peg—hardwood, nothing more or less than the piece of hard fibre which is used to fasten the canvas down. To stand by it and strike it with one of the ponderous lances which our cavalry, Indian and English, carry, is no easy task. You might try a hundred times and not thrust it through. But what will you say to a man who could ride at a full gallop three hundred yards, and, while his horse rushed past it, almost like a flash of lightning, could pick up the piece of wood on the end of his spear? Yet this was the task set, and how it was fulfilled you shall see. A signal being given, an English cavalryman burst from a group at the distance named, and rushed up the course. I noticed that he did not keep his lance's head near the ground; that, indeed he held the head up, but lowered his own face somewhat, so as to see the little white mark the more readily. All depended upon his being able to strike at the precise moment when he should reach the miniature target set up for him; there was no jugglery, no trick; all depended upon a quick eye, a cool nerve, and a strong and ready arm. Onward he flew with lightning-like rapidity, not diminishing his pace one whit till he reached the peg, when, with a dexterous turn of the wrist, he struck the wood in the centre and carried it off triumphantly. Less successful was his rival who followed, or the one who came after that, the man of the 11th Hussars remaining *facile princeps* till three or four had gone, when another achieved a like distinction, and was loudly applauded. Two or three more came very near it, and then it was the turn of native horsemen. At a given signal a rider in blue turban and dress came flying towards us, his lance held rather more slanting than those of the English, and a little more loosely. He rode easily, however, with his eye fixed on the peg, and, just as he came up to it, sent his spear clean through the middle, and bore the trophy away. Another peg was fixed, and another horseman rode at it. But this time the fates were not propitious; he struck the ground a foot from the little mark, and was nearly jerked out of the saddle; another and another came on, but some went a little too high and others a little too low, three only of the party succeeding in carrying off the peg. And now came the deciding heat, for each horseman was to have two trials, and the conqueror was yet to appear. This time three Englishmen in succession struck the mark, one of whom won the prize. Of the natives there were none who struck the peg twice; each did so once in the two trials without difficulty, but none were equal to the hussar, and so the prize fell to the Englishman, and the Sikhs and Punjabees acknowleged the justice of the award with a loud cheer.

Jumping over a bar was the amusement which followed this achievement, being duly rewarded by a prize of some value, and this occupied the attention of the spectators till the arrangements for the next trial of skill, as distinguished from force, were completed. Then the horsemen who had been upon the course left it, the jumping ceased, the perspiring competitors retired, and made way for other men. What had been done in the interval was simply this. Three sticks, duly prepared, had been driven into the ground, and on the top of these three little limes, none of them larger than a respectable pigeon's egg, had been placed. At a distance of three or four hundred yards a body of swordsmen had been collected, and these, native and English, now waited to try their skill. No mean trial was that to which they were invited. It was simply this—to ride four hundred yards at a gallop, sword in hand, and to cut the three limes in halves as they passed the sticks with a sword. The first man was a trooper of the 11th Hussars; his name was Jones. He carried the ordinary cavalry sabre of the service. As he came on I noticed that he leaned very much on the right stirrup, with his head lower than the pommel of his saddle. His sword-arm was free, and the weapon loosely held. As he came by the first lemon fell in halves, the second was clipped of its rind, and the third was cut in the middle with a powerful blow that showed Mr. Jones to be one of the keenest swordsmen living. Three such strokes in less than seventy yards were not easy to deliver. Then there came another hussar of the same regiment, carrying a native sword, curved but sharp. To him the first and second lemon fell, but the third was untouched as he galloped by. A third Englishman came and missed all three, overthrowing, however, two of the stands as he swept on. Then a fourth rode up, and rivalled the feat of Mr. Jones, cutting all three lemons with the ease of a man who was aiming at a world rather than at such a tiny mark. In this way the trial of skill proceeded; three more Englishmen achieved the feat, but the rest had less success. Then came the native swordsmen, dashing along at a furious rate one after another. They, too, were very successful, four of them, as against five Englishmen, clipping the limes in half. A neater feat of horsemanship could not be imagined; Cossacks of the Don would have shuddered to see these Sikh horsemen dash along the plain. The second trial ended no better for the natives; the English carried off the prize, and even Punjabees and Sikhs shouted applause, so great was the feat these soldiers achieved. Races on foot came next, in which the Englishmen won laurels again with ease, and then the entertainment ended, the trials of strength and skill were over, the Prince went away, and the company dispersed.

CHAPTER XXVI.

JUMMOO THE MAGNIFICENT.

At Jummoo the farthest point of our journey was reached. The trip culminated in the frontier town of Cashmere, and, as was befitting, the Prince found his most splendid reception there. It was early in the morning that a party specially invited by the Maharajah of Cashmere as his guests started from Lahore by rail to Wazirabad, the last railway station in the North of India. We did not pass over the land where Porus fought and Alexander conquered, with unseemly haste. Six hours were consumed in a journey of some fifty miles. We had plenty of time to meditate upon the ups and downs of political fortunes, to gaze at Runjeet Sing's famous burial place, where thirteen faithful wives shared the tomb with their lord, and at the grave known best for its four towering minarets and its splendid wall. Save for its historic recollections, the country could scarcely be styled interesting. A constant succession of plains and ditches without monuments of any kind is not calculated to create enthusiasm, and until Wazirabad was nearly reached, and the snow-covered peaks of the Himalayas came in view, something very akin to monotony was observable. But this was not to last. The poetry of motion which a "dak gharry," or Indian stage-coach, engenders was in store for us, and very soon we were seated in two of the funniest burlesques upon vehicles that can be conceived. How we went over hedgerows and ditches, plunged into cart-ruts, and very nearly turned over; how we passed the last British outposts, took short cuts over ploughed fields, and at last arrived in sight of Jummoo, needs not to be described. It was at the moment of sunset when the town was seen. Behind it were the everlasting hills, on one, indeed, of which it is seated. All round was dense jungle. For hours the sky had been beclouded; we had not seen a bright ray all the afternoon, till at this moment the sun burst out and lit up the landscape with its marvellous light. Pink, orange, dark purple fell upon the snow-capped ridge, threw the three-peaked Tri-couta into bold relief, glittered upon the dome and minarets, the golden spires and white stone buildings of Jummoo, lightened the dark green of the jungle, and then left us in gloom. After this we entered the thicket, passed by devious ways from the altitude we had reached namely, a thousand feet, to the bed of the river Tow, where a surprise not altogether pleasant awaited us. By the light of the stars, now shining pretty clearly, we could just discern the sluggish stream at our feet. Upon a hill on the opposite side twinkled the lights of Jummoo. Our means of conveyance were elephants, which waited on their knees for us to mount and ride. It may be prejudice, it may be ignorance, but if asked for a positive opinion, I should not travel for choice on the back of an elephant at night time where the rivers have to be forded and the hills ascended. A Member of Parliament who was one of the party, finding that the howdah which he was invited to ascend was not fastened so rigidly as to absolutely warrant security against a fall, implored some other means of transit, and was eventually conveyed to Jummoo in a palanquin, which was borne on the shoulders of four men across an exceedingly rickety bridge of boats. The rest of us, however, mounted and started for the water. Down a steep bank, the elephant cautiously feeling his way, at one time deep in the mud, and the next in the water, with the elephant's head, huge as the animal was, only just clear, and its great trunk lifted high in the air, our progress was not very rapid. Occasionally the elephants would stand still as though undecided which way to go; then an advance of half-a-dozen strides would be taken, and another standstill arrived at. Sluggish as was the stream, it was very wide, and it seemed as though the opposite shore would never be reached. At length, however, we stood on dry ground, and prepared to ascend the hill. Our way lay through roads not more than six feet wide, through passages crammed with horses, camels, and men. Up steep staircases, whereon the elephants' feet slipped, and from which a fall would have been extremely inconvenient; and so through the narrow gate of the city, where the streets were thronged and Pandemonium reigned. Still there was no time to stop, for the howdahs shook violently, and threatened to turn round every moment. Some of us urged our way to the palace of the Maharajah, where tents were provided and a welcome rest was found. I am particular in thus detailing the peculiarities of the way to Jummoo, as it was over this ground that the Prince of Wales had to travel on the following day.

Day had scarcely broken, the light had hardly struggled over the mountains, when such a drumming and trumpeting as could only be heard in an Eastern city roused everybody from sleep. Every Cashmere regiment—and the city was full of troops—was in motion, every band was playing what it liked best. And when it is noted that scarcely any two instruments were in tune with each other, that some hundreds of musicians were doing their best, and that at least thirty different airs were being performed at once, some idea may be formed of the din and the clatter. Meanwhile, the Maharajah and his son, each mounted on a beautiful Arab, attended by all kinds of horsemen, and surrounded by scores of runners on foot, entered the city to inspect the preparations. More troops, too, filed in at the gateways, thousands of workmen prepared the roads, gave the finishing touches to a grand palace which his Highness has especially erected in honour of the Prince, while the police went round and shut up the shops, clouted the recalcitrant, overturned the money tables, and bid everybody be merry.

As a consequence Jummoo decked itself out in its very best, gave its finest shawls to its inhabitants, displayed a wonderful collection of flags, and received the soldiers with all demonstrations of joy. The visitors from Leh, specially brought hither to aid in the *fête*, were invited to lend the energy of their arms and the noise of their tom-toms to the general rejoicing. And if anybody was not inclined to be merry, he went where the eye of the inspector and the staff of the policemen could not reach him. As for the troops, they poured in till, with shoulder close to shoulder, they lined all the way from the river to the Prince's tent on both sides, a distance of nearly three miles, and there stood, the great shakos and heavy muskets weighing down their diminutive forms very nearly to the ground. At very short intervals their bands were placed in position, rocket-guns were in the street by scores, the artillery of the Maharajah was posted inside the gates of the city and the gates of the palace, and the populace filled up the picture. This was ready at twelve o'clock; but the Prince did not arrive till five.

Down at the river-side a very extraordinary scene presented itself. To have an idea of the *locale* take any one of the wider reaches of the Rhine, trebling the width of the river and the hills on either side. Round the natural amphitheatre thus obtained bring the highest mountains of the Alps, with their snow-capped tops. There would, of course, be no vines, but in place of these tiny trees substitute a dense jungle. Then fix on one of the nearest hills behind the river a city of white and red stone, plentifully decorated with palaces and temples, towers and golden minarets. A palace not unlike Windsor Castle, at one point of a precipice, would then suffice to represent Jummoo very nearly. Otherwise, ride along the banks of the Tow, at the moment when the last rays of the sun are gilding the peaks of the Pier-punjal range. Then we are transported back centuries upon centuries. Nothing that meets the eye has anything to do with the age in which we were living a minute or two ago; the West has altogether disappeared; we are lost to civilisation; only the East, with its barbaric splendour, is before us. I cannot call to mind any such other spectacle. A like sight may have been witnessed in the old days, and now, as then, there are in the procession which stands on the bank Persians with high Astrachan caps, long cloaks, gaiters, and sandals. They certainly have a kind of blunderbuss on their shoulders, but from the huge bell mouth of the weapon no more effective missile could be sent than those which the followers of Darius and Porus used to hurl. Then, too, there are men-at-arms here—no counterfeit specimens, but real men in armour, with little brass caps something like inverted tea saucers with a spike in the centre, on their heads, chain mail covering their ears and necks, brass breastplates, brass backplates particularly thick—brass guards for the elbows and arms—gloves of brass, and brass protections for the ribs, hips, knees, and ankles. In their hands are long javelins, at their sides curved swords, called tulwars, while from their waistbelts hang pistols of the good old pattern prized in the days when such things were first invented. They surely have no part or lot in the nineteenth century. Nor is a party of men who wear turbans, and, apparently, carry any weapon they like best, more modernised. Away with the drill which makes machines and destroys independence! Here are some warlike gentlemen who are allowed to make themselves look as fierce as they choose. But their parti-coloured petticoats, their boots, their blankets, their spears, their shields, and their tulwars all belong to his Highness the Maharajah, whose emissaries they are. And the two golden banners round which they swarm are his escutcheons. Perhaps I was wrong in saying there is nothing modern. A body of cavalry in front of all have certainly got helmets which closely border upon the headdress of the French Cent-Gardes. But that is all. Lose sight of the casque for a moment, and glance at the bodies and nether extremities of these warriors. The present is forgotten at once; the past remains. The most gentle object in view is the elephant which stands close beside you and jingles every minute or two the great bells which hang at his side. Yet even he has his peculiarities, as you discover when he reaches out his trunk towards the neck of your terrified horse, and after you hear in more detailed fashion of the ease and grace with which he has captured and killed no less than thirteen human beings during his stay at Jummoo. There are plenty of his brethren here. Thirty, in fact, are on this bank of the river, all highly decorated and painted in approved style, while across the river, well within sight, are nearly two score more, two with grand worked gold and silver howdahs, fit, as indeed they are intended, for the Prince and Maharajah. They are regal elephants, these; on their backs and tails the painter's skill has been recklessly lavished; their foreheads and trunks are masterpieces of pictorial art, and on their trunks are the faces of gods and goddesses portrayed with endless care. Even their ears are not forgotten. On the wide-spreading flaps are drawings of lions leaping upon fishes or whales encountering tigers, while on their sides are Royal coats of arms and pictures of the three feathers. Perhaps with a very strong glass glimpses might be caught of a troop of English Lancers—the 9th—who wait the coming of the Prince as he will emerge from the jungle, but this is only momentarily; they are lost immediately afterwards in the crowd of black horsemen who sweep along the bank and envelope the tiny company.

A gun from a distant hill just now wakes the echoes, and immediately afterwards a stir on the opposite bank of the river announces the arrival of the Prince. Salute after salute is fired; the Persians shoulder their blunderbusses with more pride than ever; the men-at-arms stand closer together; yonder horsemen in helmets sit straight in their huge Eastern saddles; the crowd of chieftains who have descended from Jummoo, and whose horses have brought them down to the river's edge—a bediamonded, begilded, silk-bedecked crew—form into column four deep; the tom-toms beat faster than ever; the pipes are blown more vigorously than before; while a tall Asiatic horseman gallops over the little bridge of boats which partly connects the opposite shores, then plunges into the water, and so up the banks to where the soldiers are waiting, and bids them prepare for the Maharajah Sahib and the Prince Sahib. No need to tell them—they have all prepared, their eyes twinkle with pride and curiosity, for are they not the bravest of the brave, and is not the sight they are to witness the grandest in the world? Just now the elephants on the other side are seen to kneel one after another, as they then receive their riders, and as they turn to descend into the river the horsemen of the Maharajah, headed by the 9th Lancers, gallop across to the shore we stand on. Very slowly the Prince's elephant places one foot after another in the water, so carefully that the howdah scarcely sways at all, as with measured tread it feels its way through the bed of the river. Following close behind comes the elephant of the Maharajah; then those carrying the Prince's suite, together with Major Henderson, the former Resident, and Colonel Jenkins, who, during the temporary absence of the Major with the Prince, fulfilled the duties of Resident, and fulfilled them well. Preceded by the motley soldiers, the Royal procession wends its way round the side of the hill on which Jummoo stands, now passing by the edge of a precipice and now going between the jungle, till at last it comes to the foot of the last ascent before the gate of the city is reached. But what a climb it is! Scarcely less steep than the staircase of an ordinary London dwelling-house. Indeed, it would be impossible for us to ride up it were it not that it has been cut into wide stairs, and paved with rough boulders—boulders, by the way, upon which the feet of horses slip horribly, to the constant peril of riders. However, up these steps must the procession go—elephants, horses, footmen, and all. Night, too, is coming on—has caught us in. As we pass between the long lines of soldiers who are armed with flintlock muskets, they stand close shoulder to shoulder and salute as we go by. Nothing more funny was ever heard than the way in which the National Anthem is played by musicians of all descriptions, placed at intervals of about two hundred yards all along the line of route. They have probably never attempted it before they were ordered to rehearse for to-day. They play with energy, at least, though to our ears the result is appalling. But at the instant when our thoughts run in this wise, they are turned sharply in another direction; for suddenly the city above and the hedgerows around break out into a blaze of flame as thousands of torches, lamps, and fires are kindled simultaneously. No wonder the horses fly among the terror-stricken soldiery, no wonder the elephants execute a fandango on the steep staircase. Yet, somehow or other, although several are thrown from their seats, we all get up and pass through the narrow gate of the city, where we are received by a salvo of artillery from brass guns not twenty yards distant. The artillery and scores of bands massed near the gateway have been too much for the procession, and the conspirators are struggling to get away from the elephants and horses. On we go; the Lama priests are true to their post on the top of the house, and fully maintain their ancient reputation as noise-makers as the Prince passes by; the healthy, broad-chested, strong-armed gentlemen of Leh, who never wash, are also in fine form, and play with all their reputed vigour. They are easy victors over a brass band opposite—the street is just twelve feet wide—which is trying "God save the Queen" in a newly-discovered key. The horses are clearly of this opinion; for they rush from the musicians of Leh into the very arms of the bandsmen of Cashmere. However, we stay not: our path lies between more bands, more soldiers in extraordinary costumes, more crowds of delighted people who gather in the shop-fronts and on the tops of the low houses, and gibber with unqualified pleasure at the unearthly din. And so we come to the foot of another ascent which leads to the new palace which the Maharajah has built for the Prince. Again we are received with artillery, clatter, and shouts, aided also by bouquets of rockets, which seem to shoot up at our very feet, and thus enter the camp, where, 'mid tent pegs, ropes, pitfalls, and obstacles of various kinds, we find our way to appointed places, and dismount. The Prince is conducted to his apartments by the Maharajah, and time is given to prepare for the State dinner of the evening.

CHAPTER XXVII.

SPORT IN CASHMERE.

To be a sportsman in Cashmere, as in Spain, you must not be burdened with sensitive feelings. You will not enjoy the programme if you are a prominent and conscientious member of the Society for the Prevention of Cruelty to Animals. Still you must go as a dutiful guest to see the entertainments your host provides for you, although the sight may not be in accordance with your tastes. Leaving, then, the refinement of humanity behind you, let us mount our ponies to be off in the direction of the rendezvous for sport this afternoon. You are promised polo playing, gymnastic games, and feats of skill, to which you cannot, by any possibility, object. In addition to these there is something much more delightful to the Cashmere mind; there are to be hunts by wild animals in the presence of the Maharajah. Once across the river, an hour's gallop brings us to our destination. The Prince, who has been hunting all day, and, by the way, has succeeded in killing some game, is expected shortly, so in the meanwhile you have an opportunity of examining the ground and those who are on it. At one side is a raised daïs, with a refreshment tent for the Royal party; on the right of this are some camels and elephants, and, squatted on the ground, a number of semi-nude black men from the valley across the river. At present these are not worth much attention, as other groups deserve more. There are, for instance, some scores of persons with hawks, kites, and falcons on their arms, some hooded, some not, but all anxious for flight. A little in the rear of these are some black fellows who have charge of two cheetahs like those we saw at Baroda, and two or three great lynxes, apparently very furious beasts. Sadder by far is a group of three beautiful deer, one buck and two does, two or three hares, and a couple of jackals, who lie close to each other on the ground, their feet tied, and their tongues hanging out of their mouths, possibly for want of water; perhaps owing to fear. Then, further on still, almost exactly in front of the raised daïs, are some hundred and fifty men and boys—Baltis, from over the hills, side by side with their ponies. They are here to do battle to day in presence of the Heir Apparent, and you naturally expect great things. Polo players in England will be interested in learning that these mountaineers have a very different kind of stick from that used either by the Munniporees or the players at Hurlingham, namely, a club-like weapon curved at the end, and very much heavier than those in use elsewhere. As for the ponies, they have no guards of leather, and indeed are not very good animals either. However, as these people have come five hundred miles over the Himalayas to show their method of playing polo to the Prince, you are not disposed to be too critical as yet, but wait in expectation of some wonderful work. Major-General Biddulph explains, too, that the gentlemen who are here to-day, clad in gorgeous silks of every conceivable colour—that is to say, half of them, the rest having no clothing to speak of at all—have till lately been a sad trouble to peaceably disposed folk. They only now behave themselves because they are vassals of the Maharajah; and yonder sturdy little chieftain, who is trying hard to bend his disagreeable features into a pleasant cast while an artist sketches him, was long renowned as a sort of Cashmere Robin Hood, whose followers were more wily than honest, and whose merry men were the terror of travellers. However, at such a time as this, when the Prince is stepping upon the daïs, we must let bygones be bygones, although there are at least a score of the savages glaring at the English strangers as though they would heartily enjoy a few minutes' cutting and hacking with the curved tulwars they grasp in their nervous hands. But their comrades in silk are mounting the ponies, and they, as well as we, are quickly absorbed in the interest of the game. Advancing to the centre of the open space before the Prince, these polo players make a low bow to his Royal Highness, whereupon some musicians with trumpets quite two yards long, also some sinewy tom-tom players, squat on the ground and commence an awful din. More astonishing still is the noise which the multitude who have no silk, but only rags, indulge in. No sooner do the ponies and their riders move toward one end of the ground than every savage howls or whistles to the utmost of his power. Then a sudden lull takes place; the ball is hurled into the air and sent whirling along the plain, while the horsemen go after it helter-skelter, whereupon trumpeters, tom-tom players, and howlers make more noise. So it is every time the players pass by—a blast proceeds from the trumpets, a thunder of sound from the tom-toms, and a vocal accompaniment from their admirers of no uncertain note. They are clearly delighted beyond measure to see their countrymen so gallantly attired moving before the Prince, and they could make the most hideous roaring for many hours if allowed. Somehow or other, those engaged in the game achieve nothing; they miss the ball continually, they tumble off their horses, they do not compete with opposing sides—four Munniporee players would beat twenty of them with ease. At last the Prince sends to ask if they cannot form into two parties of say five each, and try the regular game, to which, after much discussion, they agree. But it is all to no purpose, and very soon they are requested to disappear and make room for better men. They go, and the athletes in the corner take their places. The chief points about these gentlemen appear to be that they were almost naked, very greasy, and capable of almost any grotesque movement that suggested itself. Two would meet with a rush, and each placing his head between the other's legs would forthwith turn a series of spinning wheels, making us wonder whether they were really human beings. Then they would throw all kinds of somersaults while clasped in couples, fly over each other's heads, and generally impersonate the dusky goblins with whom we were made familiar in our very early days. But their chief excellence consisted in the amazing distances they could bound. Fixing a rough spring-board in the ground, they would run and jump twelve or fifteen feet into the air and alight without the slightest shock. Presently a couple of camels were brought up, whereupon one savage after another ran and threw somersaults over the camels, humps and all, coming down on the other side as lightly as a feather. Then an elephant of the largest size was placed in position for a similar purpose, and at the first attempt a man bounded comfortably into the howdah on the top of the animal's back. But the success was only momentary, for the huge creature lifted up his trunk, trumpeted with all his might, and then ran away, utterly declining to come near that spring-board any more. Another large elephant was procured, but with similar results. Every time the athlete took a run the sagacious animal would turn round and hold out his trunk in a threatening manner, blinking his little eyes and snorting in so defiant a fashion, that, after some vain attempts at blindfolding him, the experiment was given up, and way was made for less manly sports.

I have already described to you cheetah-hunting as practised in Baroda. It is not an economical way of chasing deer, and I do not know that it is a very refined class of sport. But it is very seldom the cheetah succeeds in catching his prey; so that the spectacle of a savage beast tearing the neck of a handsome deer is not often afforded. The Maharajah of Cashmere was, however, quite determined that there should be no lack of amusement in that direction, and the way he managed it was this. The spectators, including the athletes and the Baltis, were requested to form a wide-spreading circle, embracing, perhaps, two acres of ground. Of horsemen, ladies, officers, gentlemen, and natives, there were sufficient to do so; and, all being now in readiness, the deer which we saw lying on the ground an hour before were carried by their legs to the centre of the ground, and deposited there. Similarly, though with the greatest possible care, a cheetah was brought up to the daïs, patted, caressed by its keepers, and admired by the visitors. At length one of the deer, a splendid black buck, was released and urged to run. Poor beast, his numbed limbs and dazed eyes scarcely admitted of a great deal of motion, and it was really some time before he could understand what was required of him. But when at last the struggling cheetah was held near him, he did comprehend that he was expected to do something, and accordingly began a slow trot towards the left-hand side of the daïs. He might, perhaps, have gone about two hundred yards when the leopard was let slip, and there is little doubt he would have been caught at once but for the timely interposition of a little dog, which at that particular moment got in the way. Now, I believe a cheetah likes dog-flesh as much as venison, especially when there is less trouble in getting the former than the latter, and the unlucky puppy was chased without loss of time. But it was all to no purpose: the terrier was too smart for the heavier brute, and after a little running in a circle the pursuer gave up the attempt. All this while the wretched buck had been looking for some loophole to escape. He might as well have tried to fly to the clouds. And as ill-luck would have it, at that very moment when the cheetah had crouched down in the grass, chagrined at losing the dog, the buck, endeavouring still to find an opening in the crowd, came within a yard of him. Then the fierce creature sprang up and was after him. Round they went, the one striving for life, the other for blood. In terror the deer ran to the side of the circle, hoping perhaps to leap it and get away, but without effect. Slowly the cheetah came up with his prey, although the buck, now frantic with fright, skirted the little circle inside the crowd with wonderful celerity, till at last the leopard succeeded in springing upon the hindquarters, entwining its forelegs round its victim's loins. Then followed the most sickening scene I have ever witnessed. The Prince and his suite, though they loved sport, murmured with vexation as the gasping terrified deer struggled and groaned so loudly that its pitiful cries might be heard by everyone present. Slowly the cheetah climbed on its back, though at one moment there was some hope that the beautiful creature would escape; for the former, somehow or other, failed to fasten its fangs in the buck's neck at first, and the two rolled on the ground together. I will do the crowd—that semi-fashionable, semisavage crowd—the justice to say that I believe if the buck had got clear this time they would have opened to let it pass. But this fit of mercy came too late. The strength of the deer was failing fast—another plunge, another roll, another loud groan and cry, and then the end came. The cheetah's teeth pierced the neck of the overpowered buck, there was a tearing noise, a final struggle, and then the bloodthirsty beast was seen sucking away the life of its motionless victim. It may be said that at one point, namely, on the extreme left of the daïs, there was an open passage through which the deer might have passed, and perhaps did go at first; but behind this there was a strong line of beaters, and the fact that the buck was driven back into the circle is sufficient proof of its inability to escape. The next amusement was the production of some lynxes and a jackal. This did not end satisfactorily, according to Cashmere ideas. The first lynx, on being let loose, absolutely fraternised with what should have been its prey, by rubbing its nose against that of the jackal, afterwards quietly trotting back again to its keeper; and, by the time that the second lynx was let loose, the jackal having found an opening in the crowd, made purposely, I fancy, by some of those who did not care for the spectacle of death, trotted off too, thinking, probably, that there was really nothing of interest to wait for. This was somewhat discouraging, and so a plump hare was held forthwith to the noses of the lynxes, and then untied and set free. But the little animal also got away, for the lynxes were anything but hungry, and as sport seemed to be on the wane, a couple of falcons were sent in pursuit, which, after several swoops, succeeded in killing him. It was an open plain, there was no cover very near, and the terrible birds soon disposed of their chase. This ended the "fun." The guests and the Maharajah entered their carriages, and we galloped in the rear towards Jummoo the magnificent.

It must not be supposed that there was a lack of objects of rational interest in Jummoo. On the contrary, the capital of Cashmere is perhaps more deserving of a visit than any other place the Royal party has been to, not even excepting Kandy or Benares. We were altogether in a new world, to which the habits and customs of Europeans had not extended. We saw the Asiatic in his own home, untrammelled by the laws of more modernised races. In fact, a party of those attached to his Royal Highness, discovered, in the course of a short morning's tour, some of the strangest religious curiosities of Asia. Our principal object in setting out was to witness the Lamas or Thibetan Buddhist priests. The yellow-robed ecclesiastics of Kandy had told us when in Ceylon that the Thibetan fraternity differed only from them in the colour of the dress they wore. We were desirous of judging for ourselves, and our observations led to the following conclusions: that in almost every particular the Ceylon and Asiatic Buddhists differ essentially; that while the former wear yellow robes and wash frequently, the latter seldom or never divest themselves of their dingy red habits, and certainly do not use water at all. One amiable old gentleman, whose grimy face, long matted hair, excessively objectionable cap and cloak, told their own tale, owned that he had never taken off his gown since first he adopted it, now many years ago. "Why should he?" he asked of an interrogator. Whereupon somebody suggested that a plunge in the Tow at the foot of the hill might be advisable. To which the holy man replied by a simple, artless smile, which indicated doubt and unwillingness combined. The priests of the South performed their devotions almost silently, those of the North made as much noise as possible. There was no idol on the Buddhist altar in Ceylon, certainly no objectionable pictures were there, and I did not remark any oblation beyond a quantity of flowers and some coin of the realm. But in the North there were idols in plenty. There was also a work of art, to say the least, out of harmony with English tastes, and certainly with our ideas of sacred propriety, and there was "food for the gods" enough to feed all the religious men who sat round the altar. The whole business, too, was different. Our first interview with the Lamas was a somewhat curious one. Guided by the sound of brass instruments, cymbals, clappers, tom-toms, and whistles, we climbed up the side of a dilapidated house by means of some old boarding, and so reached the roof, where, seated in a tent open at the end, were ten burly priests proceeding with their devotions. The picture referred to hung opposite the entrance; and before it were piles of sweetmeats, brass cups full of oil, corn, grain, and flour, an idol; an indescribable instrument on a stand, a lighted lamp, and some pieces of gold cloth. Squatted on their haunches, these ten gentlemen were singing and playing, one amongst them having the words of the song before him and leading the melody. How dreadful the din was which they made I cannot describe; until you have heard the Lamas sing you can have no idea of their powers. To one a most important task was committed—the turning of the praying-wheel, an apparatus unknown to the Cingalese—and the way in which he whirled round the rattling machine showed him to be a great adept in the sacred art.

Passing from the midst of these devotional people, we went on to the chief Hindoo temple of Jummoo, just at the moment when the doors were being opened for the faithful. An attempt to enter was at first vigorously opposed by some Fakeers, who hurried up with their dismal countenances, and insisted on our taking our boots off. To this we objected, and as a result we were followed by a hostile crowd to the doorway, over which we did not attempt to pass, for the whole temple was visible from the entrance. The principal idol was Vishnu, who was bedecked with a golden robe and wore a Pope's mitre. On his right hand was a goddess wearing a mitre also, while on his left sat another female divinity, who had apparently not risen to the dignity of a head-dress, and was, in consequence, obliged to do without one. There was nothing of importance to see beyond this, so we went away, and as we did so a very conscientious person took a bowl of water, and sprinkling the steps on which we had stood, washed away the defilement which the stone had contracted from our infidel feet. The next evening the Lamas danced before the Prince, and the Hindoo priests passed his Royal Highness in procession. Space forbids my attempting to describe the State dinner, at which the Prince presided—the Maharajah, as a good Hindoo, studiously keeping out of sight—or of the Nautch dance which followed. Nor can I give more than passing mention of the fact that, after two days' stay at Jummoo, his Royal Highness departed in similar fashion to that in which he arrived, and on his way back to the North-west breakfasted with the English officers at Sealkote, opened a bridge at Wuzirabad, driving in with some ceremony a silver rivet with a golden hammer; attended a native *fête* at Lahore, and the next day paid a visit to Umritzur and its golden temple.

CHAPTER XXVIII.

AKBAR'S CAPITAL.

The Prince was well received in the city of Agra. It is worth narrating how the descendants of the Mussulmans and the sons of Timour the Tartar met the Shahazada, and after what fashion they saluted him.

The records of distant ages are dim. Little is known of the gentlemen who one after another ruled this favoured spot. Not that we are wholly ignorant of their eccentricities and playfulness. Pleasant stories, conserved in marble, tell their own tale of amusements and pastimes in which a Henry the Eighth would have revelled. But what was their manner in regard to the more solemn acts of life, history fails to narrate. I mean by solemn acts the reception of some friendly monarch, some neighbouring king. Yet I do not refer exactly to the actual durbars, the presents, the pleasant words of welcome, but to what occurred before the potential visitors arrived. Take, for instance, the reception of Ali Merdan by Shah Jehan. Did the Monarch of Akberabad issue fresh regulations every twenty-four hours for a fortnight before the great Persian arrived? Did he sit on his peacock throne in the palace and rehearse the smiles and the bows he intended to make? Did he make the elephants learn their parts, and have the camels put through their facings? I think he must have done something of the sort, for at Agra there was a love of rehearsal which cannot be found anywhere else, and it must have descended from somebody or other.

Having witnessed the preparations for the Prince all over the peninsula, I can say with some certainty that nothing like the arrangements at Agra were witnessed elsewhere. At Bombay, Colombo, Madras, and Calcutta they discussed and diverged, issued edicts and cancelled them, set up arches and pulled them down again, gave orders and rescinded them, and very generally worried themselves and everybody else to the verge of insanity; but that was all. I do not believe the priests of the Temple at Kandy had a full dress rehearsal with the exhibition of Buddha's tooth; the gentleman who read the address at Madras had got it all off by heart; but I am sure that the managers of the Bankapore entertainment were not clear as to what would be done. Even at Lahore there was a pleasant uncertainty up to the last moment, and, indeed, even then; but at Agra nothing of the sort existed. All had been arranged to work like a clock. For a week before the Prince arrived everybody had been placed in full review order. The soldiers had lined the roads, their bands had taken up their positions, the gharry drivers had been thrust into fields and out-of-the-way places, and the public had been hustled and pushed, penned up, and belaboured with all the energy incident to an actual festival. The elephants had been marshalled outside the railway station gates; their drivers had kicked and yelled, and beaten the animals, just as it was desirable they should do when the grand day came; the trees of the gardens of the Taj had been partially illuminated; even to the ball, a battalion of Sepoys had been despatched "to see how six hundred people would look," as an official explained. The only thing which appears to have been left out of the rehearsal programme was an experimental supper. And all this was easily achieved in a happy community in which everybody knows his place, where a colonel would not dream of offering his arm to a general's wife, where the exact position of a commissioner at table is defined, where assistant magistrates are held to be the exact equals of captains, and settlement officers are looked down upon by district judges. The only thing to be taken for granted was that everybody who knew his place and his work did according to his lights, and thus, of course, Agra must "receive" like clockwork.

At length, however, the expected day arrived, and the city went out to meet the Queen's son. The hour of entry was fixed for four o'clock in the afternoon; everybody was in position by one. And lest, after all, somebody should have forgotten his lesson, the parts were all rehearsed again. The elephants—there were nearly a hundred of them—were placed in line, formed into column, and then marched back again. The Sepoys were brought to their places, and drilled on the spot with unrelenting energy. The Bengal Cavalry passed and repassed over the ground till the faces of the riders were recognized by the crowd, and the people in their starchy gowns and their big turbans were "regulated" for three hours without any regard for exhaustion on the part of their active preceptors.

There was one thing, however, which refused to be bound down by the programme, and, accordingly, sadly bothered the manager of the entertainment. We were all, as I have said, in our places; the police had got every wheel of the city mechanism into working order; the native musicians, on native-made platforms of extraordinary description, were tom-toming to their hearts' content, in accordance with rules laid down, when—whew!—a whirlwind sprang up and nearly choked us all. It came over the arid plains by the riverside, over the dry sandy bed of the river itself, down the roads and through the gardens, stirring up the dust in great clouds, and plunging it into our very midst, till no one could see across the road, and even the gentleman who had to read the address was nearly choked. It was all to no avail that the police waved their staves, and the inspectors galloped about. The wind would not be still. It whirled the surface of the plain into the streets and into the station itself; it snatched away umbrellas, and tore down awnings; it hid officers from their men, and the public from the constables; and it kept up this merry game with the officials of Agra till the Prince had entered and reached his destination.

I have mentioned native music-stands. They were certainly, till the dust-storm came, well worth looking at. Have you ever taken part in a wedding festival in the North-West? If so, you will remember that, as aids to the splendour of the procession, figures of ladies and gentlemen, of great artistic beauty, are often borne aloft. It is not in the exact similitude to nature that the charms of these images lie. On the contrary, it is generally the practice to portray humanity not as it is, but as the Hindoo artist thinks it should be. Consequently there is that pleasing divergence from sameness which we call variety—a result exceedingly pleasant to the native mind. What matters it indeed if a gentleman is represented with four arms instead of two? Why should we always be bound down to one nose or one head? There was a really admirable lady dressed in silver, and presumably stuffed with straw, whose head had four mouths, eight eyes, four noses, and two very fine ears. She was placed at one end of a decorated platform, whilst at the other a gentleman wearing a red elephant's trunk kept watch and ward. Between them were squatted all the friends and acquaintances of a wealthy Hindoo, all of them waiting to welcome the Prince. They had brought with them musicians also, celebrated players upon the cymbals and bones, noted performers on the tom-tom and reed whistle, some friends who knew how to blow great brass horns, and a couple of dancing ladies, who jumped about to the sound of the music as long as they could. Nor were they at all alone in their glory; there were, indeed, ever so many of these musical stands along the line of route. Happy were we to whose ears the sound of the sackbut and lute never reached; happy we who could see the energetic gentlemen with the cymbals, but could not hear them. Happier still, however, were the owners of the stands themselves as they sat, with clasped hands and radiant faces, in the very centre of all the din, proud of themselves, proud of their friends, but prouder still of the noise they were making.

But this was not the only special feature of the reception. The arrangement of the Europeans was very picturesque. Tribunes rising from the ground tier above tier were apportioned to the visitors who had flocked into Agra, and ladies in bright dresses, and gentlemen in brilliant uniforms, filled the seats in anticipation of events. All was, indeed, arranged for an exceedingly pretty spectacle, when the wind rose, and the dust came on. The elephants were splendidly painted and caparisoned; thirty Rajahs and chieftains were in their gold and silver howdahs at the station; there were retainers with the very funniest headgear, and some with no headgear at all; there were soldiers who carried matchlocks and warriors who clutched javelins and pistols; the bands were ready; the address was there—when the whirlwind came on. And so it chanced that, after all, the reception at Agra lost much of its beauty. Let it not be supposed that we saw nothing; on the contrary, between the dust clouds we caught a good view occasionally of Lord Charles Beresford's elephant behaving contumeliously, of the Prince holding to the howdah with one hand and bowing with the other, of Lord Aylesford and Lord Alfred Paget abreast on gigantic animals, and a crowd of Rajahs in the rear. But who could enjoy the scene? We had just fixed our binoculars for a good gaze at the features and dress of the youthful Rajah of Dholepore when a blast of wind obscured him from view, and the next potentate we saw was the Rajah of Chickari or the Jaghidar of Alipuia, of the existence of whom we were to that moment profoundly ignorant. But vexation was all to no purpose. The wind cared not a jot for the rage of spectators or the mortification of the simple-minded ones who wished to be seen in the procession; and we were glad at last to take shelter in our carriages, and drive away home as fast as frightened horses, bad drivers, an uncertain road, and coming darkness would allow. Besides which, there was an entertainment in the evening, to which the police "invited" early attendance, and hence our exertion.

CHAPTER XXIX.

A TOMB AND A TOWER.

It is, after all, very questionable whether even a comet obtains a satisfactory view of the universe. Its journey is extended, but it is too rapid; there is too much to be seen for a flying inspection to suffice. Perhaps the Prince thought this as he quitted Agra, for he determined on visiting the Taj Mehal twice, and the second time by moonlight.

In an Indian clime, at this season of the year, there was no need to consult the weather. Clouds may be left entirely out of consideration; if the moon was there we were sure to see it. She was visible when we arrived at Agra—a fine full one, too—lighting up the landscape with a brilliancy of which you in England, and even the dwellers at Rome, know nothing. Perchance it may have occurred to you in time gone by to roam inside the Coliseum when the moon's rays broke through the ruins and lit up the place with a ghastly glare. The selenograph imprinted on your memory at such time may still appear to you the most beautiful picture you ever saw. But those Roman beams had, after all, to penetrate through the mists of the Roman marshes, and, though unknown, parted with some of their finest rays, as they swept the damp air away. The moon at Agra had no such trouble. Unimpeded by watery particles, it shot through the clear, crisp, atmosphere a flood of such brilliant light, that the marble of the Taj became etherealised, and to the wondering spectator looked as though it would suddenly rise up and fly off. It was a singular sight to look through the grim red sandstone gateway and watch the Royal party as it filed along the marble terrace-walk which leads to this marvellous tomb. Fountains were playing; the music from a band situated nobody seemed to know where, but not far off, echoed and re-echoed against Taj and mosque; the great cypress trees cast their dark shadows over the pathway, and vandycked it with sharply-defined forms, and the perfume of innumerable flowers filled the air—it was an entry into fairy-land. No oil-lamps disfigured the trees, no limelight blinded the vision; the Taj stood unornamented in its own wonderful grandeur, just in front of those who were fortunate enough to visit it. As we approached, a glow of heat was felt by everybody. The hot sun playing upon the white marble all day had left it still palpably warm to the touch, and even now at midnight the air was warm with the unexhausted caloric. This was, however, no drawback; for, though the days are sultry, the nights are piercingly cold, and the genial temperature was rather to be courted than avoided. Still it would not do to stand constantly close to the building.

To see the Taj you must go to each of the four corners of the great marble platform on which it stands and note its huge spandrils in bold relief, the jewelled arches as they are illumined by the moon, its wondrous dome and grand minarets. Indeed, it is necessary to go up on those very minarets in order that the full beauty of this architectural gem may the better be seen, that its rich landscape setting may be fully appreciated, that the slow-flowing Jumna close by may take its part in the picture, and that the sleeping city of Agra, its fort and its temples, may also have their place.

To me it was a source of much gratification that I had spent some hours in the daytime inspecting the grandest of all buildings in the world, and that after that nothing could mar the memory of its great beauty. A great white marble tomb, built after the similitude of a Turkish mosque, its walls inlaid with precious stones, its front inscribed in Arabic, with the praises of the great woman in whose memory it was written, its huge white dome glistening in the bright sun, the tombs below and the false tombstones above, the resting-places of Shah Jehan and his lovely wife—such was the picture I saw. Nothing on earth equals it. The spandrils may not be in proportion. I believe a Scotsman who visited it at the same time I did proved successfully to another Scotsman that one of the arches was a quarter of an inch too high and another a quarter of an inch too low. I am aware that gentlemen whose knowledge of Eastern architecture is as small as the knowledge of critics usually is have given at least eight satisfactory reasons why the Taj must not be considered perfection; but I do not care a bit. I love the marvellous screenwork cut from white marble, which, with its eight sides, encloses the two tombs. To me the resting place of the First Napoleon in the Invalides seemed the merest pretence at magnificence when I had looked for a moment into the dim vaults below ground; and when I was led to the top of one of the minarets, and gazed down upon the work of the great Shah Jehan, thought of the millions of money expended in its completion, of the thousands of workmen who toiled here for years, of the sightless crew which issued from yonder gates when the top stone had been added, and the decree which went forth that not one of the workmen might ever see again, lest some other potentate, jealous and envious, might essay to build a structure as handsome in some foreign land—I felt that here was a spectacle for the Prince worthy the fatigues and trials of his whole journey. One fact was very satisfactory—the Joneses, Browns, and Robinsons had not been allowed to write their names or carve their initials on the tombs. They did, in days gone by, chip out the precious stones when nobody was watching; but now they cannot do even that, and are obliged to leave the building without recording their visit in any way. Peace, disappointed scribblers! it is one of the few places your vagrant pencil has not desecrated.

I do not think there was much talking that night as we

passed from point to point, and looked again and again at the wondrous building which the Shah Jehan erected. Hearts were too full of admiration to admit of frivolity or careless thought; we were gazing upon a scene the like of which we had never witnessed before. One idea seemed common—that to enjoy a trip to India the Taj at Agra should be the last place seen. Else with what comfort can you look afterwards upon the inferior resting-places of Akbar, Adum Khan, Suftur Jung, or even Humayon's tomb? To you, as an exacting and scrupulous archæologist, the sepulchre of the Great Mogul at Secundra may afford many delights; the purity of its architecture will please your eye and help you to point many an historical and perhaps useful moral, as a patriotic Englishman. Again, the grave of Humayon may have pleasant memories, in so far as it was the place where the mutiny received its final blow, the spot where the scheming, traitorous old King of Delhi was led away into captivity, and where his three wicked sons were led out to execution by the gallant Hodson. But after you have once seen the Taj, the grandest marble domes, the prettiest Motee Musjid in India—and what a number of these pearl mosques there are!—sinks into insignificance. You regretfully turn back to the Taj, and its beauty overtops them all.

There is another structure of great grandeur, but it is wholly dissimilar from the gem of Agra. It likewise received a parting visit, though not by moonlight.

Not a score of miles from Delhi stands a high tower, the top of which may be seen from any part of a circle of many leagues. Who built it and why it was constructed no one can tell. Yet it is claimed with equal force by both Hindoo and Mussulman, who both have some dozens of reasons to show that to their ancestors belongs the honour of having erected the highest pillar in the world. I do not, however, propose to solve the doubt, the only matter of importance to such as were invited to visit the Kootub being that it belongs just now to the English, and is an exceedingly pleasant retreat as well as a great architectural marvel. It was early in the day when, in well-appointed carriages, we found ourselves passing through the Delhi gate, and so along the road which goes by the tombs of Humayon and Suftur Jung. How the magnificence and squalor of the East intermingled, how pariah dogs and old women howled for food under the very shadow of marble domes, curiously inlaid and sculptured walls; how mud huts surrounded these masterpieces of art, and gilded minarets alternated with the poorest of straw thatches, need scarcely be told. A couple of hours brought us into the gardens of the Kootub, under the shade of the trees which environ it, and the tent which had been erected for the refreshment of such as had been specially favoured.

It was not without some satisfaction that we learned our proximity to the very centre of the world. There could be no doubt at all about it, for a large number of the very holiest men to be found in this part of India, whose word could not by any possibility be doubted, consulted their most trustworthy oracles ever so many years ago, and placed the matter at once beyond a question. In those days there lived the Rajah of Prithie, who, being somewhat anxious to remain King of Delhi as long as possible, and leave the throne in the family of which he was at once the head and principal ornament, called round him the most pious Brahmins whose acquaintance he had had the honour to make. I do not know what form the *fête* to which he invited them took; but from what I have seen of holy men of late I should infer that a feast was at least one part of the entertainment, and that the exhibition of some of the coin of the realm was another. Any way, they appear to have been satisfied, for, on his presently asking them what he had better do to obtain a permanent seat on the somewhat shaky throne, they at once put him into possession of a most valuable secret. Just under the piece of ground on which they were sitting was the head of the serpent which supported the world; there could be no mistake about it; they knew it for certain; and if the Rajah of Prithie would only make a long iron pillar and drive it into the earth in such a way as to transfix the head af that recondite snake, he would reign forever and a day, and his children after him. How he made the pillar, how they had another great feast, how the iron was driven into the ground and actually caught the serpent exactly in the very centre of his head and transfixed him, may easily be imagined. The only regrettable circumstance is that the Rajah was not satisfied when the Brahmins told him all was right. He wanted to make sure for himself, and would by no means be convinced by those pious men—in fact, he was determined to have personal evidence that the snake was caught. So, like another misguided gentleman who killed the goose that laid the golden eggs, he pulled the pillar up when, to his astonishment, the end was found to be covered with blood; proof positive that the Brahmins had been right after all. But, although he had put the iron in the right place at first, it by no means followed that even a Rajah could catch the serpent twice. Thus it happened that, the next time, the animal got away; and, sad to relate, the Rajah of Prithie very shortly afterwards was upset by an enemy, and lost not only his throne, but his eyes, ears, and head into the bargain. Still, a venerable old gentleman, who was making a chupatty close by, informed me that there is no doubt the pillar extends many hundred feet into the earth, and is within an inch or so of the centre after all. I did not think it necessary to tell him that General Cunningham some years bored the ground close by it, and found the end of the pillar was only fourteen feet below the surface—he would have disbelieved me, and worshipped it all the same. What was infinitely more unpleasant to him was my refusal to contribute to the support of the shrine of which he was the presiding genius.

Not far distant from the tower is a wonderful well, and thither we were taken. Constructed in the shape of a tank, about 30 feet square, and about 120 feet deep, this well contains generally about 40 feet of water. For drinking purposes the spring is, doubtless, valuable; but it is much more beloved by the natives for a very different reason. To jump from the top down into the dark pool 80 feet below would apparently be certain death; at any rate, on looking down into the tank you would not easily believe that the spring could be made with the slightest chance of safety. Yet the Hindoos of the village close by step up, and offer to make the attempt for a very small present. Indeed, before you can say yes or no, a dozen men and boys have stripped off all save the smallest possible waistcloth, and are standing on the edge of the well ready to jump. A moment later, and an aged savage has taken the leap. For the first fifty feet his arms are extended wide and his legs are far apart, but just then he clasps his ankles together, brings his hands close to his sides, and, striking the water with a fearful crash, disappears. It is but for an instant, however; out of the inky depths comes that old grey head, and you see the man is swimming towards the wall, and that he intends to climb up the side of the tank to a hole about twelve feet above him, through which he can creep into an adjoining reservoir, and so come to earth again. He is scaling the wall, when a little lad of some ten years makes the fearful spring. For a moment you shudder involuntarily; for the little waif of humanity has, to all appearance, jumped out too far, and is in danger of striking some stonework. But no! he misses the rocky points by about a yard, his little hands and feet close together just as did those of his predecessor, and he falls like a pebble into the water. Will he come up again? You wait nearly two minutes, and no little face is seen. Can he be drowned? you anxiously ask. Is it possible that no effort will be made to save him? You turn round and look eagerly for a swimmer to jump in and rescue the child if possible, when at your elbow stands the naked, grinning little imp, his head and body dripping with moisture. It seems that under the surface of the water a trap-door communicating with the reservoir in similar fashion to that by which the old man climbed out is found, and that by this the boy has escaped from the well; the silence of the men at the top being only another trick to arouse the sympathy of the white sahibs. After this they jump in one after another as rapidly as possible, almost falling in pell-mell on the top of each other, as though the eighty-feet spring were the merest bagatelle. Round they come through the trap-doors to earth again, dripping, steaming, shouting, and so down into the well again; but we have had enough of it. Little did the beneficent constructor of that tank think what use it would be turned to five hundred years later on. Fresh clean water, indeed! To what better purpose can it be turned than as a means of getting money from sightseeing travellers?

Still, the Kootub itself was, after all, the object of our visit, and thither we bent our steps very soon afterwards. To reach the tower it was necessary to go through a City of the Dead, a great space covered with tombs, which were erected many hundred years ago, and have now fallen into decay. It was easy to see how beautiful was this Mohammedan cemetery when Akbar reigned at Delhi, and the nobles of the land were buried one after another under the marble domes which are now crumbling to dust. Then the trees, of which one now only finds the thick, leafless stumps, were young saplings; the broken ground was covered with flowers; the fountains, of which only the remains are left, played with full vigour; and what is now a desert blossomed as the rose. Those days are gone, and in place of the dead Mohammedan, scores of squalid Hindoos and pariah dogs inhabit the tombs, crouching for shelter from the sun in the summer, and the rains in the wet season, behind the ruined walls, and only emerging to beg of the stranger as he passes by. I do not know which were the more objectionable, the dogs or the people—all were so utterly loathsome and unclean. Perhaps the animals were, after all, most bearable, for with a stick or stone we could frighten them away. But not so the pestilent crowd of human beings, who followed close upon our heels, now exhibiting sores and deformities, sightless eyes and useless limbs, and now cursing us for our want of appreciation and sympathy. I am afraid that some of them ultimately got encouragement from some of the younger travellers, who forgot that, so long as this degraded tribe can obtain alms, they will refuse to work for a livelihood.

At length, the foot of the Kootub was reached, a tall circular column nearly twice the height of the Campanile at Venice, and quite as large round as that square pillar which all the travelled Browns, Robinsons, and Smiths know so well, and which bears their honoured names wherever the space to write a word could be found. Indeed it was impossible to forget Venice all the while we were at Delhi or Agra. How could we forget, for instance, that famous Bridge of Sighs and the dark passages below where the old nobles passed on their way to strangulation and worse, when, following a torch-bearer, we explored the foundations of Akbar's Palace, and saw the well in which he drowned his troublesome wives, and the dark cells into which assassins entered in the dead of the night and perpetrated nameless cruelties upon innocent men and women? Was it not about the same time, too, when that wicked old Council of Ten sent despairing victims through the dismal secret door which the panels hid so nicely, that Akbar was disposing of his enemies in those dark passages of Agra? Akbar—Doges, all are gone; but the monuments of their genius and the memory of their crimes live after them, and show that the civilization of Venice and the barbarity of India were not very dissimilar, after all.

As for the Kootub, it was impossible to ascend its 375 steep steps without being amazed at the untiring energy which must have been employed in a work so tremendous. It does not reach to the heavens, as did the Tower of Babel; yet it is twenty times as high as another pile, which was intended to be a rival, and was actually begun some few yards distant from it. Just as no one knows who raised the great pillar of sandstone up which we climb, so no one can tell who began the rival work which ended so disastrously. But the two remain; the grand column, with its six storeis, its ornamented galleries, its countless inscriptions, its wonderful sculpture, and, close by, the ruined abortive attempt at building, overgrown with moss and rank weeds—the one a model of perseverance, the other a monument of unsuccessful ambition. But there is little time for moralising, the steps have to be climbed, till at last we stand on the little platform at the top, scarcely eight feet in diameter, and look down upon the country below Then what a panorama bursts into view! The City of the Dead is at your feet, the city of the living, teeming, crowded Delhi, only fifteen or twenty miles away; the tomb of Humayon apparently so close that you imagine it would not be very difficult to throw a stone on to its marble dome; the burying-place of Adum Khan, where his widow placed his remains after he had been twice thrown from Delhi battlements by the order of the Emperor; and farther away still, the camping ground of that gallant army which held the Ridge in those famous fights when Delhi was in the hands of rebels, and the fate of English rule in India hung in the balance. How full of food for historic thought was every inch of that remarkable landscape!

CHAPTER XXX.

NATIVE COURTS AND PRISONS.

I did not find that the Prince of Wales visited a court of justice during his stay in India. His Royal Highness consequently missed a spectacle which is so purely Indian in its characteristics, that a description of the way in which wrong is set right and right is maintained in the country districts of the Empire should be given. I do not refer to the higher courts, over which Chief Justices or Judges preside. There the terror to evil-doers is pretty much the same sort of person he is at home, sits in a robe, and if he does not wear a wig has at least bands round the neck, and the look of a lawyer stamped on his face. But in the small towns and villages this is scarcely the case.

Justice here is administered by collectors, magistrates, joint magistrates, and assistant magistrates—a goodly array of young gentlemen whose knowledge of jurisprudence is mainly derived from the occasional perusal of a kind of law catechism which is supplied by the Central Government. This is by no means their fault; they come out to the country as civil servants, after passing a somewhat stiff examination in most of the subjects with which they will not be required to deal. They are not barristers, they know nothing of English law; but to some extent they are made acquainted with the rudiments of Indian practice; they have a slight—very slight—knowledge of Hindostanee, and thus equipped they are sent into the various districts to fulfil the somewhat varied duties of revenue officers and magistrates. At certain periods of the year they travel from village to village to try cases, collect taxes, measure land, make reports, and generally look after the tract of country through which they pass. Many of them are very young, say between twenty-one and twenty-six years of age; most of them entertain the profoundest contempt for the natives, and all of them are endowed with powers such as a Bow-street magistrate of a dozen years' standing would never be allowed to use. What would Sir Thomas Henry say to a youth of twenty-two being allowed to order a man twenty lashes and two years' imprisonment? Theoretically, these sentences are all subject to revision: they are always recorded in a book, with a short reason appended. But in the course of four months' careful enquiry, I could only discover four instances in which the sentences had been revised by the collectors, and in one of these cases the punishment was increased. Very often an appeal to the High Courts, however, puts a stop to injustice; and it is in setting right the vagaries of these youthful administrators of law that the centres of justice are mainly engaged. That there are great difficulties to be contended against, no one can deny. The impossibility of placing faith in what native prosecutor or witnesses on either side may say, the certainty that more or less perjury is mixed up in every statement, and the knowledge that any amount of evidence on either side can be obtained for a few annas, places the magistrates frequently in a great dilemma, and this may possibly account for some of the mistakes that are made.

I will take you into a court of the ordinary kind, where a typical case is to be tried. It is a large, square room, very plain, very bare of furniture. Its only ornaments are a table, at which a very youthful magistrate sits, and two forms, one at his side, the other in front of him. At the door is a crowd of chattering, noisy natives, who are arranging what is to be done in the case about to be heard. Inside the room there are two native policemen, three moonshees, or native scribes, seated close to the magistrate, and in the centre of the room a miserable-looking lad of the barber caste, waiting for judgment. The Daniel at the table eyes him sternly for a moment, whereupon the barber-prisoner clasps his hands in the attitude of petition, and assumes the nearest approach to penitent submission which he can call up in his inexpressibly ugly face. His offence is a curious one: he has nearly cut off a woman's nose—the police say he is mad, and ought to be locked up, and here he is for examination. If the truth were really told, it is probable that the statement of the lady who prosecutes would be as follows: "I am unhappily burdened with excessively large eyebrows—at least so my friends and my own judgment tell me. There is not much in my appearance to recommend me; my clothes are ragged and dirty; my face is by no means pretty; but these are things over which I have no control. With my eyebrows the case is different—I can get them trimmed for a few cowrie-shells if a very low-caste barber is applied to, and hence I employed Motia. Our agreement was, however, unfortunately, not successful—he did not trim my eyebrows satisfactorily. I refused to pay him; and he then attempted to cut my nose off. I think he is a little mad—he certainly is very violent." All this would be rendered in the native language, were the prosecutrix inclined to tell the truth. To an uninstructed mind there would appear no reason why she should fail to do so; to those who know India, however, there is a very great reason indeed. That lady in rags has, curiously enough, all the objection in the world to anybody knowing she has her eyebrows trimmed. Were she a Mohammedan she would not mind a bit; were the barber a high-caste Hindoo, she would be less squeamish. As it is, she will not admit for a moment that she sent for Motia to improve her personal appearance. She must tell quite a different story to that. So she borrows somebody else's baby boy, a little urchin of some two summers, the crown of whose head has been recently shaved in approved fashion, and, carrying him in her arms, shuffles into the court. Just before she arrives, the prisoner has been making a statement which somewhat tallies with the truth, saying that he was just finishing the lady's left eyebrow when somebody jogged his elbow and made him cut her nose. The police, at whose instance the man has been brought up—for the prosecutrix is quite opposed to the action—however, deny that he was jogged at all, and declare that he is mad.

It now remains to hear the woman's story, and she begins as follows: "I am a poor woman, and have one little boy—this one (holding up her neighbour's child). I saw that his head ought to be shaved, so I sent for Motia and asked him to do it. Motia is a very careless man, but a very good man indeed, very good. Motia was not thinking of his work, I believe, for just when he ought to have been looking at the child he was looking at me; and when the boy moved Motia's hand slipped, and so his razor cut my nose." "Is that the truth?" says the magistrate, though that is a needless formality, for the lady has previously promised, her right hand in the air the meanwhile, that she will "tell the truth according to righteousness and nothing else." "Let me see your nose," continues the embodiment of justice. The woman comes forward, uncovers her face, and shows a gash which certainly no slip of the hand from such a razor as Motia owns will account for. Yet what is to be done: the woman, whose forehead has evidently been lately shaven, denies that her eyebrows were touched, says quite indignantly that she would not let Motia shave her face for any consideration. Thereupon a native doctor is sent for, and is asked whether he knows anything of the prisoner. "Yes, Sahib, I have examined him," is the reply, for the doctor prides himself on his English, "I find him very funny man; he laughs very much when he has no right to laugh; sometimes he stare at things you not stare at at all. I think he not got all the mind; he not violent, but strange." It is clear that the man cannot be punished for laughing when he ought not, or for not possessing "all the mind." So more witnesses are called for, and they come in one after another. Each tells a different story—some confirm the eyebrow shaving story, but say that the child jogged Motia; some swear to the tale that it was the child's head that was being shaved, while one old lady, unfortunately, lets out the secret that the body does not belong to the prosecutrix at all. Not a single version of the case agrees; the police reiterate what they said at first; the woman with the gashed nose contradicts them flatly; while the prisoner, staring at the wall, and so confirming the doctor's remarks, waits calmly while the opposing parties fight the matter out. At length the youthful magistrate delivers a Solomon-like oration. He finds that Motia cannot be sent to gaol because the chief sufferer will not pursue him, he finds that he cannot punish the woman because she is not legally before him, and he finds that the police have made a muddle of the whole business—and all this he first of all says and then writes down in the magisterial book before him. The crowd of witnesses thereupon file out, and justice is satisfied.

Of course when at Agra the famous gaol under the care of Dr. Tyler could not be missed. Consequently the Duke of Sutherland, attended by a large party of the Prince's suite, paid this abode of 2,500 criminals a visit on Thursday morning. I was not so fortunate as to accompany them; but an hour afterwards I received a courteous invitation from Dr. Walker, the Inspector-General of Gaols in the North-West Provinces, to join him on a tour of inspection. A few minutes afterwards I found myself in a comfortable wagonnette, and shortly after that received by a guard of honour, composed of the company of Sepoys whose business it is to guard the gaol. It is needless to say that we were accompanied on our rounds by five soldiers. The attempted murder of Dr. Tyler only two months ago warrants every precaution, for the most desperate ruffians in India are confined here for life, and they are not to be despised.

Once inside the prison walls, how forcibly we were reminded that we were in an Eastern land! A beautiful garden, shaded by the huge leaves of the plantain-tree, was before us; fruitful herbs were in plenty, and what in England would have been a desert, blossomed as the rose. There was little to remind us of the precincts of a prison. True, that here and there a gentleman in heavy fetters tied up a lettuce or earthed up a cauliflower. But you might see his fellow anywhere else in Agra. It was truly a pleasant place, albeit the ante-room to a dungeon. Our first introduction to the prisoners was an entry into the department where small boys were confined—some scores of little ignorant imps, who, squatting on the ground, were just then engaged in eating their mid-day meal. Their two hours' morning lesson over, they were about to work at carpet making—an occupation at which, I learn, they are great adepts. Passing by these we came to the yards in which the female criminals were kept—young women who had committed theft, and old ladies whose ideas of vagrancy were not consistent with those of the local magistracy. In one section were those who had committed heinous crimes, and were in prison for life. How squalid, how wretched were the countenances of this unenviable company can never be learnt by you at home I do not refer to the dresses; the ordinary grey prison garb had little about it that was repulsive. Nor do I allude to the modern badges which each wore, attached to a chain passed round the neck, and held up in obedience to command. But what a story did those fifty faces tell! Tales of infanticide, under singularly revolting circumstances; of poisoned husbands and fathers; of murders both by strategy and force. One aged matron, whose toothless gums and sightless eyes told of approaching dissolution, had been there ever since the year of grace 1837—her crime was the murder of her children and their father. Another, a very young woman, had just entered upon her term for the destruction of a brother and father. There they sat, some spinning wool, some nursing their children—a helpless crew, to whom hope never comes, before whom yonder barred gates would never open.

From such a spectacle we turned sick at heart, and were not at all sorry when we entered the place where young men were employed at mat-making—gaining what they never knew before, an honest livelihood. Nor was the next ward less admirable, containing the cooking ranges of the establishment, and bakery of the gaol. A scene of animation followed, but of a lucrative and satisfactory sort. On a raised platform, at a pace of fully three miles an hour, were forty-eight rapscallions turning round a huge capstan. Two abreast they marched at quick step, not to the sound of a band, as sailors do at sea, but to the time marked out by a warder, whose whip encouraged the tardy, and invited them to activity. They were no useless servants, however; on the contrary, the capstan they so rapidly moved gave off four horse-power, which we found to be utilised in driving wool-carding and spinning machinery, at which a number of other prisoners worked. Round went the wheel, the machines moved merrily, and wool for all the looms in the prison was being prepared. How much was needed may be guessed when it is known that some scores of prisoners were employed in making cloth for all parts of India, some with hand looms, others with larger machines moved by hand and feet together. There were carpets, too, waiting for wool, curtains, tablecloths, all kinds of things demanding more material. Well might the forty-eight be encouraged; theirs was no idle task.

But it must not be supposed that they were the only ones employed in hard labour. Many scores were grinding flour with the old-fashioned Eastern mills, pumping water, working at printing presses, and cleaning the cells. Where, however, more refined and more remunerative labour could be adopted, it was given out; and thus it was that we presently found ourselves in a great factory for manufacturing what are known as

Persian carpets. To my surprise it was under the care of an English convict, none other than Captain Lyat, who, only four months ago, was convicted of forgery and sent to prison for two years. Of his case I say nothing; but certainly his shop was in wonderful order. His men were all at work, making money for the Government, and, indeed, earning a good deal. Their task for the day consisted of six inches of carpet two feet wide—a carpet which, by the way, is sold for about £1 a square yard when manufactured, and quite treble that sum in England. It was here that we had the pleasure of seeing a Dacoit who for many years had been the terror of the North-west Provinces, and was now undergoing a sentence of seventeen years; a gentleman of most forbidding countenance, whose leg irons testified to his irremediable badness. In this way we came to cells where dangerous criminals were shut up; the yard for English convicts, now happily nearly empty; and so to the gardens once more, having seen the finest prison in India, and probably the best governed one in the world. Will it be believed that the profit on materials supplied for prison labour at Agra last year exceeded £4,000? There are few gaols in England that could show such a balance-sheet.

CHAPTER XXXI.

AN EASTERN PARIS.

In the record of Royal entries to Eastern cities the chronicler has to be careful lest, by awarding the palm of superiority to any one reception, he may find himself unable to give to the next one its proper meed of praise. As the first place to receive the Prince of Wales, Bombay had certainly a great advantage; the magnificent landscape of Ceylon lent undoubted charm to the festivities at Kandy; the absence of all foolish and needless etiquette at Calcutta rendered the Royal landing on the banks of the Hooghly memorable; at Delhi the grandest military spectacle we had witnessed was presented, when the Shahazada passed the Jumna Musjid in the sight of a score of thousands of people the Himalayas of Cashmere, the broad River Tow, the ascent to Jummoo on the hill, the barbaric music and the strange Asiatic costumes marked the procession in the far North as strikingly grand. We have again seen a magnificent spectacle, and this time the *locale* is the Paris of India—Jeypore.

I do not know who it was that gave to the city which Jey Singh built this happy title. Comparatively few travellers have visited it, for only lately a line has been laid hither from Agra. It was far from the civilised world, the home of an independent Prince, of whom almost as little was known as of the Grand Lama of Thibet. But times have altered; that modern civiliser, the railway, has grasped Jeypore, brought it within a ten hours' ride of the city of Akbar, and three days ago the Prince of Wales entered it with greater ease than Gwalior or even Jummoo. And now no more appropriate name could be given to the capital of the Maharajah than that of the

Paris of India. They say that Jey Singh was an enlightened man—that he was filled with an idea that even narrow streets on the top of a mountain were not so healthy as wide thoroughfares on a plain, especially when that stands at an elevation of fifteen hundred feet above the level of the sea; that large houses well ventilated, and a good system of sewerage, were preferable to small houses, no drains, and plenty of cholera; and that, seeing all this, he left his Royal Palace and built another. He then invited his people to quit their mud hovels for the roomy mansions which he erected, and without more ado constructed such a city as is not to be met with elsewhere in the world.

Nor is this a mere phrase—a vague, exaggerated idea; for the main thoroughfares of Jeypore are 111 feet wide, and intersecting each other are respectively two miles and forty yards, and one mile and a quarter long. These again are crossed by a third main street nearly two miles long, and thus the city is divided into six perfectly equal portions. Even in these the streets are fifty-five feet wide; and each house has a garden, each house a family tree. Nor must it be supposed that the buildings are unworthy of the streets. Erected by one designer, they are composed wholly of stone; and though the handsome frontages vary, and the eye is thus relieved, one idea runs through the whole. There is not a mud cottage—not one of any kind within the walls which surround Jeypore. It is a city of palaces, the fronts of which are artistically dyed pink and white. Even on the smallest dwellings the same care has been bestowed as upon the largest; handsome flights of steps run up to the minarets and domes, the flat roofs, and the upper rooms of the buildings; the parapets are artistically designed; and it is as though a huge palace had been framed for the residence of a king.

A Royal residence there is beside, or rather in one part of the city, but it scarcely exceeds in beauty the palaces in which the people live. In its surroundings it is magnificent, but then all these—gardens, lakes, fountains, and marble walks—are open to the people. They may not own the alligators which swarm on the water's edge, but they may see and feed them, and what more can the monarch himself do? To them may not belong the fee simple of the orange groves and paths overhung with cyprus, myrtle, plantain, and palm, but they may walk in them, and pluck the rich, juicy fruit; the fountains and the marble walks may not be at their disposal, but they are for their use; they inherit the pleasures of the locality without any of its responsibilities. And if ever they are inclined to be ungrateful and rebel they have only to look towards the hills upon the ruined dungeons of old Ambair, to be reminded of the days that are past and of the better times that are come. I call it a new city, but that is not strictly correct. Will it be believed by London vestrymen that it was in 1728 that Jey Singh made Jeypore a handsomer spot than our metropolis of to-day, and that for a hundred and fifty years the city of Rajpootana has had wider thoroughfares and better drainage, prettier houses and larger gardens, than any rival in civilised Europe?

It was in such a scene as this, then, that the spectacle of February the 4th was cast.

We take a carriage and drive through the streets while the day is yet young and the period of the Prince's arrival some hours distant. The houses on each side of the street are seldom more than two stories high. The lower portions have mostly open shop fronts, the upper are almost wholly composed of stone lattice work. In the former the men of Jeypore are seated by thousands; in the latter the women of the city are assembled, peering through the screen which hides them at the preparations for the entry of the Prince. Here, as elsewhere in India, the crowd is dressed in gay colours. Perhaps scarlet predominates, but there are yellow, light green, light blue, light red. Anyway, the people are attired in the brightest costumes. The very arrangements of the streets aided to make the sight a stirring one. When in London we went to the procession, it may be of a newly-recovered Prince or a newly married Princess, there were many things to be taken into consideration. It might rain or snow, or a hundred things may militate against a comfortable view. But in Jeypore there was no such troublesome thought. The Prince could only enter on an elephant; the bright, blue sky above forbade the suspicion of rain. So the natives who wished to be spectators, and there were many thousands of them, thronged the pathways, sat in the shop fronts, got behind windows, perched themselves upon the roofs, and filled the staircases, with the assurance that they would all have a good view of the Maharajah's guest.

There were nine residents in Jeypore, however, who were not allowed to witness the Royal entry, albeit that their dwelling-place was not a hundred yards from the Prince's route. Nine residents of Jeypore, in cages, not so much because they were wicked in the past as that they might possibly be troublesome were they allowed to mingle at present with the crowd in the streets. It was well they were so confined, for few more savage than they were ever seen. I have in different parts of the world visited zoological gardens, and wondered at the animals collected therein, but never did I see such fearful beasts as were these nine. There was a tiger fully twelve feet long, which had made twenty-five hearty meals off as many unoffending men, women, and children. There was a tigress which, as often as she saw Europeans, waxed furious and frantic, and endeavoured to tear down the slight cage in which she was pent up. There was an old tiger whose powers and propensities were such that even Jeyporeans had thought fit to vote him a double set of bars, eating half a goat, and growling as though he would leave it and spring into the street every moment. There was a lank tiger which, it was said, could spring further than any of its kind in the world—an acrobatic, athletic, wiry beast, that once, some months ago, lept up into a tree, and took therefrom a thoughtless Shikaree, who imagined that at the height of fifteen feet from the ground he was perfectly safe, and could laugh any savage animal in the kingdom to scorn. And there were three more, about each of which terrible tales were told of ravaged villages, plundered flocks, and desperate struggles before they were enticed into traps, and thence conveyed to the Maharajah's cages. Two leopards, who appeared to have arrived at the border of frenzy, completed the nine who alone in Jeypore were not invited to bid the Prince welcome. All the rest were there; even the convicts, with their heavy leg irons, were allowed a glance at the Royal guest—a day of happiness in a life of gloom.

But perhaps the most curious section of those who came to cheer the august visitor were the members of a tribe with which you in England are somewhat familiar, and everybody must have heard of the Nagas, the unruly children of the hills in Central India, the gentlemen against whom an expedition was lately sent, and some of whose villages were very recently burned. Well warned by that timely chastisement, and suitably admonished as to the necessity of good behaviour, these reckless, wild men were invited to do honour to the Prince. Nor was their duty merely the passive one of suffering the procession to go by without molestation. Their part was the active one of adding to the glory of the entry in a more pronounced manner than even their prototypes of Ceylon, the Veddahs of the hills of that island.

Before, however, I tell you what they did, let me tell you what they are like.

It was early in the afternoon when I visited their encampment for the purpose of making acquaintance with these singular creatures. My introduction was the fiat of the Maharajah, my protection the generosity of the people themselves. For, though they will occasionally murder a European, as circumstances lately showed, they are generally friendly, and, unless provoked, are fairly civil. I think that the exhibition of a lead pencil which would make a palpable mark upon paper was the magnet which attracted them into a circle—the rest was easy. In a few minutes they were persuaded to form up into two lines of about fifty apiece, and there stand while some of the party were sketched. To be drawn--to appear in a picture—was to them a new sensation. The only difficulty was to keep them from settling the moot point as to who should be selected by an immediate appeal to the arms they carried. Such a reference would have been most inconvenient. Each had a curious kind of blunderbuss, which, however, was by no means the most important part of their equipment. The formidable sword they carried was the principal weapon. Picture to yourself a blade five feet long, the handle of which is a great steel arm-guard, such as the knights in England wore as gauntlets in the "good old days;" give to that sword a flexibility compared with which the Toledo blade is stiff and unbendable, and sharpen it till it equals the steel of Damascus, and you have the Naga's falchion. Hand this to a fierce gentleman whose whiskers are mixed with his turban, and meet in a knot at the top of his head, and whose countenance is as objectionable as that of any Thuggee or Dacoit in India. In his waistcloth place a dagger of formidable size, give him a shield of metal or hide, round his naked legs put spangles and rings, on his feet a hard leather shoe—and you have a Naga ready for anything. Or in place of the dagger arm him with a spear fourteen feet long and a pistol or two; he can take his place in the ranks before us. To complete the party some would have to wear nothing but a waistcloth, while to others might be given jackets of tiger-skin, or singular coats, with great epaulettes and protections for the back of the neck extending higher than the ears; some, too, should have linen tied round their faces as though they had toothache. Such were the gentlemen who came to take part in the procession.

Their work was a simple one. If they understand anything, it is the use of the sword. It is their constant practice and amusement, and, in case of disputes, the approved way of arranging the difficulty. Does one gentleman think that another has unlawful aspirations for the possession of his wife? Then he invites him to take his weapon and his shield and decide the question of ownership at once. There is no veto in the way of such a proposition. The respective parties place themselves in position, give a preliminary caper for the amusement of their friends, and then cut and thrust till one or the other, or perhaps both, are run through. They have none of the scruples as to shedding blood which beset the ordinary Hindoo. They are, as a matter of fact, a kind of depraved Buddhists. "We do not worship in a temple," one of them said to me, "but we pray with a book to our god." The fact that Buddha disapproved of fighting, however, never troubles them; they love their swords and like to use them.

Like to use them, indeed! At the very mention of such a thing twc stepped into the pathway and began a friendly combat. One was an elderly warrior, with huge eyes and a yellow face; the other a stripling, who had painted most of his body blue. With an exhilarating flourish, they struck each other's shields and then began. Round and round they went, now rushing close to each other and stabbing, and now falling on their knees and clashing their blades together with all their might. Sometimes the points of their swords would go within an inch or two of their faces; sometimes it seemed as though their optics would be picked out cleaner than by any vulture. But no! not even a feather in the peacock's-tail plumes which they wore in their turbans was injured; they were both as safe as a mongoose from a cobra's bite. And when, with great reluctance, they were persuaded to leave off, two more went at it, and clattered away as merrily as the others. Thus couple after couple fought, like the knights in days of yore, challenging each other to feats of dexterity—sometimes rolling in the dust, sometimes chasing each other with every sign of fierceness, now imitating defeat and now victory.

At length, however, we persuaded them to stop. But their entertainment was not yet finished, and they were determined we should see what they could do. So then there rushed forward a savage, who carried a stick from which hung by iron chains several wooden balls covered with spikes, and, without more ado, he swung them round so close to my head that I wished myself comfortably at home in an arm chair once more. Flinching would have been more serious still, so with great effort I stood firmly while the spiked balls whirled round my helmet and came past my face. I am told that gentleman can send any one of the six balls within a quarter of an inch of any given object. The whole business was most troublesome, as those who wanted to "form a group" for the artist were legion and all who were there were erratic and wilful At last when everything appeared to be arranged, some jealous Naga, whose face was not a fortune, and whose appearance was certainly not prepossessing, proposed that they should dine; whereupon a mutiny arose, which all our efforts to quell were unavailing. In the end the great food question led them to rise in a body and troop off to their tents; and such were the gentlemen whose special business it was "to fight the way of the Prince" into Jeypore.

It was nearly dark; the policemen, armed with great cudgels, had amused themselves for hours with thrashing the populace first from one position to another, and then back again; the thousands in the shop-windows, behind the lattice-work, and on the roofs, had chewed as much betel-nut as the vendors with baskets could produce for the occasion; and the few Europeans who were in Jeypore had taken up their position on the top of the Medical Hall, opposite the palace gates, when a bouquet of rockets and a din of tom-toms announced that the

Maharajah was going forth to meet the Prince. A moment later, and his Highness sallied forth on horseback, preceded by a small body of the Nagas, who ran in front of him for a little way, fencing and capering in most approved fashion. They stopped when they came to a huge tower which stands in front of the city, and about whose builder a curious story is told. Jey Singh, it is said, erected it in order to look into somebody's harem. Thence the Maharajah proceeded alone, in all the glory of ordinary potentates, with horsemen and footmen, but no Nagas.

Fortunately we had not long to wait for the grand spectacle, and that little while was beguiled by a conversation with a Fakir who chanced to go by, and whose acquaintance I made. He was a very holy man, as will be easily understood when it is explained that his hair, matted in tails, hung below his waist; that a quarter of an inch of mud covered his face and neck; that he had painted that mud a striking pink and yellow; that round his eyes were bright blue rings; that he wore about his otherwise naked ribs a rope which had never been untied since the first day it was fixed there fifteen years ago; that he had stained his legs a dull grey; and that his nails had been allowed to grow to the length of an inch beyond the toes. Indeed, his sanctity was palpably acknowledged by all the other Fakirs in Jeypore; and when he stalked along the streets on the extremity of his heels—that was his favourite method of locomotion—shook a club from which were suspended a number of little bells, and yelled out, "Yo ho! yo ho!" they made way for him as a man of whom the gods were peculiarly fond. "Why did you become a Fakir?" was the question put to this amiable gentleman. "Because I love my God very much, and because it is the easiest way of getting to Heaven," was the reply. "You are certain to go there, are you not?" "Yes," said the Fakir, "I'm going there very fast, and so will you if you give me some backsheesh," saying which he held out a cocoanut shell, and, receiving a small coin, gave the club another shake, shouted out "Yo ho!" and continued his march once more.

Just then, darkness fast coming on, a salute of guns proclaimed that the Prince had reached the railway station, and was coming into the town. Of course we all prepared to receive him, and the police thrashed the crowd with renewed vigour. At length, through a triumphal arch on our right were seen the running footmen of the procession, shuffling along with a lot of irregular cavalry in the rear. Very irregular indeed were these horsemen, very irregular were their almost unmanageable steeds, too; but they came on knocking down a few natives, perhaps, but still covering the ground as directed. Probably they were the more careless of doing harm for the reason that, with admirable forethought, the good Maharajah had ordered to be swung from one-fourth of the Venetian masts that decorated the streets a very special and effective charm against the wiles and snares of the Devil which had been given him by the excellent priests of the Sila Deva Temple at Amber. This consisted of two half-squares crossed, and coming from such a source could not fail to be useful; yet it made the irregular horsemen more irregular than ever.

As to the procession, it seemed to me unique of its kind. Perchance it was because there was not the slightest European element in it. All was Jeyporean in every particular—the runners, the cavalry, the tom-tom beaters who followed in crowds, and the festive gentlemen who were trying to play "God save the Queen" on wooden whistles. The little band of Europeans on the housetop were lost in comparison with the thousands of visitors below. It was a grand pageant of the East. What else could be said of the men in red turbans and long red and yellow gowns, who, bearing banners, rode by the side of two elephants that carried huge flags? Where else, save in India, could be found such javelin men as those who came along with great silver javelins held high in the air? And, then the chieftains, who came next, Rajahs, Sirdars, Nawabs, all mounted on magnificent horses, and surrounded by crowds of retainers. How they scurried along, maintaining no sort of order, but simply heralding the coming of the Prince, as they mingled with each other, and urged their steeds forward! Not inferior either in appearance was the calvacade of led horses which followed—animals magnificently caparisoned, whose saddles were cloth of gold and round whose necks hung hundreds of gold and silver coins. Next there were horsemen in double lines, armed with spears and attired in Rajpoot costumes, while in the distance could be seen, slowly coming under the archway, torch-bearers with a great blaze of lights.

We might regret that the day was fast closing in, we might wish for the sun and the warmth of the morning, but for an Eastern spectacle could anything be more fitting than the gloom of evening and the torchlight? The torches were advancing in two lines on the pathways, in the road were the elephants on which the Prince and Maharajah rode, and in front of these huge beasts were our friends the Nagas, fighting their way in the most approved fashion. It is difficult to describe the effect produced by these capering wild men in that fitful blaze, as they jumped and thrust and ran and fenced under the trunks of the two elephants that were coming up the street. No knightly appearance had they just then; they danced like demons, and struck at each other with their brands. You could hear the clash of their weapons as they rung on the shields. You could see them falling on the ground as though mortally wounded, rolling over and over, and then springing up again, sometimes maintaining a mimic battle in line, and sometimes a running fight, shouting, crying, yelling, as though the combat were real and their energy not assumed. Just behind were the Prince and the Maharajah, behind them again the Royal and Raj suites, on a long line of elephants numbering nearly a hundred, and in rear of all an escort of cavalry. The people did not cheer, yet they smiled a pleasant assent to the doings of the day. They could not be called enthusiastic, but they were as satisfied with the pageant as it was fair to suppose they could be with anything.

CHAPTER XXXII.

TIGER SHOOTING AND A DURBAR.

Jeypore is noted for tigers. Let me describe how the Prince shot his first tiger in the Jeypore jungle.

First of all it is necessary to dismiss from your minds any apprehension of dangerous propinquity to the lord of the Indian jungle. To stalk a beast of this description on foot in a dense wood, when it may spring upon the sportsman at any moment, or to follow it along a nullah, or dry river-bed, alone, when evening is fast approaching and the tiger can see him while he cannot see it, is a feat of some danger. Equally dangerous is it to track the brute to its lair, it may be in some deep, dark, cavernous hollow, as did that model of bravery, Sir Richard Outram; but such was not the peril to which the Maharajah of Jeypore exposed the Queen's son. Indeed, so fearful was his Highness lest any evil should befall his Royal guest that no precaution of safety was neglected, and no chance of danger left.

The jungle outside Jeypore, especially in that direction which was selected by the Prince, is not very dense. There is a ridge of high hills in horseshoe form protecting Jeypore from the great Western Indian Desert, the sands of which press even into the town. Climbing these you look down upon a wide, expansive treeless plain—a great yellow, drifting level similar to that which one witnesses on the Egyptian frontier. Ever and anon the wind whirls a sand-storm into the air, and sends it up the hills, through the gorges, and so by the passes inside the walls of Jeypore. A merry game is that which the wind has with the drifting dust of the desert. On these wide-extending desolate expanses neither tiger nor leopard can live; their only shelter is the range of hills—the home of game of all kinds, driven thither by the sand. That there are great numbers of these terrible fugitives a glance at the ground over which we are climbing will readily show. Here is the footprint of a tiger, there the mark of a cheetah; we can see where the cushions of those heavy feet pressed; it needs no imagination to know that the animal had claws. You may have heard of the Gulta, of the far-famed Temple of the Sun, and the glorious view to be gained of the desert, and of the far-distant hills of Ajmere. If so, climb over the boulders and stones till an altitude of some seven hundred feet is reached; and then! Then you look down into a precipice of wonderful grandeur—a straight descent to the lowest level, and thence right across the desert, seeing nothing but sand in front, and nothing but high hills to the right and left. Behind is Jeypore, spread out like a map; round it are the jungles in which the tigers hide.

But it is on the range where you stand that their favourite home is found, and looking away to your right you can easily descry a green house of two stories—a house with a flat roof and a parapet—on the side of one of the hills. Passing along the ridge a large number of natives become apparent who have been sent out to beat the woods, and to drive the game down to yonder shooting-box. Moreover, the Prince and Maharajah, several of the Prince's suite, and some of the most famous native shots are all on that roof comfortably hidden behind the loop-holed wall. A Jeypore Shikaree avers that the tiger which the Prince is to shoot will be driven within twenty feet of that house, and that the dangers of the sport are only for those who may chance to be within range of somebody's rifle or in the way of an unexpected leopard. However, the spectators wait, although the day is sultry and the sand is hot. You are not invited to the top of the house; indeed, no ones knows of your whereabouts; and it is too late now to discover yourself, for at any moment the tiger may be driven down, and the rifles of the party behind the parapet open fire.

Driven down, indeed! All over the hills is a noise which might well frighten the boldest beast in the jungle were he here. There is sure to be something, too; since for many days past—three months, I am told—strong wooden cages, with live goats inside them, have been placed on the hills to attract the tigers. How the great growling brutes have rubbed their noses against those hard teak cases; how they have waited till day-light came, and then, sullenly picking up the the stray pieces of flesh which were scattered about the ground, have sought a friendly bush in which to hide themselves from the fierceness of the sun, might be easily told. They are not far off, depend upon it; the increase of shouting on the left bodes the coming of the prey. Suddenly a great rush, followed by a leap—the bound of a frightened animal—is heard, and then a huge tigress is seen close to the house. Close to the house? Not more than twenty feet from it, clearly in sight, ready for the Royal gun. Bang! bang! It may be that the first shot has not hit it, but the second has, for see! the tigress is making for a hillock, and is passing out of sight. She must not escape, however, or the Prince will not kill to-day. Some effort must be made to reach her in her hiding-place, the haven to which in her terror she has fled. So a trusty elephant is brought—an elephant which would dispose of the largest tiger in India in a minute with the greatest possible ease—an elephant which has been in the jungle on such expeditions a score of times before, and that knows as much about tiger-hunting as Major Bradford, the great tiger Shikaree, himself. Up in the howdah, quite out of danger, accompanied by one or two of the finest Jeypore shots, goes the Prince to despatch the wounded tigress. Very cautiously, and making a wide detour, the Prince goes round, till at length he comes opposite his victim, when, with rifle raised, he pours two shots into the struggling brute, and lays her dead. A minute after, and the suite are on the spot to congratulate His Royal Highness. Nor is the little Maharajah behind-hand in his praises. The Prince receives their felicitations graciously, a grand triumphal procession is formed, and back into Jeypore goes the Shahazada with his first victim. That the tigress on being skinned is found to have been the prospective mother of three cubs, is considered a matter for further rejoicing.

A real Indian Durbar has but seldom been seen during our progress through India. For reasons best known to the advisers of the Prince, the gentlemen who had the distribution of the fire-engines, medals, organs, albums, swords, photographs, rings, and snuff-boxes, which comprised the miscellaneous collection on board the "Serapis," thought fit that these delights of the eye should be transferred from the Royal hands to the possession of the recipients in private. We heard occasionally of a Maharajah receiving a gold pin and a walking-stick in his own house; once or twice we witnessed the affixing of a medal in the sight of the crowd, but not often. The stately display of Eastern and Western magnificence was not often achieved, and it was therefore with feelings of pleasure that we looked forward to the promised Durbar at Jeypore.

How it was held may now be narrated.

In the new palace of the Maharajah is a stately apartment, which, according to Indian fashion, is called the Dewan-i-am. Here, at stated intervals, the councils of the Raj are held; here the Rajah dispenses some justice and occasionally a little mercy; here there is a great daïs erected, on which a throne usually stands, and round it meet in solemn conclave the dignitaries of Jeypore. In the evening, long before the tiger-shooting party had returned, there had gathered in this great hall the rajahs, chiefs, sirdars, and head men of the nation, each dressed in his most splendid uniform, wearing the Rajpoot turban of state, and adorned with all the jewellery which he possessed. On the daïs were two thrones; and on either side were six long rows of nobles seated, perhaps in all twelve hundred notable grandees, the Prime Minister of the Maharajah having the first place on the left-hand side of the Heir Apparent. On the right-hand was a row of chairs in which the Prince's suite were to sit. The place was brilliantly lighted; in a gallery in rear of the daïs were such European ladies and gentlemen as desired to witness the ceremony; and in a court-yard into which one end of the room opened was a band of musicians.

It would have been amply worth the while of a stranger to traverse that vast hall and note the costumes of those who were assembled there, what curious swords they carried, what strange shields, what grand arrays of jewels they boasted, and what handsome robes they wore. There were men with such a profusion of gold, in turban and cloak, that it might well have been doubted whether more of the precious metal could, by any possibility, have been added to the needlework. There were some with grand pearl bead work of immense value and singular beauty. Hours might have been spent in a survey of the curious shawls from Cashmere and the far North, the Centre, and the East of India—such cunning needlework as the rich men of the land are most renowned for. But hours could not thus be spent, for the Prince was coming up the steps into the Dewan-i-am, led by the Maharajah—a little, bent man, wearing spectacles, a gold-embroidered cap and gown. Of course, the great assembly received the Prince upstanding, remained so while he took his seat on the daïs at the right hand of the Maharajah, and while his suite flocked in, in no very regular order, and occupied the places assigned them. All sat down when the signal was given, and the Durbar was opened. Then Major Henderson came forward, and accompanied by Mr. Lyall, the Governor-General's Agent for Rajpootana, together with the Resident here, led up, one by one, and introduced to the Prince the principal nobles of the State of Jeypore.

A pretty spectacle was that which we now witnessed. Chiefins in all their magnificence coming forward one after another to the foot of the daïs, handing a card, on which their names were inscribed, to the Resident, and then, when announced, ascending the steps, presenting an offering of a gold piece of money to the Prince, with a low bow, waiting while he touched it, Eastern fashion, and then, with many indications of humility and loyalty, with much patting of the forehead and many bows, retiring backwards and making way for other chiefs. I did not notice that any distinction was made. In coming up the steps they were received by the Prince sitting, and each retired backwards. But when the presentation was over two were called up and presented with a medal by his Royal Highness, a word being said to each indicative of the approval of the Queen of England. I fancied they looked a little puzzled at the ceremony, and wondered whether it conveyed a title such as Mr. John Jones or Mr. William Smith receives when a sword is placed on his shoulders and he is told to rise; but it was a cheap mode of decoration, and was, at any rate, a distinction.

I know that there are those who will contend that this was not a Durbar in the right sense of the word at all. There was one old gentleman whose liver had suffered the variations of an Indian climate for seven-and-twenty years, who was dreadfully irate because the Prince did not take his gold pieces and give something in exchange. But when I suggested that the money —gold mohurs—would have been almost useless to His Royal Highness, even if an attendant had, by the close of the presentation, filled a small bag with them, and that the only equivalent present which the Prince could have made in return would have taken the form of a number of telescopes or concertinas, that old gentleman's wrath took another form, and he declared against the visit and all its belongings. While he was thus inveighing, however, another ceremony was going on, and Lord Alfred Paget was called up, presented to the Maharajah, and wreathed with a garland of flowers; similarly, too, Sir Bartle Frere's neck was adorned, and then a noble went round, accompanied by an attendant, who carried a huge basket of blossoms, and threw a wreath over the necks of the suite and the hussar officers who accompanied them. Then there was some conversation, the band played Brinley Richards' Welsh air, and the Prince, shaking hands with the Maharajah, left the hall for the dining-room.

The scene of the banquet was not artistically beautiful. I have before remarked on the disadvantages and defects of Indian decorative painting. There is a freedom about it, an absence of regard for economy, a lavish waste of colour, which, however satisfactory to the Eastern mind, does not fill the traveller with delight. The ceiling of the "European room," close by, was undoubtedly a great success; but then it had been designed by an Englishman, and if nine-tenths of the chandeliers and lamps in the apartment could have been thrown out of the windows—if a selection could have been made from the musical instruments in the room, comprising a musical snuff-box, an organ, a piano, a harmonium, a whistling mechanical bird, an accordion, and a drum, it would have been still further improved; but to make the banqueting hall look better one would require to take down the ceiling and put up another with only one-hundredth part of the paint upon it. Still, if the room was not tasteful, the table was prettily laid in Russian fashion, and the banquet which followed was not unworthy of it. Much more pleasant still was the arrival of the Maharajah just as the ladies were leaving, and his taking a seat at the right hand of the Prince. Unlike the ruler of Gwalior, he of Jeypore, however, is no speaker; and thus it was that he proposed the healths of the Queen and the Prince successively in one word, drinking a full bumper of champagne to each, and then beaming through his gold spectacles on the assembled company. How the Prince replied is not matter of singular importance. The most notable thing his Royal Highness said was that he thanked his host for giving him the opportunity of shooting his first tiger—a remark which was, of course, heartily applauded by every courtier present.

And then, with cigars and hookahs, a quiet half-hour was spent—comparatively so would, perhaps, be the better expression, for to beguile the time, the Maharajah had ordered in a juggler who had certain eccentricities of no mean order. This worthy could put a decanter of water on his head, and, by the simple movement of his eyebrows, work it round the nape of his neck, over his ears, past his nose, and so up to the apex of the skull once more; and it was a highly entertaining diversion to watch the decanter slowly moving round the edge of that vagrant juggler. Then a gentleman was introduced who, similarly to one at Calcutta, essayed to play two little trumpets with his neck. A kind of "There is no deception, gentlemen" expression pervaded this worthy man's face, and the Maharajah proceeded to explain that this performance was called Nasataranga, and that it was achieved by the swelling of the veins in the player's neck, and thus by the forcible propulsion of air through the tubes of the trumpets. But the player had not counted upon the guests; at any rate, he had not quite expected to meet Dr. Fayrer, for when that gentleman took down a candle from a girandole, and attempted to hold it before the end of one of the trumpets, to see if any air was really blown through, the player, who saw his "occupation gone," resisted, and could only be compelled by a direct order to submit. Whereupon he did so with a very ill-grace; no air came through, and in the end he was pronounced a ventriloquist and an impostor, and told to begone.

All this being happily settled, an adjournment took place to a courtyard, where a tedious Nautch dance took place, amongst the performers being an ancient dame of some fifty summers, whose only qualification appeared to be that her eyes stared more violently, her feet moved more irregularly, and her twirling and jumping were more erratic than anybody else's. However, a native told me that she was the greatest *danseuse* in Jeypore, so I forbore to make further comment. If her dancing was ridiculous, the music was as bad, and so was a performance on musical basins which followed, so that on the whole nobody was particularly sorry when his Royal Highness called for his carriage, and gave the signal for departure.

The Sunday following was spent in a visit to the ruins of Ambair, the Royal party picnicing among the ruins of Jey Singh's ancient city, and visiting the Temple of Silla Deva, where once men were slaughtered, but now only goats; and a very eminent Brahmin sang a sacred song in his loudest and most discordant manner. Next day the Prince departed for Agra once more, this time with a view of proceeding to the Terai, with a portion of his suite, on a three weeks' shooting excursion.

CHAPTER XXXIII.

SCINDIA'S WELCOME.

It was early in 1872 when, one evening, remembered still by all who, coming from the mother country, reside in Gwalior, a distinguished company assembled to dine in the Palace of the Maharajah Scindia. The banquet over, decanters of wine were circulated, glasses filled, and silence procured; whereupon the ruler of the State entered, a huge silver bowl in his right hand, and essayed to make a speech. Its language was Hindostanee, but its subject-matter British. In terms of loyal affection Scindia spoke of the Sovereign to whom he owed allegiance, whose troops had rescued him from the blood-thirsty Tantia Topee, whose representative had restored him to his throne. And then, without pause, he told his hearers how that good Queen's eldest son, once stricken by fever, had at length recovered, and, amid loud shouts, proposed the health and long life of the Prince of Wales. How Sirdir and Chieftain vied with Resident and English official in obeying that call need not now be told. Next morning came the news that Lord Mayo was killed, and all that day minute guns told of Scindia's loyal grief. From that time to this the ruler of Gwalior has been one of the most trusted of the feudatories of the Queen; and that he should receive special recognition at the hands of the Prince was therefore to be expected. At length the long-talked-of Royal visit to his dominion took place.

Looking from my coign of vantage on the back of an elephant. I saw on both sides of the street that, although it yet wanted some hours to the Prince's arrival, the inhabitants were perched in their windows, and gazing complacently into the road. The natives were chatting together, patting their scarfs, adjusting their white turbans, or squatting on their haunches, full of joy at finding themselves so respectably attired, and so unmistakably the observed of all observers. They were in the very van of the procession, too; to the keeping of each had been entrusted a bright silver javelin, and the ladies of Gwalior were looking at them through the blinds of the upper windows, or, more adventurously still, were popping their heads out every now and then, and peering between their fingers at the gallants in the road. What mattered it to them that for seven hours they had to wait in the broiling sun? Was not the approval of these recondite damsels a full reward? If they did not think so, those who followed them, and wore red turbans and long yellow coats, did; for if ever contentment was portrayed, it was on the faces of these last-named owners of ancient matchlocks. They also sat down in the centre of the road, hardly deigning to move when the broad feet of the elephants threatened to annihilate them, willing to do and suffer anything rather than lay down their muskets and flee. A little further on were some scores of camels, all standing two by two in expectation of orders; behind these again were fifty of the Maharajah's horses, all gaily caparisoned and led by servants in uniform. Then there were men carrying red flags, and others with white silk banners; there were more javelin-men, and more who bore matchlocks; then a number of elephants, and after that chieftains and attendants galore. This end of the procession was hard by the old palace of Scindia; its head was scarcely half a mile from the new one just built.

It is not easy to tell you how excited the good people of Gwalior were at all these preparations. They were simply beside themselves with joy at the prospect of seeing the promised show. Apparently they had invited all their friends, too, not charging for good seats as the more practical people of Birmingham or Sheffield would have done, but turning their stores upside down, desiring their friends and acquaintances to come and rejoice in the very best windows they had got. Merry they were beyond a doubt, after the fashion of their kind, sitting closely together, clasping their hands and beaming with silent delight all the day long.

At the new palace itself a different scene was occurring. There the Europeans of the district were taking their places in corridors situate over the grand gateway in expectation of the pageant. Hundreds of native workmen were putting a finishing touch to the interior decorations, hundreds were outside hanging up lamps for illuminations. The building, which was as yet barely finished, looked like nothing so much as Buckingham Palace repainted. From the railings outside to the flagstaff on the roof there was scarcely any difference, only that, in place of the stone quadrangle inside, there was a handsome garden, prettily laid out in European fashion, boasting a splendid fountain and some beautiful marble work. But Buckingham Palace has no such apartment as Scindia's great drawing-room. Upon this the ingenuity of a distinguished gentleman named Fellowes had been wholly exhausted; its Persian carpet, upon which two thousand people might comfortably stand, was of the richest hue and the most costly work; over the back of the gilded chairs hung the rarest cloth of gold; its furniture was of the newest and the best. On the walls were handsome mirrors; all its pillars glistened with gold; the dome-like ceiling, nearly a hundred feet from the floor, was chased with delicate tints and gilt, and if there was a chandelier too many the light was all the brighter. I have not seen a drawing-room so beautiful in India, and cannot call to mind its equal anywhere. Branching away from this were corridors leading to the rooms wherein were gold toilet services, baths of silver, all kinds of contrivances for making life delightful, even to bottles of scent whereof the labels proclaimed that they were "The Prince of Wales' own Bouquet."

HUNTING IN THE TERAI—CROSSING A NULLAH.

How what but a week or two since was an unfinished mass of stone had been converted into this palatial retreat, one could not imagine, unless upon the supposition that the 7,000 workmen who had been employed had worked with quintupled energy, or that Scindia had for a moment or two got hold of the veritable wishing cap. Anyway, there the palace was, with a grand garden in front as well as one in the centre, all the rooms furnished, guards of honour mounted, the mechanical singing birds whistling melodiously on the drawing-room tables, servants all in their places, and nothing wanting except the Prince, then on his way to Gwalior, on the high road. For as to Jummoo, so to Scindia's capital, no railway runs; but some seventy and odd miles have to be traversed by carriages which do not always avoid ruts and holes. The Prince, however, did not suffer from the rugged track; he had a comfortable carriage on light springs, which heeded none of these things: nor, indeed, were we who had to sit in the humbler dakgharry so uncomfortable as when on the rougher road to Jummoo; yet seventy-two miles, in the morning by horse conveyances, is not the happiest prelude to an elephant ride of seven miles, and it was well that Scindia's palace boasted armchairs and lounges in plenty for the weary ones who were hourly expected—the more so as a State dinner was fixed for the evening, at which the Prince must be present. Gradually the day declined, the ladies and gentlemen in the corridors took tea, the lamps which were placed on every line of the palace were lit, darkness came on, and still the procession waited. At length a sound of cannon was heard, and presently the shouting of crowds announced that the Prince was really at hand; by the light of inumerable torches we could discern the moving mass of colour as it pressed towards the palace gates and waited the approach of the Shahazada.

Nor was there now long to wait. The wind blowing on the verandah brought with it the sound of tom-tom and reed, of trumpets and of cheers. A long line of lights, too, was seen approaching. The Queen's son was very near. On came the procession; the javelin-men, preceded by players upon the instruments which the Hindoo loves, holding their spears aloft in the air, and moving with no unconsidered shuffle, but a stately tramp! and on came also their companions with their matchlocks, the camels and the horses moreover, the steeds prancing just as the stately animals do when in an Eastern wedding procession they precede the bridegroom. Nor were the men with the banners less conscious of the dignity of their position. No matter to them that the evening was advancing; it was the first time in their lives that they had had so much honour. The white sahibs up in the corridor might be impatient, but they were not. The palace courtyard would end their dignity, and they were in no hurry to reach it. But the Royal elephants must come on, and at last they were in sight, each bearing its own lanterns, and moving with majestic step. On the first of them—in a bright silver howdah, upon which the lights of the torches flashed—sat the Prince, on the right hand of the Maharajah, with General Sir Richard Daly behind, as interpreter-in-chief. And following these were the suite of the Prince and that of the Ruler of Gwalior, all forming a grand array of distinguished personages. The 10th Hussars, moreover, were on either side of them; in rear were more bands, far-extending masses of cavalry, and behind all, the surging astonished crowd, hand in hand, pressing on, and wondering why the great Maharajah should thus receive the Prince Sahib. Then sounded out the National Anthem played by an English band; then English ladies waved their handkerchiefs and English gentlemen their hats; then the Prince graciously returned the welcome accorded him by a band of countrywomen and countrymen, and so passed on into the palace garden, dismounted from his elephant, was led by Scindia to the Royal apartments, and then left to preside at the feast which followed.

That India is held by the merest handful of white people is sufficiently clear to all who have travelled over its length and breadth, and, indeed to those who have not. But never was the singular nature of our position so clearly demonstrated as when we saw Scindia's army drawn up in review order under the shadow of the fort and close by his palace. We had been told that as a soldier the Maharajah has few superiors; Sir William Mansfield had years ago wished that all our brigadiers were the equal of the enterprising Mahratta; but it remained for us to see the pitch of perfection to which a native Prince could bring his troops. At Cashmere we had seen thousands of soldiers, but they were little better than barbarians; in the South, the troops of the Nizam had failed to impress those of us who entered Hyderabad territory with anything approaching awe; we had yet to see the Gwalior army, and judge of it. A great surprise awaited us.

It was scarcely seven o'clock when, on mounting our elephants and proceeding to the parade ground, we found the army of Scindia drawn up in review order. Five strong battalions, numbering quite a thousand a piece, were in the front line; in rear were three regiments of cavalry and four batteries of artillery—as admirable a brigade as could be desired in point of numbers. Ten minutes later Scindia himself, accompanied by a trumpeter, arrived on the ground, and was received by his suite, already in front of the troops. He had scarcely taken his place before guns announced that the Prince was near, whereupon Scindia went to meet his distinguished visitor, and very quickly conducted him into the field. I am afraid to say how many spectators there were. The thousands who had turned out at this early hour moved constantly from one part of the ground to the other, their gay turbans and bright dresses mingling till they looked like the colours which a well-filled kaleidoscope shows. The English were mostly on elephants, of which there were great numbers, and the tinkling of the bells which hung from the howdahs added to the brightness and pleasantness of the scene.

I need not tell you that the Prince went round the troops, and closely inspected them. Scindia follows European usages too closely to permit of such a custom being broken. It is of the march past I would speak. We had already heard of the excellence of the Maharajah's artillery, and were consequently glad to see it preparing to come by. But what will be thought at home when it is known that to the sound of "The British Grenadiers," played by a band just opposite the flagstaff, a battery of horse artillery came by, equal in drill, precision, and appearance to some of our best troops in the A brigade? Work on the "pivot system," indeed? Here was a battery which could go over the ground in a manner which would put the best artillery in France or Germany to shame. Those who in 1874 saw the gunners that Von Moltke could show went home disappointed. There was nc one disappointed here. Old soldiers who had seen a score of fights, and whose home was the parade ground, ejaculated, Beautiful! and Scindia looked proud as he left their head and took his place by the Prince's side. And yet another battery was close at hand, almost if not quite so good, the six guns going by as one, every horseman in his place, every sword in a line. Nor were the two bullock batteries which followed with heavier guns at all to be despised. The men marched past as well as the best troops in the world, and I saw nothing at Delhi to beat the drivers. Scindia may not have known why he sent his artillery past first; he may have only imitated the English, because he considered them the best models to copy; but he certainly opened the review in a way which surprised everybody present. Shall I add that his artillerymen wore a uniform exactly like the undress of the Royal regiment in England, and that at a very short distance it would have been impossible to distinguish them from European gunners? Then came the cavalry, three regiments, each containing four sqadrons, the first two being hussars, with the pivot men carrying lances, and the last lancers entirely. On they swept with marvellous precision, their officers wearing the white English helmet and the golden red-striped sash, as do the gentlemen who carry her Majesty's commission. I could see nothing in point of uniform or movement to distinguish these men from the best Punjabee cavalry we had been shown a few days before by Lord Napier. The most captious critic could see nothing to exercise his skill upon; the regiments were perfect. I for one could certainly find no fault with their movements to the tune of "Annie Lisle." The Queen's Guards may claim the tune, but even they would scarcely grudge their regimental air to such soldierly men.

But if we admired Scindia's cavalry and artillery, our praise was by no means decreased when the infantry came by. We could perceive them forming up on our left, we could see the Pioneers preceding them, we could hear the "British Grenadiers." We were fain to cheer loudly as, with bayonets in exact line, they came on with a steadiness that our best troops could not surpass. I have seen Chasseur battalions go past in far less soldierly fashion; I have even witnessed parades at Aldershot reviews that I should not have liked a severe critic to attend; but these native regiments could afford to defy inspection. The finest battalion, moreover, wore the English dress, helmet and all. I noticed that they were well shod, and that their uniforms had been carefully looked to. Even their comrades who had only the English forage cap elicited loud exclamations of praise; they could but be admired. And when they had all gone past there was but one opinion about them all—unqualified admiration. Of the gallop past I need say no more than that it was excellent.

The main interest now centred in a sham fight, and the troops were instantly divided into two equal portions, the commander-in-chief holding a ridge in front of Gwalior, while

Scindia prepared to attack it. I am not prepared to say that the result was not known beforehand. He would be a bold subject who would presume to defeat his master in presence of a Royal visitor, and a disloyal one into the bargain. But if it was arranged that Scindia should be the conquerer in his own dominion, there was, at any rate, the opportunity afforded of seeing how the troops could work in the field. There are those of us who have been present at some funny spectacles at Aldershot, who have seen batteries disposed of, and positions taken in a way which would have made us rub our eyes and wonder what it all meant, if we had not known that the whole thing was intended simply for a pretty show to amuse some potential visitor. Do none of us remember the famous battle in the Long Valley, when the Czar of All the Russias was amused by impossible cavalry charges, and wonderful artillery defeats? Let us not be too harsh upon Scindia, who wanted to please the Prince and exhibit his soldiers. At any rate, he hid his men well behind some excellent cover, and if the bullocks which drew the heavy cannon into position were exposed to rifle-fire within a few hundred yards, what of that? Do not our friends the Germans do likewise with their horses? I am told that all the men we saw were armed with old percussion-cap muskets. If so the skirmishers which appeared on the right of Scindia's enemy fired very quickly, and had better not be trusted with the Snider. Worse practice has been often made with breach-loading weapons. And as for the artillery, it may have been placed in peril now and then unnecessarily, as it moved forward to support the attack. General Lysons could tell you of a certain opponent of his who once upon Fox Hill exposed his guns in similar fashion; and Colonel Basden, at Delhi, the other day, not only endangered but actually lost his battery. Altogether there was not a great deal to find fault with. A cavalry charge at the far left of the enemy was *magnifique*, even if it were not *la guerre*, and the infantry came over the ground in admirable style, although in ordinary fighting it would probably have appeared there for the very last time.

We all knew Scindia would win, and so we pressed our elephants forward, keeping well in a line with the guns, which rattled merrily and quite woke up such sleepy people as still remained in bed within a radius of three miles. Indeed, it was hard to persuade oneself that Tantia Topee was not in yonder wood, making ready to run away, as he did in the days now happily gone. Fortunately that person is hanged, his followers, who learnt to run after their leader, have moved at such a speed that they will never be found again, and Scindia is in no dread that the result of any action he may fight will deprive him of his throne or his palace. With which cheering knowledge the efforts of the enemy to stop an advance at any point were regarded with such complacency as could be accorded by hungry men and women, who felt that the more the action was prolonged the longer a much-wanted breakfast was delayed, and eagerly desired the commander-in-chief to throw up the sponge, hoist the white flag, or surrender, in the politest Hindostanee, to the Maharajah. Some such thought appears to have occurred to the commander-in-chief himself, for suddenly he sent word to his batteries to waste powder no more, to his battalions to pile their arms, to his buglers to sound cease firing, and to the occupiers of the ridge to go home. Whereupon all who occupied the howdahs blessed his loyal discretion, and forthwith made for home to recount the events of the morning and prepare for the levee, which presently took place in the drawing-room I have described. Meanwhile the Prince galloped up to Scindia, complimented him on the appearance of his men, made a neat little speech to the soldiers also, and so departed to the palace himself.

CHAPTER XXXIV.

SCENES IN GWALIOR.

A day or two later on it was my lot to come upon a happy valley—not that which Rasselas and Dinarbas so rashly left, but the happy valley of Gwalior Fort—not much larger than the crater of Vesuvius, situated in the very heart of the famous rock which stands in the centre of Gwalior's dominions. On all sides but one it was bounded by thickly foliaged trees; but on that referred to there was hard stone, carved by the Jain worshippers of old into grotesque idol figures; and in the middle of it was a deep well. From the eminence of the fort it looked like a huge trap into which you might be decoyed for the sake of the umbrageous shade with which it abounded, only to lose your life in the almost hidden water below.

It was early in the morning, some hours before the Prince paid his visit to the fort, that I started from the Residency, where I was the guest of Colonel Hutchinson. A lofty rock, starting suddenly out of a plain, surmounted by battlements, some four hundred feet high, a mile long, and in some places half as broad—such was the place to which we were directed. Had we gone straight to the foot of the pathway which leads from the native town to the top of the hill, and at which spot two elephants were waiting to convey us to the summit, our task would have been comparatively light. But my companion was an Indian archæologist of note, a member of the Council of Orientalists, and he had heard that on the outer scrap of the rock, on the eastern side, were some Jain figures, compared with which all that had been seen by other travellers faded into insignificance: and at his suggestion I agreed to scale the side and inspect the sculptures.

Of the Gwalior caverns, and their carvings, few know any thing, and none very much. It may be that the work of exploration has not been to the taste of travellers. To reach them you must ford a somewhat rapid, though fortunately narrow, river, and then climb up the precipitous face of the rock till you are within a hundred feet of the top. Such a labour on a broiling day is not seductive, and few have taken the trouble to attempt it. In crossing the river we were fortunate. A pony was offered us, and one or other would probably have mounted and essayed to ride, when, without warning, the intractable beast rushed into the stream, and, lying down in the water, refused to move This settled the question, and we went over on foot forthwith. How we clambered up, slipping here and tumbling there, how we penetrated bushes, and clutched at stumps of trees, need not be dilated upon. At length we stood on a ledge which faced the caves and images, and were free to inspect them.

From the point where we stood we could count a score or so of sculptured figures, each nearly forty feet high. Some were sitting down, and some were standing up; they were most of them chipped and broken; but the Elephanta Caves had nothing like or equal to them, and their counterpart is nowhere to be found. I am almost afraid to say whom they represented. A guide-book, written by the learned but destructive Baber, said Parisnaut, but my archæological friend triumphantly proved, by a close argument of which I did not understand a single proposition, that they were somebody else, and I am content to leave him master of the field. I believe that the identity of these same images for a long time exercised the minds and jeopardised the friendship of at least half a dozen of the most erudite archæologists in England, and I therefore leave it in uncertainty. All I can say is that, if Parisnaut was half as ugly, his countenance would have told sadly against him in the Old Bailey dock.

But the gods themselves were not the only things worthy of

note. The carving which surrounded them was as marvellous as the forty-feet giants themselves. Round their heads were shields, over which serpents gazed with perceptible awe. Under their feet were animals of all kinds, while indescribable creatures were represented as wandering about in a purposeless but very palpable manner; and at intervals of every twenty feet or so were hollows, into which we penetrated, and found steps leading up into the rock, conducting us face to face with more divine representations; while here and there we came to a recess in the wall, wherein was found a god or goddess prone, with feet high in the air, for the devout to worship. Yet funniest of all was the admixture of Mohammedan shrines, with the Hindoo deities. Four steps only from a goddess who boasted the thickest pair of lips I ever saw, and was squatted upon a very bad imitation of a cobra, was the tomb of a very devout follower of the Prophet, with the convential ostrich-egg hanging over it, and a very bright gold cloth immediately upon it And undei the very shade of the most able-bodied god in the collection sat a Mohammeden fakir, who was just then engaged in superintending the construction of a model of a tabout, in anticipation of the great Mohuram festival now close at hand, not ten feet away from a Brahmin devotee.

There was the greatest possible contrast between the two. Had the Mohammedan harmonised with the place he was in, he should have been covered with mud, and should have whined loudly for backsheesh. He was quite clean, and if his beard was unclipped, as becomes a follower of the Prophet, his hair was trimmed. I should think he had washed his face that very morning. The only thing in which he resembled his Hindoo brother was in the anxious way in which he looked for a present at the end. Perhaps he thought the Brahminical fakir had quite enough clay on his face for any two people; perhaps he had some idea of the comfort of religion. He did not seem to lead a life of great self-abnegation. In one of the caves close by were his wife and children; the chupatty he was eating appeared to me to be as well made as the undivided attention of an otherwise unemployed man could make it, and he had as toothsome a curry as you would get at the Madras Club in his brass dish close by. The only thing he denied himself was work; he preferred to sit on a broken monument in the sun, eat and sleep, sleep and eat—only varying this programme by holding out his hand for the alms of the faithful. The serenity of his existence was never perturbed by anxiety for employment; with the exception of occasionally taking a bath he did absolutely nothing. The Hindoo was much livelier. The fates had apparently not been so kind to him. He had no chupatty, and I looked in vain for his curry; he certainly had no wife, and I should say that he had no cave either. Here he was, the nearest relation to the gods on the rock—a most estimable person, probably as objectionable an object as could be seen in a day's march, and yet he had not even a piece of betel-nut to chew. Why was he thus neglected? Nobody could say. He made noise enough to attract the attention of people half a mile off, yet, apparently, they left him to do as best he could. If this state of things were to continue, he would have to cease to be holy and actually take to labour. Is there no Hindoo Missionary Society to assist so pious a fakir?

We left him and clambered from ledge to ledge, inspecting the wonderful sculptures of the place. Most of them had been sadly mutilated by the Mahommedans; some of the images had lost all signs of serpents' heads, some of them were noseless, many had parted with both hands and feet. Yet here they stood, monuments of the work of the seventh century—a permanent protest against the supposed barbarism of that age. The execution was, in fact, most elaborate—as fine as any in India, which is the highest compliment that can be paid them.

Quitting the examination of the caves, we now descended the sides of the rock, and prepared to enter the fort by what is facetiously styled the "road." I believe the Capel Curig ascent to Snowdon has been called one before now, but why such a name should be given to the narrow pathway leading to the top of Galior Fort which rises one inch in four in most places —even more than that in some—and is so narrow in parts that two elephants can hardly pass each other on it, I cannot say. However, the fort had to be visited; and not only the Prince but all who followed him mounted to the howdahs, and presently were rising foot by foot at the rate of about five yards to the minute.

I am bound to say that the procession was not a pleasant one. Occasionally an elephant would stop, and partly turn round, and there was always the possibility that one of them might take fright and run backwards, in which event some of the party would have had an unpleasant and unsatisfactory adventure. However, at last we reached the top, and entering the narrow gates very carefully, were carried into the fort. The Happy Valley was behind us, a Jain temple before us; there was a Mohammedan mosque, now used as a powder magazine, close by, and not very far off was a temple built in the style common to Southern India, but of which there is scarcely another specimen in the Northern and Central Provinces. Under the guidance of Major Gordon and the rest of the officers of the 63rd, these curiosities were inspected till evening came on.

We were in a huge enclosure bounded on every side by a wall and a precipice; below lay the town of Gwalior, the Maharajah's Palace, and the English cantonments at Morar. Whichever way we looked the panorama was magnificent, and extended for miles. We could see the remains of the batteries which the English made when Sir Hugh Rose drove the rebels out of the fort and forced them to take shelter in the jungle. We could descry the battle-field on which Tantia Topee suffered his heaviest defeat. The walls themselves were in ruins, an agreement having been entered into with Scindia that they were not to be repaired; but through their crevices and over their sides were views of landscape such as Turner would have loved, and several of our party stayed to sketch. Unfortunately there was no one in the Royal suite capable of explaining to his Royal Highness the peculiarities of the buildings he saw, or much that is interesting might have been evolved. As it was, the most attractive place appeared to be the mess-room of the hospitable regiment which holds the place; and an embrasure about which there was a legend that in the early days of British occupation the soldiers used to smuggle in spirits from below by means of a rope and a basket at this spot and so managed to become dreadfully tipsy. Legends of Jain and Brahminical temples there were none related—not even the history of the Musjid was told; and as to learning from any competent person why old temples had been patched in places with older stones taken no one knew whence, that was, of course, impossible Still, it was pleasant to wander about amongst the ruins, and to note the wonderful stone carvings which lay in heaps everywhere, or still remain in the places where they were put in times of which we have but a very dim historical record. Indeed, a whole week, instead of two or three hours only, might have been profitably spent in examining the figures of gods and goddesses, portrayed in almost every attitude and action. But the time was limited; the grandest dinner of the visit waitep in the Fuhlbagh below, and a hurried inspection was all we could make.

It is not likely that ever Gwalior will give us trouble. Its ruler knows too well, and those who come after him are likely to learn, that the English are the best of masters. But, at the same time, prudence would suggest that it should always have at least a battery of artillery in it, which is not the case just now; that its walls should be restored and bastions erected, so that its permanent possession should always be a matter of certainty, and, at the same time, the curious temples might in some way be preserved as valuable records of an almost forgotten past.

But the State banquet which was given the Prince still remains in my memory as the grandest and most memorable feature of the entertainment which Scindia provided for the Queen's son. For reasons of space, or rather the want of it, only three of those of us who have followed the Prince's movements in the East were invited to the dinner. Scindia's dining-room is by no means commensurate with the wants of so hospitable a potentate, and a hundred and fifty covers were all that could be laid. But if the guests were comparatively few, the occasion was none the less important It had been announced that although Scindia could not, as became a good Hindoo, eat with us who profess to be Christians, his Highness would come into the banqueting hall immediately after dinner. How the feast therefore progressed, what courses and what viands were produced, it boots not to tell. The Prince—who had on his right hand the wife of General Rothway, and on his left the daughter of Colonel Hutchinson, the Resident—presided, till the cloth was removed, when a stir at the door behind the Prince told of the advent of Scindia.

I have purposely refrained from describing the ruler of Gwalior, waiting till such time as he should appear in striking contrast to those around him. The banquet brought that opportunity. Habited in white, the Star of India on his breast, with a yellow Mahratta turban on his head, a pleasant-looking gentleman of some forty-five years appeared in the hall-entrance, accompanied by a single attendant, his Prime Minister or Dewan. There could be no mistake as to who the stranger was, his quiet but regal manner proclaiming him at once, and the Prince, who by this time was aware of the presence of Scindia, jumped up, seized his Highness by both hands, and placed him at once in the post of honour, the seat at his own right hand.

Immediately upon this General Daly came up, and, taking a chair immediately behind the two illustrious personages, began to translate their respective compliments.

It was easy to see that the Maharajah was almost overcome with delight and excitement. There was, indeed, some reason. That morning his troops had displayed as fine an appearance as any in this part of the world, receiving the highest encomiums and he was now in the chief place at a table round which were gathered a more illustrious assembly than he had ever before met. For a few minutes he remained talking to his guest, while his Royal Highness lit a cigar—the signal for all present to smoke, for the ladies had by this time retired. Then up jumped Scindia, and spoke a few words to Sir Richard Daly, who at once interpreted as follows: "May it please your Royal Highness and gentlemen, his Highness the Maharajah wishes me to declare that he feels profoundly grateful to the Queen for allowing her son to come to Gwalior to see him; that he desires to express his profound loyalty to her Majesty, and to add how deeply attached he is to the English Throne—he calls upon you to drink the health of the Queen." Of course all present responded, but somehow or other there was a hitch—somebody gave a signal to the band, and the National Anthem effectually stopped all attempt at a cheer. But Scindia was not disheartened, and he was up again immediately afterwards with a bumper of champagne in his hand. This time he spoke audibly in Hindostanee. His voice was tremulous, however, with emotion, and he palpably shook with excitement. "Gentlemen," he said, "I am delighted to see his Royal Highness the Shahazada (Queen's son) here to-night. I am proud that he has come to visit me, and deeply sensible of the high honour he has done me. I wish him a long life and much happiness, and I sincerely hope that the voyage home may be a prosperous one. Gentlemen drink with me the health of the Prince of Wales." He sank down in his chair and drained his goblet, whereat everybody else did the same, and Brinley Richards' air was played.

It was now the turn of the Prince to speak, and he did his part well. Everybody upstanding, his Royal Highness, turning towards Scindia, said: "I wish to call upon all present to drink to the health of the Maharajah. I am delighted at what I have seen here, and at being able to visit Gwalior. I appreciate the kindness and hospitality of the Maharajah, and I shall not fail to convey to her Majesty the Queen the loyal sentiments he has uttered. Gentlemen, let us drink this toast in the English fashion."—ejaculating which, the Prince bowed to his host, and, waving his glass, led the cheering himself. Again and again was that call responded to, for Scindia's honest face warranted it, and his hospitality had gained the friendship of everybody. Five loud hurrahs were, in fact, shouted out before the company sat down, and they were only ended then because the Prince himself was tired of cheering. There was no formal attempt at response—that was needless. But Scindia bowed his acknowledgments, and then, rising to go, was conducted by the Prince to a drawing-room, whereupon he threw a garland of flowers over the neck of his Royal Highness, and then went to the door accompanied by the Prince and nearly the entire company. A salute from the fort proclaimed the departure, and thus this pleasant episode ended.

The festivities shortly after concluded with an impromptu dance, and then a number of us entered dakgharries and spent the night in rumbling and tumbling over the road which leads from Gwalior to Agra.

CHAPTER XXXV.

HUNTING IN THE JUNGLE.

For reasons best known to themselves, some of the advisers of the Prince decided that none of the special correspondents of the London press should accompany him into the Terai or to Nepaul, Sir Jung Bahadoor's very courteous invitation notwithstanding. However, there was no difficulty in visiting the jungle alone, even without the firman of that eccentric purveyor of Royal amusements, Sir Bartle Frere, and I am consequently enabled to give you some idea of what kind of country it was over which the Prince shot, and in which he spent some three weeks of his time in India. I may premise this by saying, that only a few of the Royal suite accompanied the Prince into this, the wildest portion of his tour, and that Sir Bartle Frere, who, was present at the less dangerous "Sports in Cashmere," excused himself from the more manly sports of the jungle and went to Peshawur. Similarly Canon Duckworth, whom we all greatly respected, went to the frontier also, and one or two others chose different courses; so that only a portion of those who had figured in Royal processions through cities and towns were present when the more serious work of ferreting out the tiger in his lair was undertaken.

Perhaps it is well that I should at once conduct you to the frontier of Nepaul, which is cut off from British dominion proper by the river Sarda. This stream is doubtless at some periods of the year a torrent of what Mr. Disraeli would designate "high consideration." When the rains swell it out, it flows down grandly and swiftly, and there is no doubt about its claims to respect. When we saw it, however, its right to admiration was not so well proved. The nullah in which it runs was almost devoid of water; it was a sluggish, hesitating stream, with just as much water as would suffice to raise it beyond the rank of a brook. At a rough guess its depth might be fixed at about six feet in the centre; and it was about twenty feet across. Here it was, then, that the Prince first entered Nepaulese territory. In front of him ran the great Himalaya range, the chief among the mountains in sight being the stately Dhwalaghiri. Time was when this great sugarloaf peak, covered as it is with snow, was accounted the highest in the world, and accordingly reverenced. But long-headed irreverent mathematicians have since then made calculations, and, despite all remonstrance, have installed Mount Everest as queen of hills. Still the huge eminence before you as you cross the Sarda is not to be despised. Twenty-eight thousand feet above the level of the sea, it towers aloft beyond any other rival within many leagues, and it were well worth the journey to its base to see its cloud-capped top and its snowy sides.

Nor can it be considered as a valuable gem in an unworthy setting; for wherever the eye turns rich verdure, great thick forests, and tall elephant grass, higher than the howdah in which you sit, is seen. One would as soon think of looking for a needle in a haystack as a tiger here, and, indeed the search would be about as fruitless, were it not that experience has shown the way by which the brutes can be reached. Place but a single torch to the base of a bunch of grass and instantly the air is full of smoke. With a loud crackle and roar the prairie burns wildly, leaving here and there a patch unconsumed. Thither have fled tigers, leopards, wild boars, bears, and all other kinds of game, and now your only requirement is a steady elephant and a sure rifle. For these jungles are by no means the peaceful places their appearance at first sight denotes. Enter any one of the little villages which dot the plain, and without much trouble you may almost invariably see the marks of the lord of the Indian forest. Some cow which has strayed a few feet from the huts is shown you, its neck marked by the four canine teeth only of the strong beast which has killed it, and purposes to return when night falls to eat it. Occasionally the skull may be found smashed by the huge forearm of the tiger, but that is not often. One terrible bite and all is over; there is no time for resistance or struggle. Even the thorn hedge by which all villages are surrounded has been unavailing to save the feeble victim. Nepaulese tigers are not to be baulked of their prey by any such device. They care no more for thorn hedges than they do for the masonry pillars which are close to the river, and mark off Nepaulese from British territory. Why should they? They are almost as numerous as the half-clad, half-starved people themselves, and much more intelligent. This, then, is the region to which the Prince went with much ceremony.

Of course Sir Jung Bahadoor met him, and in the name of the Maharajah presented a flowery address; equally, of course, the Prince replied in pleasant terms. There were very naturally references to the Mutiny, and to the services of the Nepaulese Government in those troublesome times; there were promises of future loyalty on the one side, and continued friendship on the other. Then came a review, in which Sir Jung Bahadoor's troops, drawn up in line, acquitted themselves much in the same way as the soldiers of the Maharajah of Cashmere, and then the formal reception was over. But the pleasures of the trip had only just begun. As a loyal and dutiful subject of the Queen, Sir Jung Bahadoor had determined to give her eldest son some of that pleasurable excitement which every true sportsman so dearly loves, and to this end had organized a grand hunt which should cover all that part of the jungle which contained the largest number of tigers.

I have already told you what efforts the Maharajah of Jeypore made to attract the wild game of his district to the neighbourhood of his capital; it is only fair to add that the Maharajah of Nepaul had more successfully exerted himself. All the means he could devise were put in motion, all the tigers he could drive into a good position for the Royal rifle were driven up, and all the elephants he had were placed at the service of the Prince. One unhappy result was arrived at through these very precautions. As a general rule this vast mass of elephants so intimidated the tigers that they absolutely refused to move, and were shot where they crouched for cover. Very generally the wretched animals were pointed out to the Prince, who forthwith fired at them at a safe but certain distance and so killed them. Once, however, a tiger charged his Royal Highness' elephant. Up it sprang, well nigh into the howdah in which the Prince was standing; the elephant turned its flank; the Mahout was frightened, and there was for a moment some peril. But getting into the howdah is a very different matter—for a tiger—from climbing on to the side of the elephant, and it is questionable whether the infuriated beast would, after all, have done any very great damage. However, the Prince who had plenty of rifles at hand, very fortunately had presence of mind sufficient to fire into the tiger's face, and so put an end to all further doubts by killing the wretched animal.

On another occasion His Royal Highness was present at the entangling of some wild elephants in the Nepaul jungle. But this is a sport which has been so frequently described that I need do no more than allude to it here. Generally the hunters returned at the close of the day with what in England would be called a good bag; and once the Prince of Wales shot six tigers before he came back to camp. At first, camp etiquette prevailed to a greater extent than afterwards, and no one but the Prince was supposed to shoot; but after a while this was forgotten, and very often the members of the Royal suite shot more than their master.

Useless is it to attempt to chronicle the doings of the Nepaul hunting party, for what they achieved was done with the aid of resources which were never before afforded to sportsmen, and possibly never will be again. More interesting by far is it to me to recall the delightful mornings I spent in the Himalayas, hard by Gungootra and Jumnootra, the frequent views of the land of perpetual snow, the vast expanse of mountain land, which spreading towards Thibet may be seen from the hill stations of the north of India. To such as may visit our empire of the East in times yet to come, I would recommend a trip to the hills, in preference to anything else I can think of in connection with my visit to the far East.

CHAPTER XXXVI.

ALLAHABAD AND ITS SIGHTS.

Allahabad, which was one of the last places the Prince visited, the capital of the North-west Provinces of India, is no unimportant city. If it has nothing else to recommend it to the pious Hindoo, it boasts the undying sacred tree, to worship which thousands of religious people have travelled thousands of miles and have given thousands of rupees. As an ardent admirer of the constant circulation of money, I regret to say that the object of reverence is in great adversity just now; that rupees are likely to be brought to its roots no longer; that the indefatigable priests whose business and pleasure alike it is to conduct the ceremonies which experience has shown are best fitted for such a tree are in great dread lest the services should cease for very lack of faithful worshippers; and that, in short, the famous underground temple of Allahabad Fort is in a very fair way to be shut up altogether. The cosmopolitan religionist, the lover of all kinds of worship, will, perchance, ask why this calamity overhangs so sacred a shine. Let me relate.

Many, many years ago, so far back that no one even guesses at the date, an exceptionally devout man, whose dwelling was below ground, discovered in his cave a tamarind tree which, although it never pierced the upper crust of the earth, flourished in the darkness below. He did not keep the knowledge to himself; on the contrary, he disseminated it among his acquaintances and friends; and as in those good old days there were no uncomfortable sceptics, his cave became shortly a very holy place. I do not think that tamarinds were ever supposed to grow upon that wonderful tree; the only thing the fakir urged was that shoots, delicate young green shoots, came out every spring on that recondite log, and that their appearance was the work of a highly respectable deity. Still, that was surely sufficient; it was a perpetual yearly miracle. Who that hoped for salvation, provided he were rich enough, would fail to procure one of those wondrous shoots? Besides, was not the very fort itself built close to the confluence of the sacred Ganges and the almost equally sacred Jumna? Could not the sandy yellow stream which flows from Gungootra be actually seen from the walls of the citadel as it crossed the flood of the river from Jumnootra? It undoubtedly was a fortuitous and fortunate concurrence of events which should take the pilgrim to Benares, to the golden temple and the burning ghaut; but, failing that, no journey could be more profitable than the one which should bring the devotee to the junction of the rivers and the sacred tree.

The fact was recognised. For hundreds of years the faithful from Madras and the Himalayas, from Calcutta and Bombay, from the other side of the Great Desert, and even from Ceylon, came to do Poojah in the cave and buy a sprig of the tree. Very obligingly the most pious fakirs of the district united to assist at the worship. They cut out the cave with great care, they collected the idols of all sorts and conditions of Hindoo men, and put them up in suitable places; they made, in fact, all kinds of arrangements to please everyone who might chance to appear. Did a Jain come hither, there was the well-known figure of him to adore; was Parbati the deity of the visitor, she was to be found in a most comfortable corner without the slightest difficulty; Kali of the black face, Hanaman with the monkey's tail, Silla Deva, Shiva, Vishnu, and Brahma, all were there; so that the visitor had ample and unrestrained choice. Little wonder then that the shrine was popular, or that devotees were numerous.

But reverses of fortune come to all, and the sacred tamarind tree, the cave, and the priests proved no exception to the rule. A military Pharaoh who knew not the Fakir Joseph who lived in the cave came to Allahabad Fort, and without any hesitation pronounced the tree a swindle. "It is not," rejoined the Fakir. "We shall see," replied the Major, and he forthwith gave orders that when the next spring time came no tree trunk ready to sprout should be allowed to pass the gates of the fort. Nevertheless, the priests were triumphant; the Major presently found them in full possession of a live tree and surrounded by thousands of congratulating Hindoos, who rejoiced exceedingly at the continued miracle. Still the Major was not to be conquered; he made fierce inquisition, and then found that a venal sergeant of the guard had, in consideration of the sum of fifty rupees, allowed a fresh tree to be passed into the fort in the middle of the night. Then began the troubles of the priests once more, and since that day they have continued, for, with the additional precautions taken, their efforts to substitute a fresh tamarind have been frustrated, and the old trunk, which sprouted so satisfactorily last year, shows no more shoots this spring than if it had been dead a century.

Allahabad, then, is celebrated, if for nothing else, for the possession of this once prosperous but now fallen shrine; it is, however, notable for much more. Not only was it a favourite residence of Akbar, but it was here that Nana Sahib held his court in 1857. Now, however, instead of being the headquarters of law-breakers, it is the chosen seat of law-makers and administrators, the fountain of justice for the whole of the North-West. To it come the litigants of the province, and how numerous they are those can estimate who know how fond of law Hindoos are, and how discontented and troublesome forty millions of such suitors can be.

Entering the courts of justice, you find five or six Judges, presided over by Sir Robert Stewart, the Chief Justice. Of these legal gentlemen two are, very fortunately, barristers, who, in consideration of a display of ability and fitness at home, have been sent out to India; the others are civilians. In the first court, Sir Robert and one of his brethren are hearing an appeal which may be taken as a fair sample of the cases which employ them all the year round. To an eye unaccustomed to Oriental courts the scene is peculiar. No one wears a wig, not even the chief himself. Nor have all the barristers gowns! they, indeed, are about as motley a group as may easily be found in India. Seated at a long table in the well of the court, they represent the natives of the country in more senses than one. The one at the extreme right, as you sit on the raised daïs appropriated to the Judges, is a Mohammedan, very admirably attired in a brown striped turban, a dingy yellowish green gown, and cummerbund; he has neither rings on his fingers nor shoes on his toes, and as he stands up to speak, barrister of large practice though he is, his naked feet have to meet the boards. Next to him is an English pleader, in gown and bands. A Bengalee Baboo, with the hat so well known to all who have visited Calcutta, and long, black cloak, is third; then a Hindoo *pur et simple*, with white turban, drab petticoat, and naked feet. A Mohammedan, attired exactly like his English brethren, gown, bands, and all, is the fifth; and a half-caste, or Portuguese, the last.

Just as their appearance is eminently characteristic, so is the case which they are debating. A Hindoo lady long since defunct lent various sums of money to a native gentleman also gathered to his fathers. She and he both being dead, what more natural, according to Hindoo usage, than that her descendant should claim from his that the lady had actually lent more than was originally supposed, and that therefore, the borrower's heirs were liable for more than they had reckoned upon. And what more natural either than that the other side should vigorously dispute the matter, and bring up just as many witnesses ready to swear anything as the plaintiffs had contrived to produce? All this being eminently in accord with the customs and practices of the enlightened people over whom we rule in India, it may be justly inferred that long practice has made them very perfect, and that to dismember the case from its intricacies would require all the legal acumen of the most clear-sighted Judges.

Thus it is that you find after the Mohammedan owner of the striped turban has finished his statement that an exhaustive argument begins on the meaning of some particular word in a kind of agreement which is produced. "The word *Ar* in this document," says the Mohammedan, "means mortgage, and is intended to convey the wish of the borrower to give up his land if he could not pay his debts." "No such thing," rejoins one of the Hindoo barristers, "*Ar* means nothing of the sort." "What does it mean then?" asks the Chief-Justice; whereupon a number of dictionaries are brought in, and the barristers are soon all immersed in philological research. "My dictionary gives '*Ar*, a ladle used in a sugar factory,'" says Mr. Justice Pearson. "Mine calls it 'a goad,'" ejaculated Sir Robert Stuart. "It is a line drawn across the forehead, my lord," says the Baboo barrister, "and probably refers in some distant manner to the pledge of religious fidelity which my countrymen give when they worship." "That's not right," rejoins the Hindoo; "*Ar* is the synonym for drowning, and is intended to convey the idea of being deep in debt." Whereupon the Court very sagely wags its head, and rules against the idea that mortgage is meant, and so the case proceeds. Incidentally it transpires that the interest on the original sum claimed has already amounted to five times the principal, and that in process of litigation the estate concerned has long since been swalled up. After all, it would seem that "Ar" was not a bad word to apply to that defunct gentleman's ground.

In this way the case proceeds all day. Technical objections are raised every few moments by one side or the other; there is an endless fight over words; and at last the court rises, and the question of what is meant by the document after all, or whether the gentleman who wrote it ever had the money he wanted, is left undecided. However, the lawyers are happy if their clients are not, and, as time is "no object" to any well-bred Hindoo, it is probable the litigants themselves are not greatly disappointed after all.

CHAPTER XXXVII.

ENGLISH LIFE IN THE HILLS.

Smallest of all the mountain stations to which Indians escape from the heat of the sun, Nynee Tal received a visit from the Prince, who stayed but a few hours in the hills, whilst his presence was marked by no occurrence worth noting. How different the case might have been had his Royal Highness been led to Mussoorie, let me point out.

Unlike Simla, the great summer capital of India, this eagle's nest is within twelve hours' reach by rail. Were you inclined to see the chain of snow-clad mountains from the Viceroy's Palace, you must needs submit to a five hours' journey in that most uncomfortable of vehicles, the dak-gharry—a kind of dilapidated London cab with the well boarded over—and then a perpetual ascent upon ledges more or less narrow for fifty-six miles farther, your choice of conveyance lying between a kind of palanquin, called in the language of the district a "jhampan," borne on the unequal shoulders of eight reckless savages, or a country pony the only qualification of which is that he is tolerably sure-footed. To reach Mussoorie the difficulty would be far less. You would have a rather more prolonged jolting in the dak-gharry, perhaps you might get a tumble over a little precipice, as did some travellers only a few days back; but once at the foot of the hills, in the village of Rajpore, the only remaining effort would be a steep ascent of seven miles, which on a country pony could be achieved in as many hours. I have mentioned that a happy characteristic of these creatures is their sure-footedness; and it is fortunate they possess it, for it is over no wide, easy, well-guarded road that your path lies. As a general rule, you are most of your time within a foot of the edge of an abyss many hundreds of feet deep. It is useless to endeavour to force your horse to go closer to the rock above. Experience has taught him that sometimes those overhanging stones are loosened and fall, perhaps at some time or other he has had a narrow escape from being crushed, and he resolutely declines to obey the bit. It is as much as your life is worth to spur him or to fight the question of mastery out in such a place. Most probably it is not five feet wide in all, and a sharp jerk might send you over the side. There is the remembrance of Sir Richard Temple's narrow escape on just such a ledge not many months age, when the ground over which the horse was trotting gave way, and the Lieutenant-Governor of Bengal only saved his life by springing from the saddle.

Yet difficult and somewhat unpleasant as is Mussoorie of access, it would not be wise to miss it on that account. Every step taken, every corner passed, every fresh altitude attained, unfolds to the astonished eye fresh beauties and marvels of nature. Down below is the Dhoon valley, through which runs the Jumna, on its way to Allahabad. Like a bright streak of quicksilver it divides the pleasant landscape, and gives it fertility. Nor is the valley itself unworthy your attention. Here and there it is dotted with little villages, of which that of Rajpore, through which you came, is a fair specimen. In those mud-built hovels, with straw thatches, live, all their lives through, the contented people of the plain, almost wholly engaged in the cultivation of tiny plots of ground and in the curing of skins. For round about here bear, leopard, lynx, and even tigers roam free. There are deer in plenty, with game of the lesser sort, and these harmless people, having learnt the art of dressing skins as no others can, are employed all the year round by the white Sahibs, who come hither for the purpose of shooting. It is nothing to them that the work is monotonous; that their whole lives are spent in the everlasting scrubbing and scraping of buck and cheetah skins. They are paid, and that is all they care for. What is life to them but a succession of eating, drinking, sleeping, and waking? Far from their ken lies the restless, busy world beyond, and they have no desire but to do as their fathers did before them.

Very different people are those who are carrying your luggage up the mountain side. They are men of the hills—strong, muscular, restless beings, who love nothing so much as roving and roaming. Most of them were born in Thibet, or in the stray hamlets which are to be found in all parts of the Himalayas. Their hair in front is cut short, so as not to impede the vision of their Mongolian eyes. It hangs down long at the sides as a protection for their ears. All the covering they have is a rough rug, and their feet are kept from the crags by only a straw shoe. Yet, thus equipped, they would start immediately, if directed, across even the great snow-covered ridge of mountains into Central Asia, at the risk of getting nothing more substantial than icy water for days—four hundred miles of mountain travelling. They smile when you say it is an impossibility; and three out of six of them tell you they have already achieved it. Indeed, an English officer who is near confirms their story by stating how, one bleak October, he and a companion, escorted by a hundred and twenty of these hardy savages, were safely conveyed through snow, river passes, and over steep ridges, with little more trouble or danger than we are experiencing now, and points to the fact that four men who died in process of that journey were not natives of the hills, but counterfeits, who wore warm clothing, and thought by such means to emulate the nearly naked but immeasurably hardier children of the Himalayas.

What these great heights are like you cannot as yet tell; for though the distance beneath is immense, you cannot see many feet upwards so projecting are the moss-covered cliffs. And sometimes you catch a glimpse from some rounded spur of a mass of mountains, though this is only for an instant. At length you begin to near the top, and to gain an idea of an Indian sanatorium. Perhaps the first notification is a cutting blast of a cold north wind. Then you look round, and find that you are skirting a kind of huge basin; that the ledge you are on leads slowly up to a point on which a great white building stands; that here and there other houses are peeping forth from cavernous hiding-places, and that all these various structures are upon shelves similar to that which you are traversing. You are, in fact, making your first acquaintance with Mussoorie, with all its bungalows and cottages. Perhaps you somewhat expected to find a street or road, some kind of thoroughfare on which you might amble at ease. There is nothing of the sort, in the ordinary acceptation of the terms, in the place. It is one succession of ledges and precipices. Wherever a level spot could be found, or a hill-top whereon a house could by any possibility be placed, there one has been erected. Then, to reach it, a cutting has been made in the rock sufficiently wide for two horses to pass; perhaps a slight railing has been fixed at the more precipitous parts and abrupt turnings, and all that is considered necessary has been done. If you are ignorant of the way, you will not wander about at night time alone. A false step would precipitate you into the valley below.

Once in Mussoorie, it is easy to see why wealthy Anglo-Indians should flee here to escape the sun in the plains. Seven thousand feet above the level of the sea and even more, a cool breeze is perpetually playing; the temperature is almost the same as that of England, and, were the ground only moderately even, life in this retreat would be a delight. Level it is in one direction, and in that only. Passing by the English church, which is itself perched on a point of rock overlooking a deep valley, the traveller quits the houses of Mussoorie, and enters the jungle which covers the hills. How beautiful this is, only those who have seen it know.

Gingerly picking its way, your horse leads you through forests of rhododendrons fifty feet high with stems as thick and as strong as elm trees, and branches covered with myriads of bright red blossoms—or you find yourself in a region of ferns, with the huge wide-spreading leaves overtopping your head—or a little further on you find your path bestrewn with acorns, shed from the Himalaya oak. Pheasants, startled by the unwonted sound of your horse's hoofs, fly up with a whirr into the impenetrable recesses above or down into the denser foliage beneath. Magpies chatter round you by hundreds, and parrots with bright, green feathers keep them company. You will do well not to have brought a favourite dog with you, for below are crafty leopards waiting quietly for such stray pets as may incautiously penetrate their hiding places; and your presence will scarcely suffice for its protection should a hungry cheetah cross your terrier's path. With a bound much swifter than those tame hunters of Baroda and Jummoo, the leopard gains the ledge, seizes its prey, and disappears into the thicket. Last season, at the very spot on which we are standing, the retriever of my companion was well-nigh snatched away, two strong men barely sufficing to baulk the leopard of its intended victim. Let it not be imagined that a man need fear anything. The strength of the leopard is no gauge of its bravery; and he never faces a human being unless brought to bay.

At length you emerge from the jungle for a few yards, and then what a view presents itself!

Straight away in front lie the larger mountains of the Himalayas, the great snowy range of which so much has been said, but of which so little is known. There is Gungootra, the source of the Ganges, with its four bright peaks and long connecting range, and almost touching it Jumnootra, whence flows the Jumna we have but lately seen in the valley of the Dhoon. From yonder glaciers the two streams flow, reinforced in different places and from different mountains, till they become the gigantic rivers which the Hindoos worship, which meet at Allahabad, and flow into the sea by Calcutta. Side by side they move together. You could cross them both in a single day were you but down in the valley. Indeed, there is a point at which you can see the crevices of two separate waterfalls, each of which you are told empties itself into a different river. But on this point you can scarcely assure yourself. You would have to climb over scores of mountains, each of them as high as the great Pilatus at Lucerne; you would have to press your way through jungles so dense that in the summer-time, when the rains have fallen and vegetation is ripe, they are almost impassable, and you would have to be careful not to lose your way, else you might hopelessly wander in search of your goal till you reached an uninhabited region, and there cease to exist. Still there are those who have successfully adventured, and tell you that Jumnootra, when close at hand, resembles nothing so much as a huge cathedral, that its towering peak, which reaches a height of twenty four thousand feet, is like the spire of a lordly fane, and that its snows make you almost believe that it is built of the purest white marble.

One might easily believe this sitting under the shadow of bending bamboos, close to a little waterfall which has been utilised for the purpose of lunch, so grand is the mountain which shuts in the horizon. But unhappily a lengthened look is scarcely possible, for the sun is fast setting, and what is more important still, a storm is gathering, and we are six miles from home. Every now and then the moan of wild beasts can be heard among the trees, the clatter of the birds is incessant, and our horses plunge and kick as the black clouds float towards the valley we are in. Six miles to climb up rocky path and jungle, six miles on ledge and shelf, our horses unsteady, and the rain coming on! Yet who would miss the sight of a storm in the Himalayas? The stream of light which now and again revealed the two great mountains and all their lesser kin more than compensated for the terrific downpour of rain which accompanied the vast illumination; and if the journey was tedious, the spectacle was grateful as being one we might never witness again.

Such, then, is the place to which wealthy Anglo-Indians go in the hot season, and send their wives and children. Once here, their diversions are numerous, for to the English whose life is spent in India the chief thought always is how much pleasure may be best extracted from the life they are forced to lead. Very naturally this characteristic is not left idle in the hills, and thus it is that in addition to the private social *réunion* there is always a daily assembly of all who are held to belong to society.

To effect this it is necessary that there should be a general rendezvous, and this is formed by the establishment of an Institute at every station. Thither, as soon as the sun loses somewhat of his power, in the afternoon all bend their steps. Ladies are carried in their jhampans, gentlemen go on horseback or afoot. To be absent would be about as unwarrantable a failing as an Anglo-Indian could well imagine. Nor is this without reason, for more pleasant hours could not be spent. For the stronger men, who are swift of foot and adroit of wrist, there is lawn tennis, in playing which residents in the North-West are adepts. Perhaps it is owing to the fact that in years gone by racquets were a favourite game. Anyhow, men who come fresh from England invariably find themselves no match for the residents, and have to work hard before they can cut a respectable figure in the lawn tennis court. But after all Badminton holds its own against all other diversions; and if you have any doubt as to the perfection to which this excellent game can be brought, you have but to invite the first two or three ladies who may chance to come from India to illustrate their skill, when you will quickly be convinced, especially if you chance to figure in the opposing court. They form parties which, evening after evening, from one month to another, play without ceasing. You know where to find Colonel S——; you can tell exactly at which net his wife is playing; the Commissioner will be at his post to a moment, and the Assistant Magistrate's wife will be cheerfully batting away on the spot where you saw her a week ago, at the very same hour. There is no obstacle they will not overcome to ensure their favourite game. Is the sun still too hot for them to venture out of doors? Then a bed-room is turned out, the net is stretched across, and the shuttlecock is soon flying merrily in every direction. Are they at a hill station, where all is ledge and shelf and slope? A hundred coolies are immediately set to work to hew and cut at the ground till a level place is made and roped in; then up goes the ever-appearing net, and the bats are in full swing directly.

Of course, Mussoorie is no exception to the rule. All round the Institute crooked places have been made straight, and rough places plain, rock has been actually blasted with gunpowder to make way for the all-pervading shuttlecock, and as to trees, they have certainly not been allowed to stand in the way. Only mention the possibility of Badminton, and the trees are moved off as if by magic. Nor is this altogether without its good results. How much liver complaint has been warded off doctors do not like to say. But the fact remains that fewer people in proportion go home to England in the hot weather, though money is apparently more plentiful than ever. For those, however, who do not care for such athletic exercises, there is the well-kept floor of the Institute itself; some volunteer is always at the piano; no master of ceremonies is needed, for all know each other, and partners are whirling round without intermission. Staid old men spend their time in the reading-room or at billiards; matches are even made here by thoughtful mammas, and young officers, military and civilian, are inveigled into the joys and sorrows of matrimony. I know a station in which five officers in one English regiment have thus been entrapped during the past six months, two of them subalterns.

This, then, is life in India; another side to the picture could be shown, of terrible heat and utter prostration during the six summer months down in the plains. But why think of this when the ringing laughter from the Badminton court mingles with the music in the Institute, the clicking of the billiard balls, and the soft conversation of lovers?

The journey of the Prince of Wales, so far as India was concerned, concluded shortly afterwards; his Royal Highness merely pausing on his way from Allahabad to Bombay, to pay a flying visit to Holkar, at his capital of Indore. Of the political and social results of the trip it is not my purpose to speak in this place. Suffice it to say, that owing to the united efforts of military and civil officials of India, his Royal Highness was afforded, in the course of the four months he spent in that marvellous country, an opportunity of gaining knowledge with regard to its resources and its peoples, the like of which was never enjoyed before, and, possibly, never will be again.